9.50
XX

Books by Pablo Neruda

※)(0)(0)(0)(0)(0)(0)(0

Crepusculario / Crepusculario

*Veinte poemas de amor y una canción desesperada / Twenty
Love Poems and a Song of Despair*

Tentativa del hombre infinito / Venture of the Infinite Man

El habitante y su esperanza / The Inhabitant and His Hope

Anillos / Rings

El hondero entusiasta / The Ardent Slingsman

Residencia en la tierra (1) / Residence on Earth (1)

Residencia en la tierra (2) / Residence on Earth (2)

Tercera residencia / The Third Residence

La ahogada del cielo / The Woman Drowned in the Sky
Las furias y las penas / Griefs and Rages
Reunión bajo las nuevas banderas / United under New Flags
España en el corazón / Spain in My Heart
Canto a Stalingrado / Song to Stalingrad

Canto general / Canto general

La lámpara en la tierra / A Lamp on This Earth
Alturas de Macchu Picchu / The Heights of Macchu Picchu
Los conquistadores / The Conquistadors
Los libertadores / The Liberators
La arena traicionada / The Sands Betrayed
América, no invoco tu nombre en vano / America, I Don't
Invoke Your Name in Vain
Canto general de Chile / Song of Chile
La tierra se llama Juan / The Land Is Called Juan
Que despierte el leñador / Let the Rail Splitter Awaken
El fugitivo / The Fugitive
Las flores de Punitaqui / The Flowers of Punitaqui
Los ríos del canto / Rivers of Song

Coral de año nuevo para la patria en tinieblas / A New Year's
Hymn for My Country in Darkness
El gran océano / The Great Ocean
Yo soy / I Am

Las uvas y el viento / The Grapes and the Wind

Los versos del capitán / The Captain's Verses

Odas elementales / Elemental Odes

Nuevas odas elementales / More Elemental Odes

Tercer libro de las odas / The Third Book of Odes

Viajes / Journeys

Estravagario / Extravagaria

Navegaciones y regresos / Voyages and Homecomings

Cien sonetos de amor / One Hundred Love Sonnets

Canción de gesta / Chanson de geste

Las piedras de Chile / The Stones of Chile

Cantos ceremoniales / Ceremonial Songs

Plenos poderes / Fully Empowered

Memorial de Isla Negra / Isla Negra: A Notebook

Arte de pájaros / The Art of Birds

Una casa en la arena / A House by the Shore

La barcarola / Barcarole

*Fulgor y muerte de Joaquín Murieta / Splendor and Death of
Joaquín Murieta*

*Passions and
Impressions*

Pablo Neruda

PASSIONS AND IMPRESSIONS

EDITED BY
Matilde Neruda & Miguel Otero Silva

TRANSLATED BY
Margaret Sayers Peden

Farrar • *Straus* • *Giroux*
NEW YORK

Contents

Notebook III
The Fire of Friendship

NOTEBOOK IV
Sailing in Smoke

NOTEBOOK V
Reflections from Isla Negra

NOTEBOOK VI
The Struggle for Justice

NOTEBOOK VII
Pablo Neruda Speaks

❖❱❨❱❨❱❨❱❨❱❨❱❨❱❨❱❨❖

It Is Very Early

Distant Woman

THIS woman fits in my hands. She is fair and blond, and I would carry her in my hands like a basket of magnolias.

This woman fits in my eyes. My gaze enfolds her, my gaze that sees nothing as it enfolds her.

This woman fits in my desires. She is naked before the yearning flame of my life, and my desire burns her like a live coal.

But, distant woman, my hands, my eyes, and my desires save for you their caresses, because only you, distant woman, only you fit in my heart.

The twelve prose poems on pages 3–16 appeared in *Claridad*, Santiago, in 1922

Love

Bᴇᴄᴀᴜsᴇ of you, in gardens of blossoming flowers I ache from the perfumes of spring.

I have forgotten your face, I no longer remember your hands; how did your lips feel on mine?

Because of you, I love the white statues drowsing in the parks, the white statues that have neither voice nor sight.

I have forgotten your voice, your happy voice; I have forgotten your eyes.

Like a flower to its perfume, I am bound to my vague memory of you. I live with pain that is like a wound; if you touch me, you will do me irreparable harm.

Your caresses enfold me, like climbing vines on melancholy walls.

I have forgotten your love, yet I seem to glimpse you in every window.

Because of you, the heady perfumes of summer pain me; because of you, I again seek out the signs that precipitate desires: shooting stars, falling objects.

Winds of Night

THE moon must be swaying above like the painted curtain on a stage. Winds of night, dark and gloomy winds! How the waves of the sky roar and ravage, how they tread with dew-wet feet on the rooftops. Lying asleep while the drunken surf swoops howling from the sky across the pavement. Lying asleep as distance is no more, as it flies to me, bringing before my eyes what once was far away. Winds of night, dark and gloomy winds! How insignificant my wings in this mighty buffeting! How enormous the world, how trivial the sorrow in my throat. But I can die if I wish, lie down in the night so the fury of the wind will sweep me away. Die, lie down to sleep, soar upon the violent sea swell, singing, reclining, sleeping! The hoofbeats of the sky gallop across the rooftops. A chimney sobs . . . winds of night, gloomiest of winds!

It Is Very Early

Grave tranquillity of silence. Marred by the crowing of a cock. And the footsteps of a workingman. But the silence continues.

Then a distracted hand on my chest feels my heart's beating. Always a surprise.

And again—oh, days gone by!—my memories, my sorrows, my resolves march forth, cringing and cowering, to crucify themselves along the byways of time and space.

Thus may one pass with ease.

The Leper Woman

I saw the leper woman arrive. She lies beside a clump of azaleas that smile in a deserted patio of the hospital.

When night comes, she will go away. The leper woman will go because the hospital will not take her in. She will go as the day is sinking gently in the dusk, and even the day will prolong its yellow glow to avoid leaving with the leper woman.

She weeps, she weeps beside the azaleas. The blond, blue-robed Sisters have forsaken her; the blond, blue-robed Sisters will not heal her sad sores.

The children, forbidden to approach her, have fled along the corridors.

The dogs have forgotten her, the dogs that lick the wounds of the forgotten.

The rose-colored azaleas—the only smile, the sweetest smile, of the hospital—have not moved from the corner of the patio, from the corner of the patio where the leper woman lies forsaken.

Song

My cousin Isabela . . . I don't remember my cousin Isabela. Now, years later, I have walked through the garden patio where, I am told, we saw and loved one another in our childhood. It is a place of shadows: as in cemeteries, the trees are hardened and wintry. Yellow moss encircles the waists of the huge dark-clay flowerpots toppled in this patio of memories . . . This, then, is where I first saw my cousin Isabela.

I must have looked at her with a child's eyes that expect something is going to happen, is happening, has happened . . .

Cousin Isabela, my intended bride, a channel flows steadily, eternally, between our solitudes. I, from my side, set out at a run toward valleys I cannot see; my cries, my movements, return to me, useless, forgotten echoes. You, from the other side . . .

But, Isabela, I have brushed past you many times. Because you might be anywhere! That reserved woman who, when I walk at dusk, counts, as I do, the first evening stars from her window.

Cousin Isabela, the first evening stars.

The Tent

We were repairing some rotted dock pilings deep in the heart of the south country. It was summer. At night the work gang drew close together, and exhausted, we threw ourselves down on the grass or on our outspread blankets. The south winds drenched an enthralled countryside with dew, and billowed our flapping tent like a sail.

With what strange tenderness I loved in those days the piece of canvas that sheltered us, the dwelling that strove to lull us to sleep at the end of each grueling day!

Past midnight, I would open my eyes and lie motionless, listening. Alongside me, in steady rhythm, the breathing of the sleeping men. Through an oval opening in the tent would come the strong breath of night in the open country . . . From time to time, the anguished voice of women possessed in love; at intervals, in the distance, the hallucinatory croaking of frogs, or the buffeting of the river current against the repairs on the pilings.

Sometimes, creeping along like a caterpillar, I would slip stealthily from the tent. Outside, I would lie on the wet clover, my head swimming with nostalgia, my pupils fixed on some distant constellation. The rural and oceanic night moved me to vertigo, and my life floated on the night like a butterfly fallen onto an eddy.

A shooting star filled me with unimaginable joy.

Goodness

Let us make goodness more stalwart, my friends. Good, too, is the knife that excises the rotten flesh and the worm; and good is the fire burning in the forest, that the good plow might cleave the earth.

Let us make goodness more resolute, my friends. Every weakling with weepy eyes and delicate words, every cretin with obscure motives and condescending gestures, wears goodness, awarded by you, like a locked door closed to our examination. We need to call men good who are men of honorable heart, men who are not two-faced, who are humble.

See that the word "good" makes itself party to the vilest complicities, and confess that when you have said "good," it was always—or almost always—a lie. The time has come to stop lying, for, after all, we are responsible only to ourselves, and in private we are consumed with remorse for our falseness, and, as a result, live locked inside ourselves, within the four walls of our astute stupidity.

Good men will be those who most swiftly free themselves from this terrible lie and learn to speak out with obstinate goodness against whatever deserves it. Goodness that marches, not with someone, but against someone. Good that does not toady or flatter, but gives its all in the battle, since good is the principal weapon of life.

And so, only those who are of honorable heart will be called good, those who are not two-faced, the unbowed, the best. They will vindicate goodness, which is rotting from such baseness; they will be the defenders of life and the rich in spirit. And theirs, only theirs, is the kingdom of earth.

Heroes

As if I carried them within my anxiety, I find my heroes where I seek them. At first I didn't know how to identify them, but now, wise to life's gambits, I see them pass by and I have learned to endow them with qualities they do not possess. But I find that I am oppressed by these heroics, and, exhausted, I reject them. Because now I want men who bow their backs to adversity, men who howl at the first lash of the whip, somber heroes who do not know how to laugh, who look on life as a great, dank, gloomy cellar with no ray of sunlight.

But I don't find them now. My anxiety is filled with old heroes, the heroes of old.

The Struggle to Hold
on to Memory

My thoughts have been wandering from me, but having come to a friendly path, I reject all my present tempestuous sorrows and pause, eyes closed, enervated in an aroma of faraway times and places that I have myself kept alive in my humble struggle against life. I have lived only in yesterday. "Now" has the naked expectancy of its desires, the provisional seal that grows old without love.

Yesterday is a tree with great spreading branches, and I lie in its shade, remembering.

Suddenly, to my surprise, I see long caravans of pilgrims who, like me, have come on this byway; their eyes rapt in memory, they sing songs and remember. And somehow I know they have changed only to remain the same, they have spoken only to become silent, they have opened astonished eyes to the celebration of the stars only to close them and remember . . .

Lying by the side of this new road, avid eyes filled with the flowers of other days, I try in vain to hold back the river of time that ripples over me. But what water I am able to collect lies confined in the dark pools of my heart, pools in which, tomorrow, I must immerse my aged and lonely hands . . .

Smoke

At times I am overcome by the desire to talk a little, not in a poem, but in the ordinary phrases of our reality, about the street corner, the horizon and the sky that I observe at dusk from the high window where I sit every evening, thinking. I want, and not on any universal plane, to feel the tug of the elemental cord one needs to know one is alive, sitting by a high window in the solitude of early evening.

To say, for example, that the dusty street looks like a canal in a motionless land, not capable of reflection, unequivocally taciturn.

The friction from all the activity outside fills the still air with smoke, and the moon peering from the far shore oozes fat grapes of blood.

The first light, every evening, comes on in the whorehouse on the corner. The house's homosexual comes out on the sidewalk—a skinny, preoccupied adolescent in a canvas smock. He is constantly laughing and yelping, always busy at some task: dusting with a feather duster or folding clothes or sweeping trash from the front door. So the whores come to lounge lazily in the doorway, peer out, and then go back inside, while the poor pansy keeps on laughing or dusting or worrying about the glass in the windows. Those windows must be black with dirt.

Observing these insignificant actions, I let my mind wander: Isabel had a sad voice; or perhaps I try to recall what month I came to town. Oh, how those days dropped into my outstretched hand! But only you know, my shoes, my bed, my window, only you. They may believe me dead. Wandering, wandering, thinking. It's raining, oh, my God!

Though I imagine a thin and cowering dog is sniffing and pissing along the row of housefronts, that dog is precise and real, and will never alter its imaginary route.

It seems inevitable that I must inject a little music into these letters I am scattering at random across the page. The indispensable accordion, a stairway down which drunken men occasionally stumble. But also a hurdy-gurdy pumping out its vulgar waltzes up to the rooftops.

Now, too, it seems that it is she who is coming; but what would she be coming to? The greyhounds are howling in the fields. What a long row of cowardly eucalyptus, cowardly and dour!

Remembering her, it is as if my heart were buried in the rain. Again I think it's she, but why would she be coming now? Oh, what sad days! I will go back to bed, I no longer want to look on this damp scene. Your eyes: two sleepy cups darkened by purple berries from the forest undergrowth. What a leaf, a leaf from a white vine, fragrant and heavy, I could have brought you from the forest. Everything flees from this solitude enforced by rain and contemplation. Master of my profound existence, I limit and extend my power over things. And after all, a window, a smoky sky . . . In short, I have nothing at all.

Carts totter by, rattling, scraping. As people walk past, they scribble figures in the dirt. A voice flares out behind that window. Lighted cigarettes in the shadow. Who is knocking so insistently at the door below? The mountain in the distance, a dark belt encircling the night. Nothing more fateful than that knocking, and then, steps ascending my barren stairway: someone coming to see me. Now I write in haste: the night is like a tree, its roots in me, dark and gloomy roots. Matted with blazing fruit, high, high the foliage, making a tent over the moon.

Poor, miserable bell ringer, frightening away the solitude with the clapping of his bell. The notes pierce holes in the air, then fall swiftly to the ground. You are left, alone up there, clinging to your bells.

The Ship of Farewells

Fʀᴏᴍ eternity, invisible sailors transport me through strange atmospheres, cutting through unknown seas. Limitless space has sheltered my never-ending voyages. My keel has sundered the moving mass of glittering icebergs that tried to block all routes with their powdery bodies. Later I sailed through seas of fog that spread their mists among new stars brighter than the earth. Then through white seas, and red seas, that stained my hull with their colors and their fog. At times we cruised through purest atmosphere, a dense, luminous atmosphere that drenched my sail and made it refulgent as the sun. For long whiles we anchored in countries ruled by water or the wind. And then one day—always when least expected—my invisible sailors would raise my anchors and the wind would fill my resplendent sails. And it was once again trackless infinity, the astral atmospheres that lead to endlessly solitary plains.

I reached the shore of the earth, and there they anchored my ship in a sea, the greenest of seas, beneath a blue sky I had never seen. Accustomed to the green kisses of the waves, my anchors rest upon the golden sands of the bottom of this sea, playing with the convoluted flora of the depths, and serving as steeds for the white sirens who during the long days come to ride on them. My tall, straight masts are friends to the sun, the moon, and the amorous air that comes to taste them. Birds they have never known, a rain of arrows, come to perch on the masts, score the sky, and disappear forever. I have begun to love this sky, this sea. I have begun to love these men . . .

But one day, the least expected, my invisible sailors will arrive. They will raise my anchors, now trees of seaweed in the deep waters, they will fill my resplendent sails with wind . . .

And again it will be trackless infinity, the red and white seas that stretch out amid other eternally solitary stars.

Exegesis and Solitude

I have undertaken the greatest act of self-expression: creation, hoping to illuminate words. Ten years at a solitary task, ten years that make up exactly half my life, have generated in my writing diverse rhythms, opposing currents. Tying them together, interweaving them, never finding what will endure—because it does not exist—I offer here my *Veinte poemas de amor y una canción desesperada*. As scattered as thought in its elusive variations, joyful and bitter, I have fashioned them, and I have suffered no little in doing so. I have simply sung of my life and my love for certain women, as one would by shouting greetings to the parts of the world closest to him. I sought increasingly to link my expression with my thought, and I achieved some small victory; sincerely, and consciously, I put something of myself in everything I wrote. From afar, honorable people, people I didn't even know—not clerks and pedagogues, who personally detest me—unhesitatingly demonstrated their friendliness. I didn't respond, but concentrated all my strength on damming the tides, my only concern to pour intensity into my work. I have not tired of any discipline, because I followed none: the hand-me-down clothes that fitted others were either too small for me or too large; I acknowledged them, without looking. Always a meditative man, I have given lodging, as I have lived, to too many anxieties for them to vanish because of what I write. Facing in no particular direction, freely, irrepressibly, my poems have been set free.

Published in *La Nación*, Santiago, 1924

❖❀❖❀❖❀❖❀❖❀❖

Travel Images

Travel Images

THIS, some days ago. Brazil, enormous, loomed up over the boat.

From early morning, the bay of Santos was ashen; later, objects began emitting their normal light and the sky turned blue. The shore appeared, the color of thousands of bananas; canoes came laden with oranges; macaques swayed before our eyes, and from stem to stern, parrots screeched in a deafening din.

A fantastic land. Not a sound from its silent interior: somber mountains; a torrid, vegetal horizon, secret, patterned with gigantic lianas, filling the distance with an ambience of mysterious silence. But the overburdened boats creak with crates: coffee, tobacco, fruits by the thousands; the odors seize you by the nose and pull you toward land.

That day, a Brazilian family boarded the ship—father, mother, and daughter. She, the girl, was very beautiful.

Her eyes dominate her face, engrossed eyes black as coal, serene of gaze, profoundly brilliant. They are made even more noticeable by a pale brow. Her mouth is wide, the better to display the gleam of her teeth as she smiles. A beautiful daughter of Brazil, my friend. Her being begins in two tiny feet and ascends sensuous legs whose ripeness begs to be nibbled by the eyes.

Slowly, slowly, the ship hugs the shore of these lands, as if making a great effort to wrest itself free, though drawn by the ardent sounds of the littoral. Suddenly, huge black and green butterflies rain down on the deck; suddenly the wind whistles, a warm breath from the

---

The twelve dispatches in "Travel Images" appeared in *La Nación*, Santiago, in 1927

interior, perhaps bearing tales of the work of the plantations, the echo of the silent march of the rubber workers toward the rubber trees; then the breeze dies down, its cessation a warning.

For, sailing onward, we come to the equator and the ship slips noiselessly onto a desert of water slick as oil, as if onto a millpond. There's something terrifying about encountering scalding air in the middle of the ocean. Where does this blazing ring begin? The ship steams through silent, deserted latitudes of inexorable calm. What phantasmal forms might inhabit the sea beneath this fiery pressure?

Every evening Marinech, the Brazilian girl, sits in her deck chair, facing the dusk. Her face is tinged with the hues of the sky. At times she smiles.

She is my friend, Marinech. She speaks in honeyed Portuguese; this toy-like tongue adds to her charm. A dozen swains surround her. She is haughty, pale, she shows no preference for any. Her gaze, charged with dark essences, is far away.

Now, on land, as evening falls, it shatters to pieces, it crashes as it strikes the ground. Hence that hollow sound of dusk on land, that mysterious din that is merely twilight crushing the day. Here, evening falls in lethal silence, like a dark cloth dropped over the water. And, surprising us, her footsteps unperceived, night blindfolds our eyes, wondering if she has been recognized. She, unmistakable infinity.

Port Said

To comment on passing events is to take on a certain tone. One rolls down the incline of a personal bias and presences begin to recur: the sentimental discovery, the heartrending aspects of departing or arriving; the comedian strikes sparks, the tragedian draws blood.

Sitting in my canvas chair at the bow of the packet boat, I experience no particular sensation; my expression is that of a hollow sphinx, a cartoon from which it is not easy to coax a surprise. The Orient reaches this chair very early in the morning; one day it may take the form of Egyptian merchants, dark of countenance, wearing red tarbooshes, haranguing, persistent to the point of lunacy, displaying their tapestries, their glass necklaces, soliciting for brothels.

Port Said lies alongside the ship, a row of international bazaars, launches with cheap goods for the ship trade, and, farther ashore, a horizon of truncated buildings, houses whose flat roofs seem to have stunted their growth, and the palm trees of Africa, our first, timidly green, humbled in this hullabaloo of charcoal and flour, this international exhalation, the screeching of the *donokeis*, the heavy, pulsating machinery that loads and unloads with great fiery fingers.

Port Said encompasses a raucous conglomeration of the most strident races of the world. Its narrow streets are nothing but bazaars and markets, they ring with all the world's tongues, reek with appalling stenches, are bathed in tints of green and scarlet. In that cumulus of vegetable and animal life, one wishes, but in vain, to retreat; the air, the very light, of Port Said shouts prices and propositions; the sky of Port Said, low and blue, is a ramshackle tarp, scarcely stirring over the monstrous bazaar.

From time to time, veiled Arab women with heavily made-up eyes pass through the streets. They are a rather pitiful reincarnation of the writings of Pierre Loti; completely enveloped in their dark cloths, as if weighed down by the obligation to maintain their literary prestige, they do not seem part of this violent African scene; rather, they rouse a melancholy and meager curiosity. As do the nargileh smokers; authentic beyond a shadow of doubt, sucking on that apparatus one finds to the point of boredom in every antique shop, they bear with true dignity their legendary role as disseminated in the storybooks of old. They smoke with notable nonchalance, sweating a little, bulky, dark, swathed in long robes.

Soon the ship leaves this port behind, sprawling beneath the sun of all those opulent miseries, a little lacking in the more serious Oriental décor of the films. A few stairways, an occasional cupola, the enormous earthen vessels of *The Thief of Bagdad*, and it would be with considerably more nostalgia that the ship steamed toward the Suez Canal (that cold and sterile work not quite off the drawing board of Whatman and the engineer Lesseps). The ship would be bearing away the disorientation produced by a new and hither-to unknown experience of the world, the hidden mark of having lived one more day of life amid the fantastic, the imaginary, the ineffable.

African Dance

I must write this passage with my left hand, while with my right I shade myself against the sun. Against the intense African sun that changes my fingers, one by one, from red to white. I immerse them in water; abruptly they are warm, cold, heavy. My right hand has turned to metal; with it (concealed in a glove) I shall triumph over the most terrifying boxers, the most daring fakir.

We are at anchor before Djibouti. The boundary between the Red Sea and the Indian Ocean is invisible. The waters cross this barrier of letters, of names on a map, with the unawareness of illiterates. Here, at this very point, waters and religions blend together. The first Buddhist salmon swim indifferently past the last Saracen trout.

Then from the depths of the littoral leap the most entertaining black Somalis to dive for coins, in the water and in the air. An episode described millions of times, but which actually goes as follows: the waif is olive-skinned, with long Egyptian ears; his mouth is white, a single steady smile; and his protruding navel obviously has been stamped by a French coin pitched too forcefully from a deck. These boys are a swarm of dark bees, and occasionally they catch a piece of silver on the fly; most of the time, they retrieve it from the sea and bring it up in their mouths, thus accustoming themselves to a diet of silver that makes the Somali a human species of a metallic consistency, one that rings like a bell and is impossible to shatter.

Djibouti's European sector is white, low, and square: dice on a glossy oilcloth. Djibouti is as sterile as the spine of a sword: those oranges come from Arabia; those pelts, from Abyssinia. In this country bereft of maternal instincts, the sun's rays fall vertically, riddling the ground. At this hour, the Europeans bury themselves deep inside their houses shaded by palm trees, they immerse themselves in their tubs, smoking amid water and fans. The only people in these streets perpetually bright as a flash of lightning are the unconcerned Orientals: silent Hindus, Arabs, Abyssinians with squared-off beards, naked Somalis.

Djibouti is mine. I have conquered it, walking beneath its sun at the most feared hour: midday, siesta time, the hour whose fire stamped out the life of Arthur Rimbaud, the hour when camels, their humps grown small, turn their tiny eyes from the desert.

The desert borders the native quarter. Tortuous, flattened, crumbled, and parched materials: adobe, miserable bulrushes. A variety of Arab cafés where half-naked men with haughty faces lie smoking on rush mats. At the turn of a corner, an ambuscade of women, multicolored skirts, black faces painted yellow, amber bracelets: the street of the dancing girls. In clumps and clusters, clutching at our arms, they want, each of them, to earn the foreigners' coins. I enter the first hut and recline on a Persian carpet. At that instant, two women enter from the rear. They are naked. They dance.

They dance without music, treading on the great silence of Africa as if on a rug. Their movements are slow and cautious, they would not be heard even if they danced among bells. They are shadow. Shadow like the hard and burning shadow now forever superimposed on the firm metal of their breasts, the stony strength of arms and legs. They fuel their dance with internal, guttural sounds, and the rhythm becomes faster, frenetic. Their heels strike the ground with weighted splendor; an uncentered magnetism, an irascible dictate, drives them. Their black bodies glisten with sweat, like wet furniture; their upraised hands shake sound from the bracelets, and with a sudden leap, in a last whirling tension, they lie motionless, the dance ended, collapsed on the ground like limp rag dolls, the hour of fire passed, priestesses humbled by the presence they have invoked.

The dance is over. Then I call the smaller, the more gracile, dancer to my side. She comes: with my white Palm Beach jacket I wipe her night-black brow, my arm embraces her aestival waist. Then I speak to her in a language she has never heard, I speak to her in Spanish, in the tongue of the long, crepuscular verses of Díaz Casanueva; in that language in which Joaquín Edwards preaches nationalism. My discourse is profound; I speak with eloquence and seduction; my words, more than from me, issue from the warm nights, from the many solitary nights on the Red Sea, and when the tiny dancer puts her arm around my neck, I understand that she understands. Magnificent language!

The Dreams of the Crew

IMPASSIVELY, the boat continues its forward course. What is it seeking? Soon we will make Sumatra. That diminishes its speed, which becomes imperceptible, for fear of foundering suddenly in one of the soft boscades of the island, of awakening in the morning with elephants, perhaps duckbills, on the bridge.

It is night, a night that arrived energetically, decisively. This night wants to lie on the ocean, a bed with no gorges, no volcanoes, no passing trains. There it snores in its freedom, without pulling up its legs at frontiers, without shrinking back at peninsulas; it sleeps, the enemy of topography as it dreams of freedom.

The crew lies stretched out on the bridge, to escape the heat—unseeing, in disorder, bodies scattered about as if on a battlefield. They are sleeping, each wearing a different dream as he would his clothing.

The gentle Annamese sleep on their backs on blankets, and Laho, their corporal, dreams of wielding a gold-encrusted sword; his muscles move like reptiles beneath his skin. His body aches, he exhausts himself in the duel. Others dream of warriors in dreams hard as a stone spear. They seem to suffer, eyes forced open by the sharp pressure. Others weep softly, a hoarse, lost moan, and some dream dreams smooth as an egg, whose membrane ruptures with every sound, every emotion; the contents spill like milk across the deck and then re-form, the shells adhering, without substance, without sound, while the dreamer lies engrossed. And there are others.

Laurent, true seaman of the Mediterranean, lies stretched full-length in his striped jersey and red belt. The Hindus sleep with their eyes blindfolded, separated from life by that bandage of condemned men, and one or two place their hands gently over their hearts, defending themselves valiantly against dreams as if against a bullet. The blacks of Martinique sleep voluptuously, creatures of the day. Mysterious India, a siesta of palm trees, cliffs of congealed light. The Arabs secure their heads to keep them fixed in the direction of the dead Mohammed.

Alvaro Rafael Hinojosa lies, eyes closed, daydreaming of seamstresses in Holland, of schoolteachers from Charlesville, of Erika Pola from Dresden; his dream is decomposition of space, liquid corrosion, void. He feels himself slipping down a spiral, swallowed like a butterfly in a giant ventilator; he observes himself penetrating the solid distances of earth, the briny passages of the sea; he believes himself lost, weak and legless, trapped in interminable transmigration; seeking to return, he butts his head against age after erroneous age, substituted ages, regions from which he flees, though hailed as a discoverer. In a rage, he races from one point in time to another, the wind whistling around him as if around a projectile.

The Chinese, half prostrate, have put on their frozen, stiff masks of dream and walk through sleep as if deep inside armor. The tattooed Corsicans snore, sonorous as seashells, exuding an air of diligence, even in sleep. They hoist sleep as they do the rigging of a ship, by dint of muscle and their office as seamen. What's more, their boat is most secure in dreams, it barely wavers in celestial time; in its rigging perch angels and equatorial cockatoos.

Dominique lies on the deck. On his ankle, tattooed in blue letters, is *Marche ou Crève*. On both arms he has a hand clasping a dagger, which signifies valor; on his chest, the portrait of an ungrateful Eloise, glimpsed through a tangle of hair; in addition, tattooed on his legs are anchors that ward off the dangers of the sea, doves that prevent one's being trapped on the points of the compass, that help a man set his course and guard him in his drunkenness.

There are those who sleep without dreaming, like rocks; others, whose faces display astonishment before an unbreachable barrier. I unroll my mat, close my eyes, and with infinite care my dream launches itself into space. I fear I may wake the sleeping. I try not to dream of tinkling bells, of Montmartre, of a phonograph; they might awake. I will dream of small women, the quietest of women. Of Lulu, or, better yet, Laura, whose voice one reads, whose voice is the voice of dream.

Colombo, Sleeping and Awake

AFTER ten o'clock in the evening (British time), Colombo expires. I was in Colombo at 10:05 p.m., hoping to raise at least a death rattle. But Colombo had died suddenly, it was a city without shadow or light; it was Valparaiso at night, or Buenos Aires. It was a geometric port: its white angles held not the least relationship to the Oriental axials sultry with heat and odor. It was a bas-relief of a hieratic population, hard, without breath, without drink. Not a woman's face, not a shadow of a happy song. Adios.

I returned the following morning. The dead had risen from their tombs, the dead in strange colors and clothing. That shudder of resurrection had the scale and effect of a whirlwind. If one scrabbles in that indifferent earth, the secret vitals of Ceylon will lie exposed beneath the sun, its deafening sounds, its raucous kettledrum voice.

I am being transported in a ricksha pulled by a nimble Singhalese who, as he runs, reminds me of an ostrich. The native city boils on all four sides as I pass among the 280,000 inhabitants of Colombo—an hour of flowing color.

The milling multitude has a certain uniformity. The dark, brown-skinned men are simply dressed in the side-wrapped skirt that covers them almost completely, their national *vetil*. The women, almost all of them wearing blue or royal-purple stones in their pierced noses, are dressed in heavy tulle; around their shoulders, many-colored shawls. Among the barefoot throngs, from time to time one sees Englishmen in high boots, Malayans in velvet slippers. The people of Ceylon are oddly beautiful; in each regularly featured, ardent face, two strong eyes of impressively grave gaze. There seems to be neither misery nor pain in this indifferent world. Two old men stride by with heads erect, their steady charcoal stare is haughty, and the half-naked street urchins laugh confidently, asking nothing, with no hint of begging.

The shops in the small white Hindu houses encroach upon the sidewalks, spilling strange wares onto them. The barbershops are particularly astounding: the client and the barber, facing one another, squat motionless on their haunches, as if practicing a patient rite. The barber glances at me calmly as he runs a startlingly long razor over his adversary's head. The shirtsleeved moneylenders, here called chettys, stroll about with the long beards of monarchs, and an air of impassivity; young men of religious mien pass by with vivid dots of gleaming saffron daubed between their eyebrows; others, more well-to-do, affix, in addition, a diamond or a ruby. In every shop, rubber, silks, tea, and, in all sizes, ebony elephants with ivory tusks, some of precious stones. For three rupees I buy one the size of a rabbit.

This colorful medley, like a tree with each leaf different in tone and shape and season, together forms a vast ambience of dream, of old storybooks. From books, too, from the yellowed pages of poetry, come the crows which by the hundreds roost on the cornices of the native quarter; they light on the sidewalks, flutter from one side of the street to the other in short flights, or hunch motionlessly, over the doorways, like numbers of an unknown quantity.

I was unable to enter the three-hundred-year-old Brahman temple of Colombo, with its baroque exterior encrusted with a thousand mystical figures, warriors and women carved and painted in blues and greens and reds, goddesses of nine arrogant faces, and elephant-headed gods. A saffron-painted bonze impedes my entrance, and my gestures of removing my shoes or reaching for a few rupees are ineffectual. Hindu temples are forbidden to foreigners, and I must content myself with watching and listening to fragments of ceremonies. Before the doors, two believers burst huge coconuts on the stone paving and offer the white flesh to the god Brahma. A bell rings, signaling the moment of the ritual flower libations; the bonzes hurry to prostrate themselves, lying on the ground as if mortally wounded.

The most beautiful part of Colombo is the market, that feast, that mountain, of Eden's fruits and leaves. Millions of green oranges are piled in heaps, tiny Asiatic lemons, areca nuts, mangoes, fruits with difficult names and unrecognizable savors. The betel leaves mount up in gigantic columns, beautifully arranged like bank notes, alongside the beans of Ceylon, whose pods may reach a meter in length. The enormous market is in constant flow, its extravagant produce seethes, the sharp perfumes of the fruits, the piles of vegetables, the exalted colors brilliant as crystal, are intoxicating; behind every pile stand young Hindu boys no darker than South Americans, who watch and laugh with more astuteness, with a greater sense of personal importance, with a bearing superior to that of our own people. Apart from this, one is at times startled by a resemblance; suddenly a tattoo arist approaches who looks exactly like Hugo Silva, or a betel vendor with the face of the poet Homero Arce.

The boat is leaving Colombo. Before us, the huge cosmopolitan port with merchant ships from every latitude, and in their midst, a white British cruiser, silvery and slender, as flawless and smooth as a tooth or a knife. We leave it there, facing the island forests, the pitch of pagoda roofs, amid the odor of spices from the submissive land, looming like a sign of cold menace.

Then: the scattered Singhalese boats with ocher and red sails, so narrow their crew must stand, straddling the gunwales. Erect, naked as statues, they seem to emerge from the eternity of the water, with that secret air of all elemental matter.

A Day in Singapore

I awake: though I enter, reality lags behind; the mosquito netting of my house is a veil, a subtle tissue. Beyond it, things have assumed their rightful places in the world: sweethearts are receiving flowers; debtors, bills. Where am I? From the street rise the odors and sounds of a city, humid odors, piercing sounds. On the white wall of my room, lizards are taking the sun. The water in my lavatory is warm; equatorial mosquitoes bite my ankles. I look at the window, then the map. I am in Singapore.

Yes, because to the west of the bay, beyond the brown-skinned Malayans, live the dark-skinned Hindustanis; straight past my window, the Chinese, truly yellow; and to the east, the rosy-skinned British—a progressive modulation, as if it were here that skins began to change color, here that gradually some chose Buddhism, some rice, and others tennis.

But, actually, the capital of the Straits Settlements is China. There are some three hundred thousand pale and almond-eyed souls who have renounced their pigtails, but not their opium or their national flag. Within this city there is a huge, boiling, bustling Chinese city. It is a domain of large signs with beautiful hieroglyphs, mysterious alphabets that span the streets, emerging from every window and door in splendid red and golden lacquer, an interlude of authentic Coromandel dragons. Naturally, they are the perfect harbingers of new enigmas from that opulent land, and though they may advertise the best shoe polish or the impeccable hattery, one must endow them with occult meanings and be suspicious of their outward appearance.

Magnificent multitude! The broad streets of the Chinese district barely allow for a poet's passage. The street is market, restaurant, gigantic piles of salable goods, and sellers. Every doorway is a plentiful shop, a glutted storehouse unable to contain its merchandise, which spills onto the street. What a jumble of groceries and toys, launderers, shoemakers, bakers, moneylenders, furniture makers in that human jungle; there is scarcely room for the buyer; on either side of the street, food is heaped on rows of long tables, blocks and blocks of tables, occupied at every moment of the day by patient rice-eaters, by distinguished consumers of spaghetti, long spaghetti that sometimes drapes across a chest like ribbons of honor.

There are blacksmiths squatting on their haunches to work their metals, itinerant fruit and cigarette vendors, minstrels who make their two-stringed mandolins hum. Hairdressers, where the client's head is transformed into an unyielding, lacquer-varnished castle. There are stalls with fish inside bottles; corridors of grated ice and peanuts; puppet shows; the keening of Chinese songs; and opium dens displaying their signs on their doors.

SMOKING ROOM

The tinkling of a bell announces the approach of blind beggars. Snake charmers lull their cobras to the sound of their sad, anesthetizing music. An immense spectacle of ever-changing multitudes, repeated a million times: smells, hullabaloo, colors, thirst, filth, the ambience of the Far East.

It is in the European quarter that one sees the seething intermingling of races from remote countries that have stopped in this doorway to the East. Hand in hand walk Singhalese with long hair and long skirts, Hindustanis with naked torsos, women of Malabar with precious stones in their nostrils and ears, Moslems in their truncated headgear. Amid them all, the Sikh policemen, all equally bearded and gigantic. One seldom sees a native Malayan. He has been replaced in all the desirable forms of employment and is now a humble coolie, an unhappy ricksha man. Such is the fate of former pirates: behold the grandsons of the tigers of Malaysia. The heirs to Sandokan have died, or become resigned to their fates; they are wretched in appearance, gone is their heroic mien. I saw the only surviving pirate ship in the

Raffles Museum, a ghost ship from Malayan mythology. From its mastheads hung wooden figures of hanged men; their terrible masks stared toward hell.

Erect dragonflies, policemen direct traffic with wings of cloth falling from each outstretched arm; streetcars and trolleys slip softly across the gleaming asphalt. Everything has an air of corrosion, the sheen of years of dankness. The houses bear great scars of age, of parasitical vegetable growth: everything is spongy, worm-eaten. Walls have been ravaged by fire and water, by the white sun of midday, by the equatorial rain, brief and violent, like a grudgingly given gift.

At the other end of the island of Singapore, separated by a narrow strait, is the sultanate of Johore. For about an hour, the car rolls along the recently opened highway through the jungle. We find ourselves surrounded by a heavy, accumulated silence, by astounding vegetation, the titanic enterprise of the soil. Not a glimpse of sky; the violently green foliage, the impenetrable web of trunks cover everything. Climbing vines resembling the *coille* curl on the breadfruit trees; straight coconut palms, bamboo thick as elephants' legs, reach toward the skies for nourishment. Traveler's-trees open like fans.

But the most extraordinary thing is an auction of wild animals I saw in Singapore. Recently trapped elephants, lithe tigers from Sumatra, fantastic black panthers from Java. The tigers pace in terrifying rage. These are not the aged tigers of circuses, these have a different bearing, a different coloring. One is striped brown like earth, a natural tint only recently part of the jungle. Small elephants doze in a compound like a bullpen; twin disks of gold glint from the jet pelts of the panthers. Four tiger cubs sell for two thousand dollars; a thousand for a gray python twelve meters long. Barking orangutans hurl themselves in fury against the wall of their cage; bears from Malaysia play like children.

And from the oceanic islands, arrayed in fiery plumage, a union of sapphire and saffron, the prize of every ornithologist, a splinter from a glittering quarry, a bird of paradise. Made of light: for no purpose.

Madras, Contemplations at an Aquarium

O NE morning, a Hindu juggler and snake charmer settles himself on the boat. He plays a strident, lugubrious melody on a gourd, and like an echo, a dark serpent with a flattened head coils from a round basket: the dreaded cobra. Bored in its repose, it now tries to strike at the charmer; at times, to the horror of the passengers, it tries to venture onto the bridge. The virtuoso does not stop with the snake: he makes trees grow and birds appear before everyone's eyes: the crescendo of his tricks builds to the point of incredulity.

Madras gives the impression of being a sprawling, spacious city. Low, with large parks and broad streets, it is a mirror image of an English city, then suddenly a pagoda or a temple discloses its ruined architecture, instinctual remnants, darkened traces of an original splendor. Now, for the first time, the poverty of the natives is apparent to the traveler: the first beggars of India advance with stately step and the mien of kings, but their fingers close like pincers on the tiny coin, the anna of nickel; coolies sweat and strain through the streets, dragging heavy cartloads of supplies; one is all too aware that this is a man taking on the harsh burden of the beast, the horse, the ox. As for the oxen, these small Asiatic animals with their long horizontal horns are like toys; they are surely stuffed with sawdust, or they may be apparitions from the bestiary of the temples.

But I want to praise in the most glowing terms the tunics, the dress, of the Hindu women, which I am seeing here for the first time. A single piece of cloth, which then becomes a skirt, and is draped with supernatural grace diagonally around the torso, enveloping the wearers in a single flame of gleaming silk, green, purple, violet, rising from the rings on their feet to the jewels on their arms and necks.

37

This is ancient Greece or Rome—the same air, the same majestic poise, the golden Grecian frets on the cloth, the severity of the Aryan face, seemingly reclaim them from a buried world, purest of creatures, formed of tranquillity and time.

A ricksha carries me along the Marina, the pride of Madras, broad, asphalt-paved, its English gardens interspersed with palm trees, its shoreline the extensive waters of the Gulf of Bengal. Large public complexes dotted with trees, tennis courts with dark-skinned players —more accurately, enthusiasts. Overhead, the sun of the first month of winter, a terrible sun that beats down, unaffected by that cold word "winter." Sweat pours down the cleft of my richsha man's bronze spine; I watch it trickle, thick, glistening threads.

We are on our way to the Marine Aquarium of Madras, famous the world over for its extraordinary specimens. Truly, it is extraordinary.

There are no more than twenty tanks, but they are filled with unexcelled sea monsters. Here are enormous shelled and sedentary fish, buoyant tricolored medusas, canary fish, yellow as sulfur. Here, too, are small, supple, whiskered creatures: lively swimmers that communicate an electric shock to any who touch them; the trochoid dragonet, whose large fins and defensive trappings liken it to a knight at a medieval tourney, with great fringes of protective frills and fans. Butterfly fish glide in their sunny tank, flat as soles, with wide blue and gold bands, and umbrella ribs descending from their spines. Here are fish like zebras, like dominoes, hooded and masked at a submarine ball, in electric blues, frets outlined in vermilion, eyes of precious green stones encrusted in gold. The coiled tails of the sea horses cling to their transported coral.

The sea snakes are impressive. Brown, black, some rise like petrified columns from the bottom of the tank. Others, in an eternal martyrdom of motion, undulate without pause, perpetually.

Here are the sinister cobras of the sea, identical to land cobras, and even more venomous. One survives their bite for a few minutes only and ah, pity the fisherman who captures such sinister treasure in his nocturnal net.

Beside them, in a small grotto, the morays of the Indian Ocean, cruel eels of gregarious nature, forming an indistinct gray knot. It is useless to attempt to separate them, as they scale the tall tanks of the aquarium to rejoin their clan. They are an ugly clump of witches, condemned to torture, moving in restless curves, a true assemblage of visceral monsters.

There are tiny fish only a millimeter long, of just one scale; clever and curious octopuses, living traps; fish that walk on two feet, like humans; fish that dwell in the night of the sea, somber, cloaked in velvet; singing fish whose school gathers at their song; contemporary examples of Angel Cruchaga's fish, a diluvial fish from remote ages. Motionless in the bottoms of the tanks, or whirling in eternal circles, they give the impression of a forgotten, almost human, world: fish with decorations and disguises, warriors, traitors, heroes, they revolve in a mute chorus, desirous of their profound oceanic solitude. They slip and slither, pure matter, color in motion, as beautifully shaped as bullets or coffins.

It is late when I return from this ever-changing museum. In the doorways of their houses, Hindus, squatting on the ground, slowly eat their curry from broad leaves: the women revealing their silver ankle bracelets and bejeweled feet; the men melancholy, smaller and dark, as if crushed by the enormous dusk, the religious pulsations, of India.

On the launches in the semi-darkness of the breakwater, fishermen, with absent, awed expressions, dexterously weave their nets. In each group, one man is reading by flickering lamplight; his reading is a humming, at times slightly wild and guttural; at other times the sound emerges from his lips in an imperceptible prattle. He is reading prayers, sacred praises, ritual legends, Ramayanas.

Beneath his protection, the subjugated and the downtrodden find consolation; reviving cosmic and heroic dreams, they search for paths to oblivion, and food for hope.

Winter in the Ports

I is sad to leave Indochina behind, the land of soft names: Battambang, Berembang, Saigon. From the entire peninsula—not flowered, but fruited—emanates a consistent aroma, a tenacious saturation of custom. How difficult to leave Siam, to say goodbye forever to the ethereal, murmuring night of Bangkok, the dream of its thousand boat-covered canals, its hills, each with its drop of honey, its monumental Khmerian ruin, as graceful as a dancer's body. But even more difficult to leave Saigon, a delicate city filled with enchantment.

This semi-Westernized area is an oasis in the East: one notes the odor of hot coffee, the temperature soft as a woman's skin, and nature, which tends toward the paradisiacal. The opium sold on every street corner, the Chinese firecrackers exploding like machine-gun fire, the French restaurants replete with laughter, salads, and red wine make of Saigon a city of mixed bloods, a city with a perturbing allure. Add to this the Annamese women adorned in silks, kerchiefs forming an adorable headdress, tiny, exquisitely feminine dolls subtly reminiscent of the gynaeceum, gracile as spirits of flowers, approachable and amorous.

But what a violent change those first days on the China Sea, sailing beneath implacable constellations of ice, with a terrible cold raking one's bones.

Disembarking in Kowloon beneath a stony drizzle is something of an event and something of a foray into a land of Eskimos. The passengers shiver in their scarves and mufflers, and the coolies unloading luggage wear, incredibly, Macfarlanes of straw and burlap. They resemble fantastic penguins on some glacial shore. The quivering lights of Hong Kong stud the theater of the hills. At dusk, the tall

American buildings fade somewhat, and an unfathomable multitude of roofs nestle beneath sheets of thick fog.

Kowloon! I gaze upon the streets where only recently Juan Guzmán both absorbed and created a life of decisive solitude, the frightening isolation of a British colony, and the avenues seem to retain something of his writing, something elegant, cold, and somber. But there is a reverberation at the very edge of the waters of the canal: it is Hong Kong, vast, dark, and glittering as a newly harpooned whale, alive with sound, with mysterious exhalations, with incredible whistlings.

And now one finds oneself in the midst of a swarming city of tall gray walls, with no hint of China other than advertisements in that inscrutable alphabet: the tumult of some great Western city—Buenos Aires or London—whose inhabitants have acquired slanted eyes and pallid skin. The multitudes pushing us along in their path are, as a general rule, clothed in enormous overcoats, long to the point of extravagance, or in robes of black silk or satin, beneath which one glimpses heavy protective quilting. In this garb, the people seem ridiculously obese, and the children, whose heads barely protrude from such heavy bundles of clothing, take on a curiously extrahuman, almost hippopotamus-like appearance. Every morning at dawn, a dozen are found dead from the cold of the terrible Hong Kong night, a far-reaching and hostile night that demands its corpses, and to which victims must punctually be sacrificed to nourish its lethal designs.

Shanghai, with its international cabarets, its all-night metropolitan life, and its visible moral turmoil, appears more hospitable and more comfortable.

All the passengers on my ship disembark in Shanghai, the terminal point of their voyage. They come from Norway, from Martinique, from Mendoza. In all the littoral of the Orient there is no greater magnet than this port on the Whangpoo River. Here is our planet's most intense accretion, the densest human tumult, a colossal race and caste system. In its streets one's concentration wanders, one's attention is splintered as one attempts to take in the whole of the noisy wave of humanity, the bustle of the traffic repeated ad infinitum. Countless Chinese alleys empty into the European avenues like boats with extraordinarily colorful sails. In them, that is, in the jungle of hanging cloth that adorns the exterior of the bazaars, one finds at every step a lion of silk or a lotus of jade, the jacket of a mandarin, the pipe of a dreamer. These alleys, bursting with multitudes, a compacted mass of humanity, seem, rather than alleys, the route of an enormous living beast, the slow progress of an elongated, shrieking dragon.

Within the Concessions, the Bund, or financial city, stretches along the river shore, and less than fifty meters away the gray silhouettes of the great fleets of the British, American, and French navies sit low in the water. These severe and menacing presences impose security on the great port. And yet, nowhere is the proximity, the atmosphere, of revolution more noticeable. The iron portals that close each night on the entrance to the Concessions seem much too weak ever to withstand an unleashed avalanche. One is constantly aware of displays of aggression toward foreigners, and the transient Chinese, the ambiguous subject of Nanking and London, here becomes haughty and audacious. My traveling companion, the Chilean Alvaro Hinojosa, is assaulted and robbed on his first evening out. The Shanghai coolie is decidedly insolent to the white man: his Mongolian ferocity seems to crave nourishment in this age of ferocity and blood. The proposal every traveler hears in the Orient a thousand times a day: *Girls! Girls!* in Shanghai becomes insistent; the ricksha man and the taxi driver wage a fierce competition over each client, stripping his luggage clean, of course, with their eyes.

Yet Shanghai refuses to adopt an obscure colonial way of life. Its many lives are pleasure-filled: in the Far East, Shanghai is the very zenith of cabarets and roulette. In spite of that, I find a certain sadness in these night spots. The same monotonous clientele of soldiers and mariners. Dance halls where the bell-bottomed legs of the international sailor are obligatorily pressed against the skirts of the Russian adventuress. Dance halls which, like the salons of deposed kings, are too large, dimly lit; the music doesn't reach into the corners, like a faulty heating system that fails to impart warmth and intimacy.

But, as an insuperable resource for the picturesque, there is the street, the always surprising, magnetic thoroughfares of Asia. What discoveries, what a bag of extravagant tricks, what a setting for exotic colors and customs, in every district. Conveyances, clothing—everything is a strange brew stirred by the marvelous fingers of the absurd.

Taoist priests, mendicant Buddhists, basket vendors, food sellers, jugglers, fortune-tellers, houses of pleasure and tea gardens, itinerant dentists, and also the seignorial covered litters bearing beautiful, smiling women. Each bespeaks one more incommunicable encounter, one more sudden surprise to be added to all the others.

A Dead Man's Name

I met Winter in his haven, in his Late Empire hideaway. I knew him as a legend, then by sight, and, finally, intimately. Why should I be surprised that he is dead? It doesn't surprise me that a woman has children, that an object casts a shadow. The shadow of Winter was mortal, his preferences in life mournful, he was an authentic guest of phantoms, Winter. His vocation for solitude was more intense than that of anyone I have ever known, and his immersion in the spirit world totally isolated him, enveloping him in cold, in celestial vapors. Student of Shadows, Doctor of Deserts!

Don Augusto had very small hands, and eyes like blue water; he was an aristocrat from the North, a true gentleman of an older era. He came to a South of contrasts, a land of rebellious mestizos, of dark-skinned colonists, to a breeding ground of lawless Indians. That's where our delicate Don Augusto lived and grew old. He was surrounded by his books and erudition; and over everything hung a dense curtain of rain and alcoholism. Even in memory, I am terrified by those solitudes! When foul weather is unleashed in that part of the world, the rain seems kin to the devil; the waters of the river and the sea and sky couple, bellowing. A forsaken land where even letters arrive wilted, withered by distances, where hearts petrify and are altered.

All this is bound to my childhood, this and Don Augusto with his age-yellowed beard and his penetrating eyes. To me—so many years ago now—that gentleman, his mournful air, his sorrowful countenance were shrouded in mystery. I watched him every afternoon as he paced along the shore of a dim and shadowy world, his gaze turned inward, as if revisiting interior spaces. Poor, lonely man! Since then, I have seen men who live in great isolation, men depressed by life, not given to action, lost in other horizons. But none like him. No one who had such faith in misfortune, such affinity with oblivion.

Many were the times, while talking with Winter, that I listened to the howling of endless frontier storms. Other times, I saw him as an innocent against the bloody background of the upheaval of elections; then he seemed the archetype of the outlander, Don Augusto, so exceptional, so spotless, amid the hurricane of Araucan Indians and ravaging, galloping riflemen. Against a background of rain, of the lakes of southern Chile, he was more at peace, as he himself resembled this transparent and uneasy element. Behind the curtain of years, years that had slipped into months, weeks, days, into millions of hours in the same spot, grinding and bitter as the tenacity of dripping water. I remember his house, his tobacco, his theosophy, his Catholicism, his atheism, and I see him lying asleep, accompanied by these habits and anxieties. I pay homage to him and, with dread, I cross myself, seeking his blessing: "Begone, terrible solitude!"

There is something of his personality in his poetry, something in that rather meandering cadence, in that glow of patience and patina of age. His poems are like old lace destructively tattered; they are sad, with the musty smell of secret caches.

These poems are ancient eulogies, with a recurrent note, ay! of melancholy waters, a chorus of sorrowful spaces, of long-lost dreams. His poetry is the eternal trickling of a desolate sound, the loss and the restitution of heartrending essences.

But something inside him shivered with untenable desperation. I have seen him racked by uncertainty; both the dove and the scourge fed on his soul. His entire being sought a Destroyer; his sorrowful nature both denied and solicited.

I think about his silent, recumbent body beside the Pacific. Old comrades, lamented comrades!

Contribution to the World
of Apparel

THERE are territories on our planet where apparel flowers. There is a season for such clothing: a spring that lingers, a fabulous summer. The suit, gray companion to business, mundane angel, smiles. It was, to be certain, interminable, that death agony of color; finally, side by side, there was no difference between the multitudes of searing Spain and raining Great Britain. Dark masses all blending together, idolators of the raincoat, idolators of the bowler, encased in lugubrious bureaucratic garb, uniformed under the mandate of cashmere.

This dreary manner of dressing, seemingly inconsequential, has in fact profoundly damaged our sense of the historical, has destroyed the populace's feeling for splendor. Revolution, dethronement, insurrection, conspiracy—a magnificent rosary of events, even today. But it all rings hollow now, dead, smothered beneath the cloth of trousers subjugated by morning coat and umbrella.

Those words, their grand implications, are abdicating, expelled by a mode of dress totally lacking in grandeur. But, doubtlessly, they will return in the future, accompanied by a Dictator of the Robing Room, who with his dictator's heart will adore the magic of Italian opera and will restore its beautiful velvet buskins, knee breeches, and indigo-blue sleeves.

But I want to speak of the Orient, of their perpetual sartorial *saison*. I like the Chinese theater, for example; it seems to be just that: an idealization of raiment, restitution of the marvelous. Everything seems to reflect luxury, splendor of vesture. Many times, and through long hours, I have been present at the unfolding of an improbably slow Chinese drama. As if blown by the insistent, piercing notes of the flute, from the far left emerge characters with exaggeratedly majestic step. They are, in general, benevolent monarchs, venerated rulers adorned to the point of the inexpressible, bales of silks with long white beards, wide sleeves longer than their arms, swords at their waists, a ritual quill box and a handkerchief in their hands. The head is barely visible, as if chopped off, beneath a huge, resplendent headdress made even larger by a crest of plumes; a luminous, vivid, ankle-length robe hangs open to reveal blindingly embroidered breeches. From the shoulders, strips of cloth like ribbons fall to metal and lacquer buskins. This is the personage: he advances with short, ceremonial steps, as if in an ancient dance; he repeatedly tosses back his head, stroking his long beard; he steps back, he turns, as if to display the riches of the reverse side of his robes. Finally, the incarnation of solemnity, he crosses the stage, armed with a shield, a stupendous, supernatural mannequin in crimson and yellow. Then this monstrous silk phantom disappears, yielding the stage to others even more dazzling.

Often these wordless processions, these pure exhibitions of sartorial finery, last for long periods of time. Every movement, every shading of the personage's gait is devoured and digested by a public avid for the marvelous. The theatrical objective, undoubtedly, has been achieved in exalting the importance of vesture; the extravagance displayed on the actor's body has given anxiety and pleasure to a multitude.

The ordinary Chinese man on the street wears simple, uncomely clothes: a jacket and trousers; the Chinese workingman, an ant in an anthill, fades into the crowd in his common uniform; he appears worn down, polished thin by the labor of centuries, his very body as smooth as a hammer grip. And so the phantasmagorical stage enriches his life, this prodigious puppetry seemingly favors its masters.

I still recall my first impression when several months ago in Colombo I saw my first Hindustani women. They were beautiful, but that isn't the point. I adored their garments from the first moment I saw them. Those robes in which color seems to flow like oil or flame. The gown is simply a long tunic called a sari, which is wound and folded several times at the waist; it falls to the feet, almost entirely veiling the gait, the ankle bangles, the naked heels; this tunic is then draped over the shoulder with secure solemnity, and, among the women of Bengal, is worn around the head to frame the face. It creates a severe, peplum-like effect; like the chlamys, a vestige of an unquestionably serene antiquity. But its life comes primarily from its color, a vivacity of color for which words are pallid. Sulfurous green, amaranth—lifeless words; actually, these are purity, color seen for the first time. Adolescent legs wrapped in cloth of fire, a dark shoulder concealed in a wave of light combed into a long black twist in which a bejeweled rose glitters—these remain for a long time in one's memory, like passionate ghosts.

Now, Hindustani attire is inherent to their condition of nobility and tranquillity. No one wears it better than Tagore; I have seen him, and clad in his wheat-colored tunic, he was God the Father himself. The poet was playing his part in this half-didactic, half-sacred obligation of ours. I shook hands with the aged poet, majestic of raiment, august of beard.

In Burma, where I am writing this leisurely recollection, color is equated with clothing. Man wraps himself in multicolored skirts, his head in a rose-colored scarf. He wears a short dark Chinese-style jacket, very plain, without lapels; from the waist up, he is a Mongolian torero. But his lungi, his skirt, is gleaming, extraordinary, extreme; it is carmine, sorrel-colored, vermilion blue. The streets of Mandalay, the avenues, the bazaars of Rangoon seethe perpetually with dazzling tints. Amid the colorful crowds stroll the *ponyls*, the mendicant Buddhist priests, as serious as men risen from the dead, dressed in airy, vividly sulfur, sacredly yellow tunics. The throng is like a day strung with bright banners, a walking paint box; for the first time I need to call on the word "kaleidoscopic."

Here in Burma the women smoke cigars and display long cylindrical hairdos into which are tucked the ubiquitous flowers of the padauk. Since the overthrow of the Burmese dynasty, dancing girls have worn the apparel of princesses, white with jewels, indescribable, overlapping squares of cloth at the hips; these embellishments are a vital part of the athletic contortions of the popular *pue*, and make even more exotic the ineffable movements that constitute its mortal tensions.

Frequently, in this tumultuous garden of apparel, in this season of variegated dress, one sees combinations of the grotesque and the capricious. This is a park of surprises, a hothouse of vivid essences, and one's attention is absorbed in an ocean of unexpected variations, excellent and instantaneous experiments in the audacious; even, at times, beautiful nudes.

I remember once on the outskirts of Semarang, in Java, having come upon a pair of Malayan dancers performing before a sparse audience. She was a child; she wore a corselet, a sarong, and a tin crown. He was old, he followed her, moving his toes in the manner of Malayan dancers; a mask of red lacquer covered his face, and he carried a long wooden knife. Often, sleeping, I see again that sad dance in the suburbs of Semarang.

The fact is, I had found my mode of attire. I wanted to dress as a masked dancer; I wanted to be called Michael.

The Jungle of Ceylon

Felicitous shore! A coral reef stretches parallel to the beach; there the ocean interposes in its blues the perpetual white of a rippling ruff of feathers and foam; the triangular red sails of the sampans; the unmarred line of the coast on which the straight trunks of the coconut palms rise like explosions, their brilliant green Spanish combs nearly touching the sky.

Crossing the island in an almost straight line in the direction of Trincomalee, the landscape becomes dense, earth-dominated; human beings and their belongings disappear; the immutable, impenetrable jungle replaces everything. Trees knot in clumps, aiding or destroying one another, and as they meld together they lose their contours, so one travels as if through a low, thick, vegetal tunnel, through a frightening world of chaotic and violent cabbages.

Herds of elephants cross the road one by one; small jungle rabbits leap frantically, fleeing from the automobile; perfect little wild hens and cocks are everywhere; fragile blue birds of paradise appear and flee.

By night, our vehicle travels silently through the perfumes and shadows of the jungle. All around us, the blazing eyes of surprised beasts, eyes like flames of alcohol; it is the night of the jungle, seething with instincts, hungers, and desires. We shoot wild boar, beautiful leopards, and deer. They stop in their tracks before the headlights, making no attempt to flee, as if disoriented, and then fall, disappearing among the branches; the downed animal is dragged to the car, damp and magnificent with dew and blood, smelling of foliage and of death.

In the deep jungle, there is a silence like that of libraries: abstract and humid.

At times, we hear the trumpeting of wild elephants or the familiar howling of the jackal. At times, a shot from a hunter's gun rings out, then fades, swallowed by the silence as water swallows a stone.

Also reposing in the middle of the jungle, and overrun by it, lie the ruins of mysterious Singhalese cities: Anuradhapura, Polonnaruwa, Mihintale, Sigiriya, Dambulla. The gray shells of narrow stone columns buried for twenty centuries peer through the vegetation, tumbled statues and stairways, enormous ponds and palaces that have returned to the earth, to their progenitors long forgotten. Even so, beside those scattered stones in the shadow of the enormous pagodas of Anuradhapura, the moonlit night is filled with kneeling Buddhists, and the ancient prayers return to Singhalese lips.

The tragedy of the rock of Sigiriya comes to mind as I write. In the deep heart of the jungle rises an enormous and precipitous hill or rock, accessible only by insecure, risky gradins carved into the great stone; and on its heights, the ruins of a palace, and marvelous Sigiriyan frescoes still intact in spite of the centuries. Fifteen hundred years ago a King of Ceylon, a parricide, sought asylum from his avenging brother on the summit of this terrible mountain of stone. There, in his image and likeness, he constructed his isolated castle of remorse. With his queens and his warriors and his artists and his elephants, he climbed the rock and remained there for twenty years, until his implacable brother arrived to kill him.

On all the planet there is no site as desolate as Sigiriya. The gigantic rock with its tenuous, interminable, carved stairways and its sentry posts forever divested of sentinels; above, the remains of the palace, the audience chambers of the monarch with his throne of black stone, and, everywhere, ruins of what once had been, covered now in vegetation and oblivion; and, from the heights, nothing around us for leagues and leagues but the impenetrable jungle; nothing, no human being, not one hut, not one flicker of life, nothing but the dark, thick, oceanic jungle.

Orient, Origin

I find it very strange that "exotic" writers should speak in such glowing terms of the tropical regions of the Orient. There is no part of the world less deserving of allegoric or panegyric effusions; these lands require little more than constant awareness and unwavering attention. A great aura of fire, of dazzling vegetal life, has reduced man to a minuscule plane. In India, the human being is part of the landscape; there is no discontinuity between man and nature as in the contemporary West. The great cultural epochs of the intermediate or Brahman East did not sever man's roots, or flower in his stead, as was the case with Christianity. Rather, those periods stand like monumental walls, with little relation to human ills, but as powerful tributes to an all-encompassing mystery.

One is always aware of the presence of a remote past behind the cults and ceremonies of the East, and this past remains vital and charged with authority. The gods, then, are but a superior caste, which, though no longer present, continues to decree and direct from that active past, as from an invisible but not very distant city peopled with authoritarian beings. Power infuses them with infernal poisons, and, as happens with human beings, such gods are sexual and sanguinary.

Yes, only time can construct idols, and what is remote is immediately divine. Origins and eternity are antithetical qualities, the living being is immersed in the spontaneous, in the creative and destructive, while lives that endure continue on in limbo, with no possibility of beginning or end. Never lost, yet at the same time losing itself, the being returns to the origin of its creation, "as the drop of seawater returns to the sea," the Katha Upanishad tells us. To participate in the divine, to return to that indestructible energy, is that not a germ of the impossible, of ominous doctrinaire obscurities?

So then, as if suddenly wounded by this overwhelming remoteness, man has fallen, diminishing his individual intelligence and increasing his instinctive powers, apprehensive in the presence of a possible evasion or a creative spark that would attract new conflicts and disorder to his existence. Hindu societies are a decomposed detritus, but their decomposition is natural—vegetal and animal fermentation, reproduction and death.

In contrast, nothing more frenetic, grandiose, and cruel than the gods. It is depressing to see in Hindu temples the authority of the miserable dark Brahmans humbled by superhuman idolatry, crawling beneath the enormous doors and stone columns. The past has pierced their hearts, reducing them to insignificance.

Hence the outward repulsiveness of Indian societies. There man has not undertaken to be divine, like the modern Occidental; rather, he has left divinity entirely to the gods, in a tragic division from mortal labors.

I have no compulsion to write about India and Burma and Ceylon; so many causes and origins seem hidden from me, so many phenomena still unexplained. Everything seems in ruins, in disintegration; but, in fact, powerful, elemental, and vital ties unite these appearances with almost secret, almost eternal bonds.

The Fire of Friendship

Introduction to the Poetry
of Angel Cruchaga

No man who swears like a trooper, no man who weeps with great emotion, has ever been forbidden entrance to the pantheon of the poetic muses. But the man who laughs, that man must remain outside.

The dwelling of our Mistress Muses is hung with acidulous tapestries, and usually the Ladies go about garbed in mournful organdies. The walls of this somber abode are hard and crystalline, like vertical congealed water. And the harvest of their gardens does not reveal summer's hand but, rather, the depths of their dark mystery.

One needs a similar attitude, must make a similar sacrifice, if one is to visit the estate of Angel de Cruchaga y de Santa María, meet his many angels, and digest his obdurate and lugubrious food.

Like a tolling of black bells, with a prophetic and diametrical trembling and sound, the words of this magus cut across the solitudes of Chile, absorb from the atmosphere various qualities of superstition and rain. Acquisitions and age have transfigured him, clothing him every day in more somber garb, so that, if suddenly seen at night in his House, sinisterly stripped of mortal attributes, he would without doubt resemble the statue erected at the entrance to the final abode.

Like rings of atmosphere at the coming of an autumn dawn, the poems of Angel come to one frozen in an icy clarity, with a certain extraterrestrial or sublunar quivering, clad, as it were, in the skin of the stars. Like a nebulous coffer of embroideries and almost-abstract jewels, still dazzlingly bright, that produce an unhealthy sadness, they seem to adapt immediately to what one has seen and felt before, to the ancient and the bitter, to darkly sensitive roots that pierce the soul, leaving there all their dolorous needs and painful oblivion.

These sweet and phenomenal coffers of Angel's poetry contain, more than any other thing, the blue eyes of women long disappeared, eyes large and cold as the eyes of some rare fish, and capable still of flashing glances as far-reaching as the rainbow. Definitively stellar substances, comets, an occasional star, slow-moving celestial phenomena have left their heavenly aroma there and, at the same time, the smell of used adornments, rich carpets worn thin, yellowed roses, old addresses that betray the motionless passage of time. Objects in this astral empire are warmly feminine; they gyrate in circles of dark splendor, like the bodies of beautiful drowned women floating in stagnant water, awaiting the ceremonies of the poet.

The living and the dead of Cruchaga are characterized by an overwhelming disposition toward death, they have lived so purely, hands somberly crossed upon their breasts, in such a crepuscular atmosphere, behind such an abundance of stained glass, at such an unhurried corporeal pace, that they most closely resemble water plants, dank and motionless florescences.

Episcopal colors and changes of light alternate in Cruchaga's dwelling, and this duality of lights repeats itself in an eternal ritual. In the atrium of the angels there is no sound or movement of dance, but a silent populace with often shadowy voices and masks. From one boundary to another, the movement of the air repeats sounds and moans in a despairing, muffled chorus.

Illness and dream, divine creatures, a blending of boredom and solitude, and the aromas of certain flowers and certain countries and continents, have found in the rhetoric of Angel a more ecstatic home than in the world of accustomed reality. His geographical mythology and the silvery names like veins of cold fire weave through the matrix of the stone of his favorite, his only, statue.

And among the repeated mystic symbols of this desolate work, I occasionally feel him brush by me, acting upon my surroundings with infinite dominion.

Batavia, Java, February 1931

Federico García Lorca

How does one dare select one name to stand out from all the others amid the vast forest of our dead! The humble tillers of Andalusia, murdered by enemies older than memory, the dead miners in Asturias, the carpenters, the bricklayers, the salaried workers in city and country, as well as each of the thousands of murdered women and slaughtered children, each of these fiery shadows has the right to appear before you as witness from a great unhappy land, and each, I believe, has a place in your hearts, if you are free of injustice and evil. All of these terrible shadows have names in our memories, names of fire and loyalty, pure names as ordinary, as ancient and noble, as the names "salt" and "water." Like salt and water they have again become one with the earth, one with the infinite name of the earth. Because the sacrifices, the sorrows, the purity and strength of the people of Spain are at the heart of this purifying struggle—more than in any other struggle—in a wintry panorama of plains and wheat and rocks against the background of a harsh planet for which snow and blood are competing.

Yes, how dare choose one name, one alone, among so many who have been silenced? Because the name I am going to utter among you holds in its dark syllables such mortal richness, is so weighted and so fraught with significance, that to utter it is to utter the names of all those who fell defending the very essence of his poems, for he was the sonorous defender of Spain's heart. Federico García Lorca! He was as much a part of the people as a guitar, happy and melancholy, as profound and lucid as a child, as the people. If one had searched

---

This speech was delivered in Paris in 1937

diligently, scouring step by step every inch of the land for someone to sacrifice, to sacrifice as a symbol, one could not have found in anyone or in anything, to the degree it existed in this man who was chosen, the essence of Spain, its vitality and its profundity. Yes, they chose well, those who as they shot him aimed at the heart of the race. They chose him in order to subjugate and martyr Spain, to drain her very essence, to stifle her most intense breath, to silence her most indestructible laughter. The two irreconcilable Spains were on trial in this death: the black and green Spain of the dreadful, diabolical cloven hoof, subterranean Spain, damned Spain, the crucifying and poisonous Spain of the great dynastic and ecclesiastical crimes; and confronting that Spain, the Spain radiant with vital pride and spirit, the meteoric Spain of intuition, of tradition, and discovery, the Spain of Federico García Lorca.

He lies dead, offered like an orange blossom, like a wild guitar, beneath the soil his murderers kicked over his wounded body; but, like his poetry, his people defend themselves, erect and singing, while from their soul pours a torrent of blood, thus to remain forever in the memory of man.

It is difficult to be specific about García Lorca's memory. The violent light of life illuminated only for a moment his face, wounded now, extinguished. But during that long moment of his life, his body shone with sunlight. Since the time of Góngora and Lope, Spain has not seen such creative élan, such flexibility of form and language; and since the time when the Spaniards in small villages kissed the hem of Lope de Vega's habit, the Spanish language has not had a poet who so totally enchanted the people. Everything he touched, even at the level of the mysteries of aestheticism—which as a learned poet he could not renounce without betraying something of himself—everything he touched rang with the profound essences of sounds that reached something fundamental among the people. When I say aestheticism, let us understand one another: García Lorca was an anti-aesthete, in the sense that he filled his poetry and his plays with human dramas and tempests of the heart, but not in the sense that he renounced the earliest secrets of the mystery of poetry. The people, with their marvelous intuition, claim his poetry, and it is still sung today as folk poetry in the villages of Andalusia. But he did not flatter himself about this propensity, or use it to his own benefit; far from it: he searched avidly both outside and within himself.

García Lorca's anti-aestheticism may be the origin of his enormous popularity in America. Of the brilliant generation of poets like Alberti, Aleixandre, Altolaguirre, Cernuda, and others, he was perhaps the only one upon whom the shadow of Góngora had not exercised its icy influence, which aesthetically sterilized the writing of the great young poets of Spain. America, separated by an ocean and by centuries from the classical fathers of the language, recognized the greatness of this young poet who was irresistibly attracted to the people and to blood. Three years ago in Buenos Aires I witnessed the greatest manifestation of appreciation that a poet of ours has ever received; enormous crowds listened with emotion and tears to his tragedies of astounding verbal opulence. In his language the eternal drama of Spain was renewed, acquiring a new and phosphorescent brilliance; love and death dancing a frenetic dance, love and death, masked or naked.

To sketch his memory, his photograph, at this distance in time, is impossible. Physically, he was a flash of lightning, energy in continuous, rapid motion, happiness, resplendence, a totally superhuman tenderness. His person was magic and dark, and he carried happiness with him.

By a curious and persistent coincidence, the two major young poets of greatest reknown in Spain, Alberti and García Lorca, resembled one another greatly, to the brink of rivalry. Both were Dionysian Andalusians, musical, exuberant, secret, and of the people. Both exhausted the origins of Spanish poetry, the millenary folklore of Andalusia and Castile, gradually channeling their writing from the ethereal and pastoral grace of the beginnings of the language to the mastery of grace, and the initiation into the thickets of the dramas of Spain. Then they parted. While one, Alberti, devotes himself with unstinting generosity to the cause of the oppressed, and lives only in the service of his magnificent revolutionary faith, the other in his literature turns more and more toward his land, toward Granada, to return there with his whole heart, to die there. There was no true rivalry between them; they were good and brilliant brothers, and we saw that the last time Alberti returned from Russia and Mexico, in the great celebration that was held in his honor in Madrid, when

Federico, on behalf of each of us, spoke such magnificent words about him. A few months later, García Lorca left for Granada. And there, through a strange twist of fate, death awaited him, the death that the enemies of the people had reserved for Alberti. Without forgetting our great dead poet, let us for a second remember our great living comrade, Alberti, who with other poets like Serrano Plaja, Miguel Hernández, Emilio Prados, Antonio Aparicio is at this moment in Madrid defending the cause of his people and his poetry.

But in Federico social restiveness took other forms more closely related to his Moorish minstrel's soul. With his troupe, La Barraca, he traveled the byways of Spain, performing the great forgotten theater of other centuries: Lope de Rueda, Lope de Vega, Cervantes. The ancient ballads and chivalric tales, dramatized, were returned by him to the pure heart from which they had sprung. The most remote corners of Castile knew his performances. Through him, the Andalusians, the Asturians, the Extremadurans once again communed with the master poets who'd been asleep only briefly in their hearts, so that the spectacle filled them with astonishment, but not surprise. Neither the ancient costumes nor the archaic language shocked those peasants, who often had never seen an automobile or heard a phonograph. For, through the tremendous, the fantastic poverty of the Spanish peasants—men that I, even I, have seen reduced to living in caves and eating herbs and reptiles—passed this magic whirlwind of poetry carrying, along with the dreams of ancient poets, grains of explosive dissatisfaction with their way of life.

In those dying provinces he saw the incredible misery in which the privileged kept their people. With the peasants he endured a winter in the open fields and sere hills, and the tragedy caused his southern heart to tremble in great sorrow.

I now recall a story about him. Some months ago he set out again through the small towns. They were planning to perform Lope de Vega's *Peribáñez*, and Federico went ahead to search the most remote areas of Extremadura in hopes of finding any authentic seventeenth-century garments that old peasant families might have stored in their chests. He returned with a marvelous bundle of blue and gold cloth, of shoes and beads, raiment that had come to light for the first time in centuries. It was his irresistible charm that had obtained it.

One night in a village in Extremadura he was unable to sleep, and arose as dawn was approaching. The harsh Extremaduran countryside was still covered in mist. Federico sat down beside some toppled statues to watch the sunrise. They were marble figures from the eighteenth century and they lay at the entrance to a feudal lord's estates, which were abandoned, as are so many of the holdings of the great Spanish lords. Federico was gazing at the broken torsos, their whiteness inflamed by the rising run, when a tiny lamb that had strayed from its flock began to graze nearby. Suddenly a half dozen black swine crossed the road and fell on the lamb, and in minutes, to his terror and surprise, they had torn it to pieces and devoured it. Federico, prey to an inexpressible fear, immobilized by horror, watched as the black swine killed and devoured the lamb among the fallen statues in the light of that solitary dawn.

When he told me about it on his return to Madrid, his voice still trembled; because of his childlike sensitivity, the tragedy of the death obsessed him to the point of delirium. Now his death, his terrible death that nothing can erase from our memories, recalls that bloody dawn. Perhaps to that great, sweet, prophetic poet, life offered in advance, through a terrible symbol, the vision of his own death.

I have sought to bring before you the memory of our great lost comrade. Many may have expected from me tranquil, poetic words remote from earth and war. To many people the very word Spain bears enormous anguish mixed with grave hope. I have not wished to increase that anguish, or to upset your hopes, but having only recently come from Spain, I, a Latin American, Spanish by race and by language, am unable to speak of anything except its misfortunes. I am not a political man, nor have I ever taken part in political contention, but my words, which many would have wished to be neutral, have been colored by passion. You must understand, understand that we, the poets of Spanish America and the poets of Spain, cannot forget or ever forgive the murder of the one we know to be the greatest among us, the guiding spirit of this moment in our language. Forgive also that among all the sorrows of Spain I have reminded you only of the life and death of one poet. We can never forget this crime, or forgive it. We shall not forget it and we shall never forgive it. Never.

Literary Friendships and Enmities

Nᴏᴛ by the stars alone . . .

It has probably not been the lot of any other writer in this part of the world to unleash such envy as has been vented on my own literary reputation. There are people who make their living from this profession, from envying me, from writing strange things about me in twisted and tenacious pamphlets and highly colorful reviews. Somewhere in my travels I lost this singular collection. I have left small pamphlets strewn behind me in faraway rooms, in other climes. In Chile I am again filling a suitcase with this endemic and phosphorescent leprosy, still ignoring the vicious adjectives that attempt to annihilate me. In other countries these things don't happen to me. But yet I return. The fact is that I love my country blindly, love all the green and bitter savor of its sky and its mud. And what love is mine to have means more to me here, and this extravagant and mystic hatred that surrounds me nourishes everything I own with necessary and fertilizing excrement. Man does not live by the stars alone.

Spain, the moment I stepped upon her soil, offered me the hands of her poets, her loyal poets, and with them I shared bread and wine in the unqualified friendship of the central years of my life. I have a vivid memory of those first hours, and years, in Spain, and I often miss the affection of my comrades.

Published in *Qué Hubo*, Santiago, April 20, 1940

VICENTE ALEIXANDRE

In a neighborhood filled with flowers, between Cuatro Caminos and the developing University City, on Wellingtonia Street, lives Vicente Aleixandre.

He is a big man, fair-haired and rosy. He has been ill for years. He never leaves his house. He is virtually an invalid.

His profound and marvelous poetry is the revelation of a world dominated by mysterious forces. He is Spain's most secret poet; the submerged splendor of his verses somewhat resembles those of our Rosamel del Valle.

Each week he awaits me, on a fixed day that for him, in his solitude, is a holiday. We speak only of poetry. Aleixandre cannot go to the cinema. He knows nothing of politics.

I set him apart from all other friends because of the infinite purity of his friendship. In the isolated sphere of his home, poetry and life acquire a sacred transparency.

I bring to him the life of Madrid, the venerable poets I discover in the countless bookshops on Atocha, my tours through the markets where I harvest huge bunches of celery or chunks of Manchegan cheese anointed with oil from the Levant. He is filled with enthusiasm for my wanderings, the long walks on which he cannot accompany me through narrow, cool Cava Baja Street, a street of coopers and ropemakers, all golden from the wood and the fiber.

Or for long periods we read Pedro de Espinosa, Soto de Rojas, Villamediana. In them we searched for the magical and physical elements that make Spanish poetry, in a courtly era, a persistent and vital current of clarity and mystery.

MIGUEL HERNÁNDEZ

What has become of Miguel Hernández? Now priests and the Civil Guard are "directing" culture in Spain. Eugenio Montes and Pemán are now great figures, and they are well suited to stand beside the renegade Millán Astray, for it is none other than he who presides over the new literary society of Spain. Meanwhile, Miguel Hernández, the great young peasant poet, if not shot and buried, is probably in prison, or wandering through the mountains.

Before Miguel arrived in Madrid I had read his *autos sacramentales*, those astounding verbal constructions. In Orihuela, Miguel was a goatherd, and the priest there lent him Catholic books, which he read and thoroughly absorbed.

Thus it happens that the greatest of the new creators of political poetry is the greatest new poet of Spanish Catholicism. He was about to return home following a second visit to Madrid, but during a visit in my home, I convinced him to stay. So he remained, very much a country boy in Madrid, very much the outsider, with his potato face and shining eyes.

My great friend Miguel, how I love you, and how I respect and love your strong, youthful poetry. Where you may be at this moment, in prison, on the road, dead, is of no consequence; no jailer, no Civil Guard, no murderer can still your voice now that it has been heard—your voice, which was the voice of your people.

RAFAEL ALBERTI

I knew Rafael Alberti before I went to Spain. I received his first letter more than ten years ago in Ceylon. He wanted to print my book *Residencia en la tierra*. He carried it on many trips, from Moscow to Liguria, and, especially, he spread it through all Madrid. From Rafael's original, Gerardo Diego made three copies. Rafael was indefatigable. All the poets in Madrid heard my verses, read by him on his terrace on Urquijo Street.

Everyone—Bergamín, Serrano Plaja, Petere, and many, many others—knew me before I arrived. Thanks to Rafael Alberti, I had staunch friends before I ever met them.

Since that time, Rafael and I have been, to state it simply, brothers. Our lives have been intertwined, stirring together our poetry and our destinies.

This young master of contemporary Spanish literature, this irreproachable revolutionary of poetry and politics, should come to Chile, should bring his strength, his happiness, and his generosity to our country. He should come so we can sing together. There is a lot of singing to be done here. With Rafael and Roces we could make a formidable chorus. Alberti sings the *tamborileiro*, the "Ebro Pass," and other songs of happy times and of war, better than anyone I know.

Rafael Alberti is the most impassioned poet it has been my lot to know. Like Paul Eluard, he and poetry are never far apart. He can recite by memory Góngora's *Primera soledad*, and, in addition, long portions of Garcilaso and Rubén Darío and Apollinaire and Mayakovsky.

It may be that, among other things, Rafael Alberti will write the pages of his life that it has been our lot to share. In them, as in everything he does, will shine his splendid, fraternal heart and his very Spanish hierarchical spirit, precise and central within the diamantine and absolute structure of his now classic writing.

DISPATCH: TO ARTURO SERRANO PLAJA
AND VICENTE SALAS VIU

You are the only friends from my literary life in Spain who have ever come to my country. It would have pleased me to bring them all here, and I have not given up trying. I will try to bring them, from Mexico, from Buenos Aires, from Santo Domingo, from Spain.

It was not only the war that united us, but poetry as well. I brought to you in Madrid my simple American heart and a bouquet of poems that you have kept with you.

You, how many of you! all of you, have done so much to clarify my thinking, have given me a singular and translucent friendship. And I have quietly helped many of you with confidential problems, before, during, and following the war.

But you have helped me even more.

You have shown me a happy and carefully nurtured friendship, though your intellectual decorum at first amazed me: I had come from the crude envy of my country, from torment. When you accepted me as one of you, you gave such a sense of security, such meaning to my life, and to my poetry, that I went with serenity to join the struggle among the ranks of the people. Your friendship and your nobility helped me more than any treatise. And even now, I recognize this simple road as the only road for intellectuals. Let the envious, the resentful, the embittered, the evil, the megalomaniacs, not join with the people.

Let them keep to their side.

With us, my Spanish friends and brothers, only the pure, the fraternal, the honorable . . . our own.

César Vallejo Is Dead

In Europe, spring is burgeoning over still another unforgettable friend among the dead: our greatly admired, our greatly beloved César Vallejo. By this time in Paris he would have had his window open, that pensive brow of Peruvian stone absorbing the sounds of France, of the world, of Spain . . . Old warrior of hope, old friend. Is it possible? And what can we do in this world to be worthy of your silent, enduring work, of your private, essential growth? In recent years, brother, your body, your soul, longed for American soil, but the flames in Spain held you in France, where no one was more alien. Because you were the American specter—Indian-American, as you preferred to say—of our martyred America, a specter mature in its liberty and its passion. There was something of a mine about you, of a lunar excavation, something earthily profound.

"He rendered homage to his long hunger," Juan Larrea wrote me. Long hunger, it doesn't seem true. Long hunger, long solitude, long leagues of your voyage pondering the question of mankind, of injustice upon this earth, of the cowardice of half of mankind. The tragedy of Spain was gnawing at your soul. That soul already corroded by your own spirit, so stripped, so wounded, by your own asceticism. Every day the tragedy of Spain bored into your boundless virtue. You were a great man, Vallejo. You were private and great, like a glorious palace of subterranean stone with a great, mineral silence and copious essences of time and matter. And deep within, the implacable fire of your spirit, coal and ashes . . .

A toast, great poet; a toast, my brother.

Published in *Aurora*, Santiago, August 1, 1938

To Eduardo Carranza

Dᴇᴀʀ Eduardo, poet of Colombia:

When through the years my thoughts have turned to Colombia, I have seen in my mind your vast green and sylvan land, seen the river Cauca swollen by Mary's tears, and, hovering over all your lands and rivers, like handkerchiefs of celestial velvet, the extraordinary butterflies of the Amazon, the butterflies of Muzo. I always see your country through a light of butterfly blue, beneath that wave of ultraviolet wings. I see your villages beneath a trembling whirring of wings, and then I see the history of Colombia trailing a comet of blue butterflies: your great captains, Santander and Bolívar, with a luminous butterfly poised like a dazzling epaulet on each shoulder, and your poets, whether unfortunate, like José Asunción and Porfirio, or proud, like Valencia, pursued to the ends of their lives by a butterfly they then left forgotten on a hat or in a sonnet, a butterfly that fluttered away when Silva consummated his romantic suicide, later to alight, perhaps, upon your brow, Eduardo Carranza.

Because you are the brow of Colombian poetry, that Colombia of a thousand brows, that sonorous land, ringing with the secret songs of virginal groves and the soaring, magnanimous hymn of Colombian poetry. Beneath the soil of your native land, the mysterious matrix of the emerald was formed, and poetry rose in the air like a column of crystal.

Allow me today to recall that fraternity of poets I had the pleasure of knowing and coming to love. You, mad Colombian that you are, would like all your friends to be with us at this gathering. Well, then,

This speech was delivered in Santiago, June 1, 1946

look; see the prodigal Scandinavian gentleman just entering through that door: it's León de Greiff, the lofty, choral voice of America. And there, beyond him, that great squanderer of coffee, life, and libraries: it's Arturo Camacho Ramírez, Dionysiac and revolutionary. Here is Carlos Martín, who just now fished up from some alligator-infested bend of his native river three poems still drenched with exotic blooms. Here comes Ciro Mendía, recently arrived from Medellín; you recognize him by his noble sailor's bearing and the sylvan lyre under his arm. And finally here is your great brother Jorge Rojas, great of body and great of heart, just emerged from his frosted poetry, from his epic submarine mission where his victories were crowned with salt of the most difficult provenance.

But here, tonight, you represent each of the beloved friends who cannot be with us.

In your poetry, congealing into a thousand rosettes, are crystalized the geometrical lines of your poetic tradition, and, along with its vigor, a sentimental, emotional air that touches every leaf of the American Montparnasse, an air of life and melancholy, of farewell and arrival, the savor of gentle love and the sweet grape.

Today you have come to our hurricane-swept land, to the oceanic storm of our poetry, to a poetry whose only norm is vital exploration, a poetry that from Gabriela Mistral and Angel Cruchaga to the newest of our poets covers our sands and forests and chasms and paths like a Greek mantle whipped by the fury of our marine wind.

With this unusual embrace and with this joyous celebration we receive you into our hearts, and we do so in the awareness that you are an honorable laborer in the laboratory of America, and that your crystalline goblet also belongs to us, because in it you have placed a vivid mirror of transparency and dream.

When I came to your native Colombia, your brothers and your companions welcomed me, and I remember that amid the chorus of that powerful fraternity, one of the youngest and most esteemed among you reproached me, in language of unparalleled dignity, for the most recent stage of my life and my poetry, which I consecrate with an iron will to the future of man and to the struggle of the people.

I scarcely responded, but I do so by being here before you, so that you see how naturally my poetic vocation and my political conduct converge. I did not answer him, because I constantly answer with my poems and my actions the many questions people ask me and the questions I ask myself. But perhaps I could answer them all by saying that in this bloody battle we wage, we are defending, among other things of purity, a pure poetry. That is, the future freedom of the poet, so that in a happy world—yes, that is the point—in a world where there are no rags, no hunger, their most secret and most deeply buried songs may burst free.

So, then, in my journey through Colombia, I did not turn away from the expressions of your aesthetic concepts, but, rather, I absorbed your inquiries, your problems, and your myths. I walked into your large and beautiful reception halls, and as the spreading dusk of Colombia filtered through the windows, I felt I had become rich among your precious jewels, and luminous in your diamantine light.

So, too, now that you have come to live and sing among us, I ask in the name of our poetry—from the tiny, naked feet of Gabriela's poem, and from the poems of Víctor Domingo Silva that so recently told the sorrows of a suffering people—today I ask that you not deny your inevitable destiny, that you set aside something from your bursting treasure chests for your people, who are also our people. Sailors on the ships of your great rivers, the black fishermen along your shore, your salt and emerald miners, the poorly housed peasants on your coffee plantations, each of them has a claim on your thoughts, your consideration, and your poetry, and what a great gift you will make to us Chileans if during your stay in our southern land, as beautiful and as sorrowful as all our America, you become steeped in the dark sorrows of the people we love, for whose liberation your courageous, fertile, and resplendent poetry will do battle tomorrow.

Enough of words, though they carry with them all our affection. Today is a festive day in your heart, and in this hall. Today, on a street in Santiago, within four Chilean walls, your son was born. Please express our affection to your sweet wife, Rosita Coronado. And to you we offer this celebration, with the paper flowers we ourselves have fashioned, with guitars and the wine of autumn, with the names of some of those we revere in your country, and with the flame of friendship that you have lighted between your country and ours, the flame you must bear on high, between stone and sky. May it never be extinguished.

Rafael Alberti and
María Teresa León

It was here that some years ago I began to speak about Spain, traveling through every town, through every nook and cranny of America, telling of the Spain that yesterday was ravaged and deeply wounded and today is, once again, forgotten and betrayed.

Today I am proud to present to you this twofold glory, this Spanish couple upon whose gilded brows blaze the aurora and the agony of their country, writ in indelible, fiery letters on the soil of Chile.

Rafael Alberti, first poet of Spain, exemplary soldier, my brother:

I never imagined, amid the flowers and gunpowder of peace and war in Madrid, amid festivity and bursting shells, in the steely air of the Castilian plain, that someday I would be standing here handing you the keys to our snow-encircled capital, and opening to you the oceanic, Andean doors of this land that centuries ago Don Alonso de Ercilla left enriched and sowed and spangled with his powerful ultramarine poetry.

María Teresa, I never imagined, when we so often broke bread and shared wine in your hospitable home, that it was to be my good fortune to offer to you in my country the bread, the wine, and the friendship of all Chileans.

Because all of us were awaiting you, Rafael and María Teresa. My people have esteemed you, not only as proud and unsurpassed intellectuals, but as pilgrims from a country isolated by blood and hatred.

No people in America felt the misfortunes of Spain as deeply as our people, and none has remained as loyal as we to your struggle and your hope. Try to forget, María Teresa and Rafael, the governments

---

This speech was delivered in Santiago in 1946

that so easily align themselves with the universal compromise of cowardice; for, as you enter Chile, you may knock at the door or at the breast of any Chilean, and the heart of a people who have never recognized Franco will welcome you. This is what every man and woman, young and old citizen of my country will tell you, even the stones on the roadways, on which the hands of the people have scribbled, with a conscience more refined than that of any Labor Minister, their curses against Franco and their impassioned love for the people's Republic of which you are the roving children and brilliant ambassadors.

In this land of poetry and freedom, we are happy to welcome you, the young creators of the poetry and freedom you defended by the side of your people. And now that finally you have reached our shores, having crossed the Pacific, that broadest of the planet's highways, given to the world by other Spanish pilgrims, may this also be your point of return, because when freedom flowers across the earth, you will have a greater right than anyone to reclaim it for Spain, as you were the first to battle for it.

Beloved brother and sister: we have loved you so long that it was scarcely necessary for you to be here for us to hear you. Wherever you were, your poetry and your courage illuminated the many lands of America. You have chosen to cross the highest snows of the planet so that at this dizzying moment in world history we might look upon the two noble faces that to us represent the dignity of universal thought. Won't you, in turn, look upon the countless faces of the people who offer you their welcome? Come singing, this is what we love; come in the springtime of our sea-rimmed land, plumb every mineral depth of the warm heart of Chile, because you already know, Rafael and María, the guitars have already told you, that when the people of Chile give their hearts, they give them wholly and forever to those who, like you, have known so supremely how to sing and do battle.

Here they are. Spain will speak through their mouths.

Picasso Is a People

Iɴ our Americas discoveries are made: on uninhabited islands or in irascible jungles suddenly, beneath the earth, one finds statues of gold, stone paintings, turquoise necklaces, gigantic heads, vestiges of countless unknown beings who are yet to be discovered and given names so that they may speak from their centuries of silence.

If on one of our islands one were to find the multiple layers of Picasso, his monumental abstraction, his rock-hard creation, his precise jewels, his paintings of happiness and terror, the astonished archaeologist would search long and hard for the inhabitants and the cultures that so productively accumulated such fabulous games and miracles.

Picasso is an island. A continent peopled by Argonauts, Caribs, bulls, and oranges. Picasso is a people. In his heart the sun never sets.

Written on the occasion of Picasso's ninetieth birthday, Paris, October 1971

This Cold Day

THIS cold day in the middle of summer is like his departure, like his sudden disappearance in the midst of the ever-increasing joy of his writing.

I am not going to offer a funeral oration for Mariano Latorre.

Instead, I want to dedicate to him a flight of *queltehues* alongside the water, the oracular screams, the black and white feathers lifting suddenly like a mourner's fan.

I am going to dedicate to him the sorrowful call of the dark-feathered *piden*, the wet, blood-like stain on the breast of the Chilean *loica*.

I am going to dedicate to him the dew-moist spur of some rugged horseman as he undertakes his early-morning journey along the shores of the fragrant Maule.

I come to dedicate to him, raise in his honor, a glass of the wine of our country, brimming with the essences he described and relished.

I come to leave him a yellow rosary of *topa-topas*, the wild, pure flowers of our ravines.

But he also deserves the secret murmur of the protective branches of the *maiten* and the fronds of the araucarias. He, more than anyone, is worthy of our flora, and his true crown, from today forward, will be found in the mountains of Araucania, woven from fragrant boldo, myrtle, copihue, and laurel.

The music of the grape harvest accompanies him, and the bountiful braids of our country girls, through corridors and beneath the eaves in summer light or rain.

Written on the death of the Chilean writer Mariano Latorre, 1955

And this tricolor ribbon tied around the neck of the guitars, the thread of the music, encircles his body like a garland, and accompanies him.

We have heard beside him the footsteps of laborers and men of the pampas, of miners and fishermen, those who work, hoe, plow, and enrich our harsh earth.

At this moment the grain is ripening, and, soon, swaying yellow wheat fields will recall the one who will not be among us.

From Victoria in the South to our green islands, in fields and hamlets, in huts and highways, he will not be with us. We will miss him. Schooners laden with the fruits of the sea will ply our waters, but Mariano will no longer sail among the islands.

He loved the land and the waters of Chile, he made them his through his patience, his wisdom, and his love; he stamped them with his words and the blue of his eyes.

In our Americas, those who govern, from one region to another, do nothing but sacrifice our native riches. The writer, joining in the struggles of the people, defends and preserves our heritage. In the future, if our customs and our costumes, our songs and our guitars, have been sacrificed, we will seek them in the treasure that men like Mariano Latorre have protected, eternal in their national song.

We will search in the bowers of his books, we will flock to his precious pages to know and defend what is ours.

The earth produces the classic writer, or, perhaps, the alliance between his books and the earth, and we may have lived alongside our first classic, Mariano Latorre, without appreciating his enduring fidelity to the mandate of the earth. Forgotten men, tools and birds, language and weariness, animals and festivals, will live forever in the freshness of his books.

His heart was a ship of fragrant wood from the forests of the Maule, sturdily constructed and wrought in the shipyards of the estuary, and in his voyage across the ocean he will continue to carry the strength, the flower, and the poetry of our country.

The Splendor of Blood

FROM exile our rugged land assumes the color of the moon; distance and days polish and soften its long contours, its plains, its mountains, and its islands.

I remember an evening spent with Elías Lafertte in a deserted town, one of the abandoned mines of the pampa.

The pampa stretched in all directions, sandy and infinite, and as the sunlight wrought its changes, the pale sands glimmered like the iridescence on the throat of a delicate wild pigeon; green and violet were sprinkled on the scars of the earth, ashes fallen from the skies, a hazy mother-of-pearl spread like a rainbow across the desert.

It was in the enormous desolate North, in the solitudes of Huantajaya. This book begins there, its pages are gritty from that sand, its world is strong, broad, and vibrant, and in it lives are etched with fire and sweat, like the spade handles of the crew that shovels the rubble. An additional color is painted onto the expanse of the pampa: the splendor of blood.

No one will be able to forget this book.

With few exceptions, those who govern have cruelly treated the people of Chile and have ferociously repressed popular movements. They have followed the decrees of caste or the mandates of foreign interests. From the slaughter of Iquique to the death camp González Videla erected in Pisagua, ours is a long and cruel history. Continuous war has been waged against the people, that is to say, against our

---

Preface to *Hijo del salitre* (*Child of the Salt Mines*) by the Chilean writer Volodia Teitelboim, May 1952

country. Police torture, the club and the sword, siege, the marines, the army, ships of war, planes and tanks: the leaders of Chile do not use these weapons to defend our nitrate and our copper against foreign pirates, no, these are the instruments of their bloody assault against Chile itself. Prison, exile, and death are measures used to maintain "order," and the leaders who execute bloody acts against their countrymen are rewarded with trips to Washington, are honored in North American universities. This is in fact the politics of colonialism. There is little difference between the massacres of Madagascar, Tunisia, Malaysia, and Korea inflicted by French, British, and North American invaders upon defenseless countries and the systematic repression inflicted here on our continent by the pitiless leaders who are the agents of imperialist interests.

But throughout this history the Chilean people have emerged victorious.

They have learned from each tragic onslaught, and have responded, as perhaps no other American people, with their most powerful weapon: organization in their struggle.

This many-pronged struggle is the center of our national life, its vertebrae, its nerves, and its blood. Countless sad or victorious episodes inflame it and keep it alive. This is why in the vast drama of Chile the eternal protagonist is the people. This book is a kind of extensive prologue to that drama, and with purity and profundity it depicts the dawn of awareness.

But *Hijo del salitre* is not simply a civilian dissertation on life in the desert, but rather an impressive and many-layered portrait of man. Shattering and epic descriptions are followed by passages of inconceivable tenderness. Volodia Teitelboim's love for his people leads him to the hidden source of songs and tears, the eruption of violent joy, the solitary lives of the pampa, the fluctuations that isolate and scatter the destinies of the simple people who live in this book.

For the writer in a capitalist world, the problems of realism are major. *Hijo del salitre* meets the criterion of creativity that is essential in the books we hope for. It does more than reject all obscurantist babbling, reactionary individualism, inanimate naturalism, and pessimistic realism. This book fulfills and surpasses the traditional canons of the novel, flooding us with its beauty and grandeur. But it also achieves another of the aims that are inseparable from contemporary creation: the chronicling of an epoch. We already know how the lying officials of the bourgeoisie have appropriated history. In a capitalist world, it is the writers who must be responsible for preserving the truth of our time: General Silva Renard or President González Videla must not escape the true judgment of history. The writers of Chile will have to write in blood—yes, in the blood of Iquique or Pisagua: in this way will our literature be born.

In the history of such epics, for which Baldomero Lillo set the first black stone, Volodia Teitelboim raises the first, the essential column. Because the sorrows, the joys, and the truths of a people are not engraved here merely to be forgotten; like many paths that join together to form a broad and well-marked route, the people are on the point of attaining their liberating organization, the Party. In this book, Recabarren and Lafertte are not static heroes, they are the progenitors of history.

With Volodia Teitelboim, and with our people, we have lived many great and hard hours. After years of exile his book reaches my hands, astonishing lives and struggles clustered like grapes and bursting with seed. From this distance, as surely as if I stood on the abandoned heights of Huantajaya, I perceive in these pages the terrible life of the men of the salt mines. I see the sands, the hills, the misery, the blood, and the victories of my people.

I am proud of my brother's creation.

Carlo Levi, Owl

As he was painting my portrait in his ancient studio, the Roman dusk slowly descended. Colors paled as if time, impatient, were suddenly consuming them. One could hear the trumpeting of automobiles racing toward the countryside, toward silence, toward the starry night. I sank into darkness, but Levi continued to paint. Silence completely engulfed me, but he continued to paint—my skeleton, perhaps. Because the alternatives were either that my bones were phosphorescent or that Carlo Levi was an owl, with the searching eyes of that bird of the night.

As I could see nothing around me, not even a glimpse of his brushes, and as he surely could not make out my nose or arms, I concentrated on thinking about him, on clothing him in my imagination. I was sure that he was covered with feathers, and he was painting with his wing tip. Because what I could hear, more than the stroke of an oiled brush on canvas, was a rasping of night-flying wings, wings that surely were sketching my outlines in that submerged painting. I protested in vain; his enormous eyes froze my words in the darkness of the studio.

Again I became absorbed in thought. In my imagination I saw him converted into a giant chrysanthemum whose huge petals were falling on the painting, endowing it with fresh or ashen yellows. Suddenly in the shadow I knew that he was smiling a chrysanthemum smile and that he was not going to allow me to leave the studio until the painting was completed. But as calm returned, I knew, too, that Carlo Levi was also a sun, that he thought and painted like a sun, strongly and clearly, his luminous force beaming ever from outer space. And I understood that this spaceman would save me with his rays, raising me finally from my cowardice, lighting my way up the steps of the ancient palace toward the street, toward the cinema, toward the starry night, toward the ocean that belongs to me.

But I also knew that I would always be there, on his canvas and in his thought, that I would never again escape Carlo Levi, his clairvoyance, his sun, his chrysanthemum, the intensely serene eyes that probe everything, every facet of life.

Such is the power of this magus. So, many years later, writing, as dusk falls, in my house by the waves of the southern sea, I feel bound to him by this same Roman dusk, by his unforgettable faculty for thought, by his consummate art, and by the wisdom of that great nocturnal bird that traversed all space but was always with us.

Rome, 1949

Our Great Brother
Mayakovsky

I do not declare myself an inveterate enemy of great literary debates, but I confess that debate is not my element. I do not take to it like a duck to water. But I am an impassioned aficionado of literary debates. Poetry is my element.

Though it is difficult to speak about Mayakovsky without becoming involved in a debate, and though this great poet soars through them like an eagle in the sky (gliding, perhaps, on the flight of his fancy), I want to speak about Mayakovsky with love and simplicity, without dwelling either on his productive life or on his unfortunate death.

Mayakovsky is the first poet to have incorporated the Party and the active proletariat into his poetry, and to make great poetry from them. This is a transcendental revolution, and on the plane of universal literature it is a contribution to contemporary poetry equal to that of Baudelaire or Whitman. By this I wish to emphasize that Mayakovsky's contribution is not dogmatic but poetic. Because any innovation in content that is not digested to become a nurturing constituent of our thought is never anything more than an external stimulus to our thought. The harsh themes of the struggle, the reiterated themes of brotherhood course through Mayakovsky's poetry; in it, these topics flower, become miraculous weapons, red orange blossoms.

This does not mean that all poetry has to be political and partisan; but, because of Mayakovsky, a true poet being born today will be able to choose a new road from among the many roads of true poetry.

Mayakovsky has a fire of his own that cannot be extinguished. He is an opulent poet, and I sense that like Federico García Lorca, and in spite of the maturity of his poetry, he still had many things to say, many things to create, and to sing. It seems to me that the works of these two young poets, both dead at the height of their intellectual powers, were those of incipient giants still to be measured against mountains. Only they had the key to surpassing themselves, and, to our misfortune, those keys have been lost, tragically buried beneath the soil of Spain and Russia.

Mayakovsky is a poet of a verbal vitality that approaches insolence. Prodigiously gifted, he calls upon every device, every recourse of the virtuoso. His poetry is a catalogue of unexpected images that continue to glow like phosphorescence. It is as often insulting and offensive as it is filled with the purest tenderness. He is a violent and gentle being who is organically both child and father of his poetry.

And to all this, one must add his satirical bent.

Mayakovsky's satires against bureaucracy are devastating, and today are being presented with ever-increasing success in Russian theaters. His sarcastic attack on the petit bourgeoisie is just short of cruelty and abhorrence. We may not agree, we may detest this cruelty directed toward people deformed by the vices of a system, but the great satirists have always written with the most irrational exaggeration. So, Swift. So, Gogol.

In the forty years of Soviet literature, during which time many good and many bad books have been written, Mayakovsky, in my opinion, continues to be an impressive poet, a towering poet. We see him from every corner of our land. We see the head, the hands, the feet, of this young giant. He wrote with all of himself, with his head, with his hands, with his body. He wrote with intelligence, with great craftsmanship, with all the violence of a soldier engaged in battle.

In these days of homage and reflection, as we celebrate with love and pride this anniversary of the October Revolution, I pause for a moment by the side of the road and I bow before the person and the poetry of our great brother Mayakovsky.

In these days during which he would have sung like no other, I salute his memory with a rose, a single red rose.

Peking, August 1957

My Friend Paul Eluard
Is Dead

IT is very difficult for me to write about Paul Eluard. I will always see him beside me, alive, his blue eyes alight with the electric depths that could see so far and so clearly.

This tranquil man was a flower of France, a tower. He came from a soil where laurels and roots intertwine their fragrant heritage. He was tall, water and stone that supported venerable vines heavy with flowers, splendor, bird nests, and transparent songs.

Transparency; that is the word. His poetry was precious crystal, water frozen in a continuously flowing current.

Poet of the pinnacle of love, the blazing bonfire of noonday: during its most disastrous days he planted his heart in the very center of his country, and it provided the necessary fire to sustain the battle.

So it was natural that he should join the ranks of the Party. For Eluard, to be a Communist was to affirm with his poetry and his life the values of humanity and humanism.

Never believe that Eluard was less a political man than a poet. He often astounded me with his clear vision and his formidable political intellect. Together we considered many issues, many men, and many problems of our time, and his lucidity served me forever.

He did not lose his way in Surrealist irrationalism because he was always a creator, never an imitator; he fired shots of clarity and intelligence into the corpse of Surrealism.

He was my friend, every day of my life, and in losing his tenderness I lose a portion of my daily bread. No one now can give to me what he gave to me. His dynamic brotherhood was one of the most precious luxuries of my life.

His blue column upheld the forces of peace and happiness. He is dead, he of the flowering hands, a soldier of peace, the poet of his people.

Tower of France! Brother!

I kneel, and I look on your closed eyes; they will continue to transmit the light and the grandeur, the simplicity and rectitude, the goodness and naturalness that you brought to the earth.

1952

The Visit of
Margarita Aligher

I was in Concepción, in the South of my country, when I read in the newspapers that Margarita Aligher had arrived in Chile.

Though between Santiago de Chile and Concepción there are hundreds of kilometers of vineyards, cattle, and grapes that in the month of March will become wine, Margarita soon arrived in the South.

It was midsummer in Chile, the sky of the South was wholly blue, like a blue banner, like a goblet. Not the tiniest white cloud. The blue sky of Chile needed Margarita Aligher because she is like a little white cloud. She is so silent that it is as if she were traveling enveloped in a cloud. Moreover, she often sits on the little cloud, and after a gathering, it gently transports her wherever she wants to go. So one day we traveled together across a spectacular landscape, I on my horse and she on her cloud. Both means of travel are necessary in this part of the country, because the roads are often rough, and the mountains give way to unexpected meadows that end in the sand of the sea.

Margarita looks at everything with an untiring, penetrating gaze. It is true that Margarita Aligher can go for hours without speaking a word, but she is absorbing everything. I have never known a person who looks at everything in such detail as Margarita.

Whether traveling at a hundred kilometers an hour or standing motionless, she looks as no other person looks. It is not the mystic or

---

Written on the occasion of the visit to Chile of the Soviet poet Margarita Aligher, 1968 sensual gaze of the romantic poet, it is an all-seeing, direct scrutiny, an inspection that probes beneath the soil, sees fruits among the leaves, and the working of the roots. She also inspects with keenness human faces and problems. We went to markets and plazas filled with townspeople. The Chileans became accustomed to Margarita's penetrating eyes, adding up and subtracting things and people and the high, blue banner of the passing days.

We also went to various painters' studios, and made a special point of visiting González Camarena's enormous mural in the Casa del Arte.

It's a huge mural some forty meters long and eight meters high. The painter told me that he had found the theme of his work while reading my *Canto general*. It pleased me that he told me this.

In one corner, the wild flowers of the Chilean copihue are intertwined with a Mexican nopal cactus. These plants are symbols of our nations.

The nopal is pierced by dozens of daggers and some of its thick leaves are lopped off, or mutilated. This, in the artist's view, symbolizes the North American attacks on Mexico, and the subsequent loss of territories.

In the background, several meters high, are gigantic faces of the different American races. Below them, as if in tunnels, lie the skeletons of the Conquistadors, and in the ore-rich subsoil the excavations of the mines. All this bursts into bloom aboveground in the figures of gods and harvests, wheat, and other representations of splendor.

This is only a superficial description. The wall with its greens and violets, its rich grays, its marvelous ochers, its metaphorical, abstract, cubist, humanist composition, is a fine example of how every school contributes, like color to light, one element that becomes part of the eternal in the rainbow of truth.

The fragile figure of Margarita, with its ethereal gentleness, vibrated among the phosphorescent planes of the fresco to take its place among the monumental and subterranean figures as if it had been painted there.

And justly so, after all, since her poetry, so airy and at the same time so profound, is part of the flora, the dreams, the life, the reality, the radiant colors her ancestral Mexico displays in the painting.

Having come from so far, from Russian Georgia, from the Ural Mountains, from Moscow, Margarita Aligher became part of our world.

She is celestial and subterranean; she creates dreams, and gazes out of the wide, eternal eyes of poetry.

Flowering Rumania, Her Poets

THE moment I arrived in Transylvania I asked about Dracula.

No one knew what I was talking about. What a pity!

That tail-coated vampire descending from the parapets of his castle of black stone! That inhumanly energetic terrorist flashing through the air like a bat!

What a pity!

All my dreams collapsed. He had dwelled here in these great fir forests, he himself terrified of the light of day, retreating and emerging to the rhythm of the attraction and power of the gloom that activated the fluttering of his shadowy cape.

What a pity!

The fact is that the Rumanian poets with whom I was traveling knew nothing about him. If I had been born in Rumania I would never have slackened in my pursuit. I would have stalked him from childhood; the membranous, metamorphosing wings would have brushed by me; I would have waited in the Transylvanian shadows for one of his golden keys to fall from the pocket of his tailcoat. Then, furtively opening the huge gates, I would have raced through his estate, I would have learned the mortal secrets of that satanic power. But none of that was possible! Dracula no longer dwells in the forests of Transylvania.

The poets around me had souls as clear as mountain streams, they saluted me with hearty laughter. Yes, I must confess it, my com-

Preface to an anthology of Rumanian poetry translated by Neruda and published in 1967 by Losada, Buenos Aires

panions, the poets of a blossoming Rumania, are not expert in matters of gloom and shadow.

The shadows of Rumania . . . The song of Rumanian streams. How many things to forget! How many things to sing about!

Unfortunately, the shadows were not just pages of paper, but harsh events, cruel chapters, interminable agonies.

Fortunately, the streams sang in spite of everything, they are singing, they will continue to sing.

Centuries of servitude, eras of martyrdom, invasions, abandonment, misery, death, insurrection, soldiering, rebellion, fire. And above this ancient Rumania molded by the transcendent hands of sorrow, behind this Rumania crucified a thousand times in each of her men, beneath this poor, medieval, folkloric, weeping Rumania, sang poetry, never attempting to disguise its eminence, sang forever in the crystal clarity of its bell.

Much of this will be seen in these pages.

The thrust of a rich and ancient literature that always expressed itself in criticism and creativity finds its continuity in today's Rumania.

Neither silence nor violence interrupted the periods between revolutions. With the death of feudalism, poetry did not disappear beneath the rubble, because the great poetry of Rumania was never shrouded in the misery and suffering that dominated the countryside.

Poetry strode easily into the new age. Its seeds stirred beneath the earth, and its flowers bloomed copiously along with the broader flowering of a people.

Poetry did not abandon its song of the streams choked in their flow from the mountains, but, rather, channeled those waters into the active humanism of the new Rumania. And it accomplished this without sacrificing either reflection or melancholy. As always, it sang of life and death, but now, too, of reality and hope. The lamentations that enveloped the Symbolist Bacovia like a mantle were stained with the smoke of the city and the blood of the slaughterhouse. The new poets of today reflect like the statues of naked gladiators the color of sun and wheat. Yet, beneath it all, this poetry continued to grow among the national roots, and you will find no verse, no line, no syllable that is not imbued with Rumanian light and darkness, with a wild and tender feeling of love for the land, for the most ancient and most modern soul of Europe.

Near Constanţa I saw a Greek marble that had recently been dredged from the waters of the Black Sea. Some frogman had accidentally discovered those white gods still listening to the song of the ancient sirens. Near Ploesti some peasants found a treasure beside a highway: dozens of golden amphoras and goblets, wrought perhaps for ancient monarchs. They are in a display case. I never saw such splendor.

Tirnave, Dragasani, Legarcea, Murfatlar are the names of ancient vineyards that moved the hearts of men in distant lands, but whose aroma was born between the Carpathian Mountains and the Danube.

Every inch of the soil and clay of Rumania pulses with the magnanimous culture that absorbed and shared treasures. Rumania's poetry was nourished by the bright light of earth, water, and air, it was clothed in ancient gold, it dreamed Grecian dreams. And it matured in the rationalism of our era, solemnly following the road of an always serious, always sonorous, always inspiring song. The ageless land of Rumania is vibrating with its factories, schools, and songs. Poetry sings in the revolution of the wheat, in the rhythm of the looms, in the new richness of life, in the security of the people, in every newly discovered dimension. Poetry sings in the old and in the new wine.

It is difficult to talk about this creation, to write about it. Why should one? What need does poetry have for irrelevant interpretation, loyalties, or suspicions? We are inundated with books that comment on poems that want nothing more than to be allowed to wander life's highways in their delicate slippers or their stout boots. But what happens to us is that we get caught up in reading what someone writes about what we have written.

So in this Age of Paper I want to present in a *natural* way these Rumanian poets as traditional as the unsophisticated songs and customs of their heritage, and as revolutionary as their humming power plants and the obvious transformation in the world in which they live.

I want to mention the venerable poet, Tudor Arghezi.

More than eighty years old, Arghezi is Rumania's grand old man, and he bears with good humor and a touch of irony the chiaroscuro of the laurels that crown a body of work that is serene and frenetic, pure and demonic, cosmic and provincial.

It was in Bucharest that I met this elderly rebel honored by ministers and workers, loved and respected by a republic that protects his freedom and his tranquillity.

It is strange that this great European poet should be known by so few, as was also the case with the great Italian Saba.

Saba was a murmuring river that gradually sinks underground, burying its marvelous channel before it reaches the ocean.

Arghezi is wrathful and heretical, seditious and strong. The black meditation of the first long stages of his career has given way in his latest books to the impetuous joy of his soul. He has ceased to sustain himself in his own solitude: in his later years he shares in the spring of his country.

But I want to name others, to thank every one of them for allowing their poetry to live with me through the long winter of Isla Negra here on the southern coast of the Pacific, and to envelop me with the strength and freshness of Rumania for these many months, in waking and in slumber.

My thanks to you, Maria Banus!

Thank you for the persistent throbbing of your love and your dreams, for the magical net in whose threads of smoke and gold you snare deep, dark recollections like fish from an abyss, or net in the air the wild butterfly of Baragan.

And to you, Jebeleanu, you who traveled to Hiroshima and gathered from that heart of ashes a pure flower transfigured in your song: may you find some spark of your generous poetry in this book. And to Mihail Beniuc: thank you for your contemplative strength, for your battle songs.

My thanks to Maria Porumbacu, to Demostene Botez, to Radu Boureanu, to Ion Brand, forgive me for what your poems may have lost of their essential strength, their amber drops, as I poured them from cup to cup. But each of you knows, I am sure of it, that I placed great love in the never-ending labor of translating your poetry.

The Rumanian language, blood kin to Spanish, is enriched beyond our own by its Slavic twists and turns. We lose our way in these labyrinths, we look upward, downward, and, finally, we clutch at the French in order not to be left in the dark. But the Rumanian tongue, far from being a kind of oblique Castilian, draws electric lyricism from the linguistic alluvia deposited on its soil. The Rumanian language is strong and resplendent, and preeminently poetic. Through Tristan Tzara, Ilarie Voronka, and others who wrote in French, Rumania contributed to its passion for the universal. We know, of course, that Eminescu and Caragiale have penetrated the barriers of language and are treasured and discussed everywhere. But from its streets and mountains the voice of Rumania has always joined in the world concert. An aspiration to the universal, the natural, and cultural growth, especially that of today, has been the pride of the contemporary cultural expansion. But the poets who emigrated in the past, and had to write in a different language, were forced to do so by the cruelty of an era. This was not the case with Europeanized Americans. The Rumanians did not go to France to imitate, but to set an example. They were Rumania's participation in the universal creation.

For more than one winter, in my house overlooking the icy ocean and countless migrations of birds, the poets Homero Arce and Ennio Moltedo assisted me diligently in the translation of these Rumanian poems.

I want to thank my two friends. Their wisdom and commitment helped me greatly. As we worked, they, as well as I, took delight from the blossoming foliage, the water and the fire, that multiplied in these multiple voices, inviting us to hear and recognize the chorus of a distant and kindred people.

They Tried to Extinguish the Light of Spain

OTHERS here have already discussed with wisdom the poetic transcendence of Federico García Lorca.

I want to begin by mentioning, and by praising, the fact that this is the first monument to his memory. And as such homage is an obligation of every country in America, honor and love is owed to this land that offers it before any other. On behalf of world poetry, I applaud the city of São Paulo, Brazil.

Federico García Lorca was the happiest man I have known in a now rather long lifetime. He radiated joy in everything, in seeing, hearing, singing, living. For this reason we must proceed in our ceremony with some caution. This is not a moment for last rites. We are celebrating the immortality of joy.

As we contemplate with sadness the photographs of that time, I am astounded by his youth, by his almost childish face. He was, as a youth, vibrant with life, the new channel of a powerful river. He squandered imagination, he was enlightened in his speech, he made a present of his music, he lavished his magical drawings, he cracked walls with his laughter, he extemporized the impossible, and in his hands a prank became a work of art. I have never seen such magnetism and such constructiveness in a human being. This marvelous and playful man wrote with a meticulous conscientiousness, and if his poetry spilled out in madness and tenderness, I know that it came from a man who had the wisdom of his ancestors, a man who had inherited all the grace and grandeur of the Spanish language. But

---

This speech was delivered at the dedication of a monument to the memory of Federico García Lorca, São Paulo, 1968

what saddens me is the thought that he was merely beginning, and that we will never know how far he would have gone if depravity had not snuffed out that enchanted destiny. The last time I saw him he took me off into a corner, and as if in secret recited six or seven sonnets that remain in my memory as incredibly beautiful models of the form. They were part of a collection that no one has ever seen, a book he called *Sonetos del amor oscuro* (*Sonnets of Dark Love*). García Lorca was an indefatigable writer, experimenter, and performer. He held in his hands the substance and tools for supreme inventiveness, to reach the most distant horizons. So when I see the beauty that he left us, and remember how his life was cut off in its prime, I think with sorrow of the beauty of which we have been deprived.

There are two Federicos: the real and the legendary. And the two are one. There are three Federicos—the poet, the man who lived, and the man who died. And the three are a single being. There are a hundred Federicos, each of them singing. There are Federicos for the entire world. His poetry, his life, and his death have spread across the earth. His song and his blood are multiplied in every human being. His brief life is not ended. His shattered heart was bursting with seed: those who murdered him could not have known that they were sowing that seed, that it would send forth roots, that it would sing and blossom everywhere, in every language, ever more resonant, ever more vivid. The usurpers who are governing Spain try to disguise his appalling death. Their official publication describes it as a *fait divers*, one of the calamities of those first bloody days. But that is not true. The proof is the fact that another marvelous poet, young Miguel Hernández, was held in Fascist prisons until his death. This was a case of direct aggression against intelligence, carried out with terrifying deliberation. A million dead, a half million exiled. The martyrdom of this poet was the assault of darkness: they tried to extinguish the light of Spain.

This beautiful, mysterious, translucent monument created by Flavio de Carvalho is a major event in our lives. But we await as well an even greater monument to the glory of Federico García Lorca: the liberation of Spain.

Farewell to Lenka

"I put on my black necktie to bid you goodbye, Lenka."

"Don't be silly, take it off."

"We wept last night remembering you, Lenka."

"How absurd! Remember instead all the times we laughed together."

"What can I say to you, Lenka!"

"Tell me a story, and then be quiet."

"To know how to tell, and for the telling, I will tell you that today the earth reminds me of your darling head, all unruly gold and threatening snow. All the time you were dying, we worked every day in Isla Negra. You almost died there. It was the only appointment you never kept. Your place at the table was empty."

As you were dying, you advanced and retreated with the pain, every wave said your name as it broke on the sands. It was your life battling and singing. Every wave ebbed and then swelled again with you. Flowered and died. Every movement between the land and the sea was you, Lenka, you coming to see me, it was you speaking again, whipped incessantly by the winds of the world. It was you at last arriving where we awaited you, it was you, dear wanderer, you who lived and died so near to us, so far.

To think about you with the foam and the sky was to dedicate to you the best things. Like the swelling of the sea came your memory, your mysterious face. So magnificently intelligent, so indulged. So industrious, so lazy, my darling girl. So fragile, and so robust. You were the essence of womanhood and an example to a million men.

The journalist Lenka Franulić died in Santiago on May 25, 1961

I will never forget that when I was being harassed, I and many others, when life was a carnival of hypocrisy, you maintained the purity of your white face, your helmet of gold, holding high the dignity of the written word. Other journalists, false masters, bayed at the scent of my poetry like bloodhounds, fulfilling their destinies as buffoons and traitors, while you embodied the translucence of truth, a truth without illusions but also without betrayals.

"You're exceeding yourself in my eulogy, Pablo. I know you."

"Forgive me, Lenka, if I am but too human. You are even more beautiful now. You are a crystal wave with the bluest eyes, so tall, so radiant that probably we will never again see the likes of your wave of gold and snow on our humble sands."

Farewell to Zoilo Escobar

THE purest heart in all Valparaiso has been stilled. As it will for every man, the earth will open to guard his body, but it will be the earth he loved, the earth of the hills overlooking the port of which he sang. He will rest facing the ocean whose waves and winds billowed in his poetry like the sails of an ancient sailing ship. There are no words that can compensate for his absence, and perhaps no voice should be raised at this time to bid him farewell and render him homage except the voice of the sea, the sea of Valparaiso.

Zoilo was a poet of the people, he came from the people, and throughout his life he bore the stamp of the bards of old, the balladeers of the sea. The happy roguishness that gleamed in his eyes reflected the high spirits of a miner or a fisherman. The wrinkles on his face were like furrows in the soil of Chile; his poetry was a guitar of Chile.

Two words will always come to mind in remembering this man's life: *purity* and *poverty*. Zoilo Escobar was solemnly pure and happily poor. But here on the site of his final resting place we poets must make it eminently clear that no one should toy with these words and distort this dreamer's life. There are those who will want to confuse his purity with his poverty, in order to justify their own indifference toward the people. But we poets do not advocate poverty in poets or in peoples, and in this, like every true poet, Zoilo Escobar was a revolutionary. He was brother to Pezoa Véliz; his poetry, from the beginnings of the century, was tinged with red. Those were the anarchical times in which Baldomero Lillo wrote our continent's first

The poet Zoilo Escobar died in Valparaiso in 1963

novel of social realism. Zoilo Escobar evolved with our world, and his blossoming voice sang the victories of emerging socialism.

Will Zoilo Escobar occupy a permanent place in our national literature? This is an irrelevant question that no one here can, or should, answer: only the ocean winds can answer. He did not fight tooth-and-nail during his lifetime to insure that his name would live on in the pantheon of our Parnassus. Instead, he gave to all of us who had known him from our youth a daily lesson in brotherhood, friendship, and love of life. He gave us a long lesson in poetry.

His renowned tenderness is something I will always remember. Many poets now dead profited from the kindness of our older brother, who had known kindness and poetry longer than we. It would be a great honor for me if those now forever silent might speak through my voice to bid him farewell now that his voice, too, has been stilled.

I bring these fragrant blossoms from Isla Negra. They flowered beside the windy sea, like his dreams and his poems.

Alberto Sánchez, Bone
and Iron

Wʜᴇɴ Alberto Sánchez died in Moscow I not only felt the sudden
pain one feels at the loss of a great brother, I was bewildered as well.
Anyone, I thought, except Alberto.

My bewilderment is explained by the work and the person of the
man who is in my opinion the most extraordinary sculptor of our
time.

Shortly after the 1920's, Alberto began to produce his vigorous
sculptures of stone and iron. He himself—his long skinny body and
lean dry face with its bold and powerful bone structure—was a natural sculpture of Castile. Externally, this great Alberto Sánchez was
wholly stone, bone, and iron, like a skeleton shaped by the harsh
weather of Castile, sculpted by sun and cold.

That is why his death seemed to me contrary to the laws of nature.
He was a product of a hard earth, a man of ore, weather-beaten from
birth. I always thought of him as one of the towering trees of my
country that so closely resemble the ore of the Andes. Alberto Sánchez was a tree, and high in his branches he harbored birds and
lightning rods, wings for flight, and tempestuous magnetism.

I do not mean to imply that our gigantic sculptor was a monolith,
stony inside as well as out. In his youth he was a baker by trade, and,
in truth, he had a heart of bread, flour and murmuring wheat. Certainly in many of his sculptures, as Picasso was the first to note, one
could see the baker at work: his masses were elongated and twisted,
creating the movement, the form, the rhythm of bread. Commonplace, like the animal and bird figures baked in Spanish villages. But

---

The Spanish sculptor Alberto Sánchez died in Moscow on October 12, 1962

the baker is not the only influence we see in his work. When in 1934 I saw his sculptures for the first time in the house of Rafael Alberti, I recognized immediately that this man was a great revealer of Spain. Those passionately free-form works were incrusted with scraps of iron, pebbles, bones, and nails that bristled from the skin of his strange animals. "Bird of My Invention," I remember he called one of his works in which these strange fragments seemed to blend into the hirsute surface of the plain. The clay or cement sculpture was scored and crisscrossed with lines and furrows like newly sown fields or peasant faces. And thus, in his own manner, with his own unique and magnificent style, he offered to us the image of the earth he loved and understood and expressed like no other.

Alberto often visited my house in Madrid before he married the admirable and beloved Clara Sánchez. Who else would this Castilian marry but a Clara (clear and bright) and a Sancha (practically a Sánchez)? And so it was until now; now Clarita has lost her Alberto and her Spain.

It was about that time in Madrid that Alberto had his first exhibition. He received one compassionate review from the officialdom of criticism, the rest relegated him to the back room reserved for the victims of Spanish obtuseness, where, as if in a cellar, such offenses were stored. Fortunately, Alberto had the iron and the grit to bear their contempt. Though I have seen him pale, and once I saw him weep, when the bourgeoisie of Madrid ridiculed his work, and even went so far as to spit on his sculptures.

On that afternoon he came to my room in the Casa de las Flores and found me ill in bed. He told me of the outrageous insults he was suffering every day of his exhibition. His essential realism, which surpasses form, the vehemence of his revolutionary plasticity into which all the elements, beginning with earth and fire, seemed to be incorporated, his colossal power, the amazing flight of his monumental concepts—all this led him toward a form that seemed abstract but actually was steadfastly real. His women were other women; his stars, different stars; his birds *were* birds of his invention. Each of his works was a small planet seeking its orbit in the limitless space of our minds and our emotions, and as it entered, it awakened unknown presences.

He was the creator of fabulous objects formed as mysteriously as nature forms life. Thus Alberto offered to us a world created by his hands, a natural and supernatural world I not only understood but which helped me to decipher the enigmas surrounding us. It was only natural that the bourgeoisie of Madrid should react violently against him. Those dullards had codified realism. The repetition of form, the bad photograph of a smile or a flower, the tediousness that copies the whole and its detail, the death of interpretation, imagination, and creation, were the apex of the official culture of Spain. Neither is it surprising that Fascism would raise its head nearby, adding its dark limitations and its rigid restrictions to further subject man.

That day I got up from my sickbed and we rushed to the deserted exhibition hall. Just the two of us, Alberto and I. We dismantled the show days before it was scheduled to end. Then we went to a tavern to drink the acrid wine of Valdepeñas. War was prowling the streets. That bitter wine was punctuated by distant gunfire. Soon war was everywhere, and nothing could be heard above the explosions.

No sooner had the war begun than Alberto, as a Toledo peasant, as a baker, and as a sculptor, gave all his strength and passion to the struggle against the Fascists. Summoned by his great friend, the architect Luis Lacasa, our sculptor, along with Picasso and Miró, made up the trinity whose art enriched the Spanish Republican Pavilion at the Paris Exposition of 1937. On that occasion a masterwork of world painting, the *Guernica*, fresh from the prolific workshop of its creator, was delivered by Picasso's own hands. But at the entrance to the Exposition, it was Picasso who stood bemused for a long while, staring at a grotesquely elongated figure, ridged and striated like a California cactus, whose soaring verticality illustrated the consuming theme of Alberto's work: the wrinkled and lunar face of Castile. This armless, eyeless Quixote was the portrait of Spain, rising vertically toward the combat in all its lean power.

Casting his lot with his country, Alberto was exiled, and took refuge in Moscow, and until the time he left us, he worked there in silent intensity.

First, during that bitter final period under Stalin, he submerged himself in realism, though not the realism in vogue during those troubled days. And he created splendid stage sets. His set for the Ballet of the Birds is a masterwork, unequaled; in it he displayed the feathered, magical beauty of the birds he loved so deeply. He also created magnificent sets for the Gypsy Theater's presentations of Spanish plays. And the voice that sings the old songs that ennoble the film *Don Quixote* is the voice of Alberto, who will sing for us forever. It is the voice of our lost Quixote.

He also painted. He had never worked in oils in Spain, but learned to use the palette in Moscow to create his realistic works. These were still lifes of great plastic purity, beautiful and spare in subject matter, tender in their appreciation of the most humble objects.

This was the realism of Zurbarán, but instead of pallid monks, Alberto painted with the same mystical exaltation strings of garlic, wooden drinking vessels, large bottles bathed in the nostalgia of Spanish light. These studies are the apogee of realistic painting, and will one day be coveted by the Prado Museum.

But I was saying that those days found Alberto just arrived in Moscow and welcomed in full brotherhood and affection. From that moment he loved the Soviet Union passionately. There he lived the misfortunes of the war and the joys of victory. Still, like rivers that bury themselves in the sands of a great desert and then emerge before flowing to the sea, it was only after the Twentieth Congress that Alberto returned to his true, his transcendent, creation.

In his studio in the University District of Moscow, where he lived so happily those last years, working and singing, there remain many works and many projected works. They constitute his reencounter with his personal truth, and with the world that this great universal artist helped to create. A world in which the harshest of materials rise to infinite heights through the art of an extraordinarily inventive spirit. The works of Alberto Sánchez, severe and magnificent, born of the intense communication between a man and his country, creations of extraordinary love between a great human being and a powerful land, will live in cultural history as monuments erected by a man who consumed himself in seeking the highest and truest expression of our time.

The Needleworkers of Isla Negra

Everything flowers in Isla Negra. The tiniest yellow flowers survive the long winters to become blue, then later, with spring, magenta. The sea flowers the year round. Its rose is white. Its petals are stars of salt.

And just this last winter the needleworkers of Isla Negra have begun to flower. Each of the houses I have known for thirty years displayed on its exterior an embroidery like a flower. Before, these houses were dark and silent; and suddenly they were alight with colored threads of blue innocence, violet profundity, red clarity. The embroiderers are simple women, and they embroider with the color of their hearts. Their names are Mercedes, like the wife of José Luis, or Eufemia, or Pura, or Adela, or Adelaida. Their names are simple names, as names should be. They have the names that flowers would have if they could choose their names. And they embroider with their names, with the pure colors of earth, sun, water, and springtime.

There is nothing more beautiful than these embroideries, illustrious in their purity, radiant in a joy that has transcended suffering.

With pride, I present the needleworkers of Isla Negra. They may explain why the roots of my poetry are deep in the soil of this place.

This popular art from the industrious hands of these women reveals how everything flowers here.

Spring in Isla Negra, here's to you!

September 1969

Pleasant Memories

Here in Isla Negra, and in houses in Buenos Aires and Totoral de Córdoba, we spent a lot of time together, the author of this book and I, as you will see. Whether beside the Great Ocean or in the groves of his Argentina, his companionship provided me with constant and invigorating happiness. My pleasure in his savage humor developed into a deep friendship and admiration for his many virtues. Both his humor and his virtue will be seen in these unforgettable pages. An era and à society in whose active turmoil this book participates—for good or ill—are on trial here.

"How can one take your country seriously?" Ehrenburg once asked me. On his arrival at the airport in Santiago, Chile, the police had seized his papers: a collection of crossword puzzles he had been working on the airplane, and a list of Chilean plants he hoped to take back to his country's Botanical Garden. "This is undoubtedly the name of a Bolshevik agent," crowed a strutting police officer. He was referring to the words *Lapageria rosea*, the name a French botanist had given the copihue, in honor of the Empress Josephine de La Pagerie. Our police—could one be anything but pleased?—know none of the best secrets, nor, one may add, even the beautiful scientific name of Chile's national flower.

One will note in these pages that same lack of *seriousness*, which is typical of a long period of Argentine history, and which might as easily be true of Brazil, Ecuador, or Panama. The narration pulls no punches, we see elegance and cruelty arm in arm, we witness the

---

Preface to *El recuerdo y las cárceles* (*Recollections and Prisons*) by Rodolfo Aráoz Alfaro, published in Buenos Aires in 1967

mutual affection of brotherhood, we are astonished by the inefficacy and the degree of excess. This book by Aráoz is also the story of a lifetime of honor. Because, like his ancestor on the last page, prisons did not break this man, nor did threats tame him.

Running through these memories are the fragrant breezes of childhood, the heresies of youth, the forays of a confident Argentine through a Europe pulsating between bloodbaths, and later wild boar hunts in Ongamira de la Sierra and Tulumba, and siestas in Totoral to the accompaniment of a chorus of croaking toads.

But beyond event and happenstance, what distinguishes this book is that it is fascinating, uninterruptedly fascinating, magical water that sings a story as it flows, a thread that weaves together story and memory. I urged Rodolfo to write from the moment I first received his vibrant and sarcastic letters, the kind of letter no one writes today because the epistolary mode has disappeared, along with the meditative ease the furniture of those days afforded us.

One thing I know, these memories are letters addressed to the future. And the future, I am sure, will acknowledge receipt. The fruit from Aráoz's vine has an acid, electric savor that will endure. And someday in the future he will be read the way we read our most delicious classics, Sarmiento, Mansilla, Pérez Rosales, with melancholy and delight, envying even their suffering.

Isla Negra, August 1967

A Few Words about
This River

El río is not exactly a book, nor is it a river. It is an excrescence of nature oozing pus and pain, a loathsome story inscribed on human flesh, on the skin of any of my Latin American peoples.

Like every Chilean, like Gómez Morel, I came into the world beneath the shadow of the highest snows of the planet. From Santiago de Chile the Andes resemble a recumbent statue we live with all year long. Fathomless blizzards sweep down from her breasts; swirling cold descends from her heights; a river is born of her frozen bosom, a river that wends its way down from the dizzying peaks into the city; it flows through the city and reaches the sea, where it finds release.

Beneath one of the bridges that span this river Mapocho (as it was called by the Araucans and the Conquistadors), tough little bands of children lived and suffered, exposed to cold, hunger, and an incredibly malign innocence.

Beneath one of those bridges the heart of Gómez Morel was shaped by total neglect that years later carried him from crime to crime, and, finally, to prison.

Though I had never met the author, I attended the birth of these pages, which a mutual friend carried in and out of his cell. The book was published several years ago without any intent of sensationalism. For its author it had but one essential purpose: to wash down to the distant sea all the pain those filthy waters encountered in their path, and thus allow the author, face to face with himself, to become free.

Preface to the French edition of *El río* (*The River*) by the Chilean writer Alfredo Gómez Morel, January 1973

The river shuddered cataclysmically and the man emerged from prison, still bound to his river.

Years have passed, and this classic story of wretchedness has gone through many printings. But always wearing its Spanish shirt, speaking not only the language but the bitter truth we shared in horror, so vividly aware of the degraded lives, of the ignominy, that stain the hands of Latin America. This is the first time the book has shown its face beyond the sea. Now it will stand face to face with elegant Europeans, interrogating them, transfixing them with its implacable glare. There is no exoticism, only human excrement, as Gómez Morel states in these pages. In the land of Mallarmé, in the garden of Ronsard (which is, however, the land of Zola as well), how will this book be received? With compassion, with rage, with revulsion, or with tenderness?

I hope that its terrible light will shed understanding not only on the life and suffering of one man but also on the lives, the struggles, and the hopes of all our peoples.

Chile, against enormous difficulties and the attacks of many enemies, is creating on this continent a new order that will counteract the realities Gómez Morel's book denounces with such spine-chilling clarity.

Take heed!

Listen! The rancorous barcarole is about to begin. It will be sung for you by a bitter river and a man who could not be conquered by evil or by suffering.

Miguel Otero Silva: The Novels and the Man

The day I went to Ortiz it was burning hot. The Venezuelan sun was beating down on the earth. In the ruins of the church, tied there with thick wire, hung the old bell that had been heard so often by the living and the dead whose lives and deaths Miguel Otero Silva relates to us. I couldn't imagine why that village with its deserted houses was still on the map. Nothing existed but deafening silence and harsh sun. And the ancient bell suspended from the sun and the silence.

I never saw *Oficina no. 1*, but I am sure that the hellish life, the unceasing ferment, the forces that create and those that destroy, a society that is suddenly self-aware and fighting for its rights: all of this still exists, as it does in the book. Because, in its desolation and its vitality, this book represents the chaotic reality of Latin America, in addition to being a searing, a poetic photograph of the skeleton and the soul of Venezuela.

The author belongs to a young generation of Venezuelans who from the moment they were born learned to live with turmoil. A long tyrannical shadow, a creeping, violent hegemony of terror, spread down from the Venezuelan mountains to reach the most remote corners of the country. Entire families were dragged off to prison. Camps and villages were decimated by malaria and poverty. Chain gangs of political prisoners were led through Ortiz, between the dead houses of that dying town, marched in silence toward a mysterious destination, which was a rendezvous with death.

Preface to the Czechoslovakian edition of two novels by Miguel Otero Silva, *Casas muertas* (*Dead Houses*) and *Oficina no. 1* (*Office No. 1*), 1963

What Miguel Otero Silva does not say is that, with chains on his ankles, he marched through these streets, through that malign silence, toward the prisons of Gómez. He was then about fifteen or sixteen.

What the writer does not tell us is that when he was older, adventurous and passionate, he lived through many *Oficinas no. 1*, many boomtowns created by the discovery of oil, the erupting and sprouting of our astonishing continent still in the process of being born. A poet of the people, generous of heart, the total Venezuelan patriot, there is no cockfight or union meeting that has not been graced by his presence, no country dance floor that has not vibrated beneath the feet that could dance the joropo better than any man, no improvement or dream of liberation that was not guarded and nurtured in the heart of Otero Silva.

For us Americans who live in the extreme south of the continent, in the cold and quiet shaken only by nature's tremors, Venezuela was a stone of mystery, a stone that weighed on the hearts of all Americans. Following the death of the tyrant who governed for forty years and went calmly to his grave leaving crowded prisons behind him, unforeseen events occurred. A noble poet, Andrés Eloy Blanco, slightly intoxicated from the unaccustomed air of freedom, proposed that the shackles and chains that were the only law the Tyrant of the Andes knew be collected. And, in fact, a whole mountain of irons was gathered and, to the accompaniment of lyrical speeches, thrown into the sea.

Those young patriots who were innocent of the ways of history thought that by drowning the instruments of torture they could bury Venezuela's sorrows. This did not prove to be true.

Instead, along with the petroleum and the North American enterprises, arose the tumultuous life described in this book, as well as a new breed of rulers: the betancourts. These men subordinated the welfare of their country to the decrees of the oil companies; they made themselves the tools of foreign greed. They threatened, they rode roughshod over, they even shot, the masses, who were merely demanding their rights. And when Cuba became the brightest star in the stormy Caribbean sky, the betancourts allied themselves with the petroleum interests to thwart, to betray, the immaculate revolution of the sister island.

It is clear that, instead of throwing the irons into the sea, they should have preserved that mountain of memories as an ever-present monument.

First and foremost, the author of this book is a true poet, a poet incarnate. His poetry has spread throughout the Spanish-speaking world. I have heard his poems recited in athenaeums and academies, and also at crowded labor rallies, in the midst of battle, on happy days and nights of darkness. The power of Otero Silva's transparent poetry embraces every realm of humanity. He names and describes the exotic flowers and plants of Venezuela, and, with the same clarity, characterizes the activities and qualities of the simple, forgotten people who come alive in his books.

These regions and these beings are implacably divided between anguish and well-being, between the past and hope for the future, between abuse and truth. It may seem schematic, it may seem only a brushstroke of light and shadow, but this division exists. Its scar disfigures the shining, sorrowful face of the Republic of Venezuela. Otero Silva's book reveals the origin of these evils, with tenderness at times, but also with pitiless realism.

Miguel Otero Silva immerses us in his world, showing us both faces of his dramatic land.

A PERSONAL NOTE: Accustomed to a life of companionship and the militancy of friendship, I am suddenly struck by the absence of a friend. Not the man himself necessarily, his physical presence. No, I miss a characteristic, something of him that lingers in the air in the vacuum of his absence.

What I miss most about Otero Silva is his laugh. The Andalusian poet Rafael Alberti, that exiled free spirit, and Miguel, have the greatest laughs in all America. Rafael sits on his laugh like a hen on her nest, incubating it until it can no longer be contained; then it shakes his whole body, ending finally in the waves of his curly hair. Miguel's laugh, on the other hand, erupts, an exclamatory bellow that ends on a high note without ever losing its richness and hoarseness. His is a laugh that in his native Venezuela echoes from mountaintop to mountaintop and, when we wander the wide world together, echoes from street to street. It is a laugh that proclaims for every passerby the right to grace and the freedom to be joyful, even in the most uncertain circumstances.

Above this serious, beautiful, and revealing book I see rising the laughter of Miguel Otero Silva, as if a high-flying bird soared free from its pages.

The Revueltas Family

I have received a letter informing me that the novelist José Revueltas is in prison in his native Mexico.

This is bitter news for anyone who knows him, and it evokes memories and sadness.

The Revueltas family is a fascinating one. Even in a country of such creativity as our sister country, they stand out as extremely gifted. The family excels in music, in writing, and in the theater. They are like the Parras of Chile, outstanding in poetry and folklore, their talent ever ripening and flowering.

One afternoon, when I returned from work, I found a stranger sitting in the living room of my home in Mexico City. I could not see his face clearly, because he had put on a small, brightly colored straw hat I had bought at a fair. Beneath its brim I could see a thick, graying head of hair, and a strong neck. The shoulders of a colossus strained the seams of a rumpled suit. Beside him were several bottles of my cherished Chilean wine, definitely empty.

This was the greatest, the most original, the most powerful composer in Mexico: Silvestre Revueltas.

As I sat down across from him, he raised his minotaur's head. Barely slitting his eyes, he said: "Bring me another bottle. I've been waiting for you for hours. It occurred to me this morning that I might die without ever meeting you. That's why I'm here. It's a bad thing for brothers not to know one another."

This letter was sent to Gustavo Díaz Ordaz, President of Mexico, in February 1969

He was capricious, immoderate, and childlike, the genial giant of Mexican music.

He spent three days and three nights in my house. I would go out to see to my business affairs and return to find him sitting in the same chair, waiting.

We reviewed our lives and the lives of others. We talked until late at night, until he stretched out on the bed, still wearing his suit and shoes. Once I saw he was asleep, I would place another bottle of wine, opened, on a table beside his enormous head.

One day, without ceremony, just as he had come, he disappeared, without so much as a goodbye. He had gone to direct the rehearsals of his *Renacuajo paseador*, a classic ballet of our times.

Sometime later I took a box for the night of the premiere. According to the program, the moment was approaching for Silvestre to appear to conduct his work. But that moment never came. In the shadows, I felt a touch on my shoulder. I turned. Silvestre's brother José whispered to me: "I've just come from the house. Silvestre's dead. You are the first to know."

We went outside to talk. He told me Silvestre had taken a turn for the worse in recent days, and that shortly before he died he'd asked them to hang on the wall facing his bed the little straw hat he'd taken with him. We buried him the next day. I read my "Oratorio menor" [from *Canto general*], dedicated to his memory. Never has a dead man listened to me more carefully, because my poem lifted him from his surroundings, from the confines of his country, to accord him the continental recognition he deserved.

Speaking of the family, I am reminded that once in Berlin I was invited by Helene Weigel, the widow of Bertolt Brecht, to a performance of the Berliner Ensemble. They were performing some nineteenth-century Russian play—in German, of course—with a large cast of ladies and gentlemen dressed for the hunt. The leading lady was beautiful, feted, fatally attractive, and very natural. I looked at the program. The actress was the sister of Silvestre and José, the dark-skinned Mexican Rosaura Revueltas. There she was, black eyes glittering and sparkling, speaking German in a European capital, the center of the most famous theater troupe in the world.

After the performance, I asked her: "How did you manage to look so fair among all those blonds? I thought you'd look like a fly in a bowl of milk. Did they use light makeup on you?"

"No," she replied. "You'll never guess what they did. They used dark makeup on all the others."

But at the moment our most important Revueltas is José. José Revueltas is contradictory, hirsute, inventive, despondent, and mischievous—a synthesis of the Mexican soul. Like his country, he moves within his own orbit, wild and free. He has the rebelliousness of Mexico, and a greatness inherited from his family.

I feel a sensual love for Mexico, with all the fluctuations of passion: burning desire and pure enchantment. Everything that happens there affects me. Often its sorrow pains me, its mistakes disturb me, and I share in each of its victories.

One learns to love Mexico in her sweetness and her bitterness, suffering with her, singing about her, as I have done, whether near or far.

And so, with the tranquillity that is the lover's right, I close with these words:

Señor Díaz Ordaz, Mr. President: I demand the release of José Revueltas. Among other reasons, because I am sure he is innocent. Also, because he has the geniality of all the Revueltas. And last and most important, because we all love him very much.

Venturelli: Alive and Well

Venturelli has been my friend for many years, although I am over fifty and he is barely thirty. He is a young giant of a man. He speaks very little. He smiles with his eyes and his hands; painters always do. We poets don't know how to move our hands. Painters leave a phrase unfinished, pluck it from the air, shape it, throw it against the wall, paint it.

Venturelli suffered from bad lungs, and for a long time was in a sanatorium high in the Chilean cordillera. That was a period filled with mystery. The painter was dying . . . but when we went to bury him, there was no corpse. We kept receiving dozens of marvelous paintings, sketches patiently illuminated in the dramatic colors that could only be Venturelli's: bleeding yellows, ochered greens.

During that time I was constantly on the move, through the streets, into the mines, along the rivers, waging my private war against a tinhorn tyrant buzzing around my country like a droning fly. From time to time, Venturelli's drawings and my poems crossed, his descending from the snowy mountains and mine ascending from the lush archipelagos. In this exchange of lightning flashes I felt that my poems were illuminated and, at the same time, that my poetry transmigrated into his painting.

These were meetings between travelers, between guerrillas. We are all travelers and guerrillas in this land where Venturelli and I were born. Chile, sword-sharp, snow-crowned, sand-covered, mortally rent asunder by ocean and mountain, land of a long golden spring beside the sea, and poverty howling night and day at the door of the poor.

So our mutual anxieties, our unique lamps, were interchanged, and from this was born our working friendship.

Then I became even more mysterious than Venturelli. I disappeared into the heart of my people, the police hard on my trail. These were the fly's police, and to prevent his finding me I moved from house to house, from street to street, from town to town. New smoke. New shadow.

I was writing my *Canto general.* We couldn't allow the pages to fall into the hands of the pursuers, so the minute I lifted my pen from the pages, they were rushed through mysterious channels to be set and printed.

Venturelli, now alive and well, directed the clandestine editing, and in the secret "cellars of liberty," as Jorge Amado would describe them, the thousands of pages were piling up that would comprise the book. There were times when everything was in danger of falling into the fly's hands. The police questioned everyone, and more than once they did it sitting on the stacked pages of my book. Venturelli was everywhere, carrying galleys, correcting proofs, fitting together the scattered sections of the book that had been stored in different hiding places, the way you reconstruct the skeleton of some prehistoric animal.

And sometime during the comings and goings of this roaming guerrilla, Venturelli added his stirring illustrations to my poems. His are the drawings of the Conquistador with the cross and sword, the small Andean Indian, the heroic hussar, the machine-gunned strikers. His, too, the crazy images from my poetry, the wine pitcher with the butterfly, the naked figurehead that once flew on a prow.

Venturelli is a great man. He is as unsophisticated and dramatic as our America. Suddenly, with him, everything is terrible. All he can see is mourning and ravens. He is forsaken. He looks into the abyss; he is going to die. Our people are going to die; we will sink beneath the weight of so many cruelties; we can't last any longer. Then, suddenly, Venturelli smiles. Everything has changed. His tortured figures have been erased by maturity: action is the mother of hope.

1955

Nemesio Antúnez

I must use geographical terms when I speak of the painter Nemesio Antúnez. Great beauty is exploration of the air, the moon, the earth. Especially, the earth.

Anyone approaching the narrow, elongated country of Chile will find in the uppermost portion the Great North, the desert-like regions of salt and copper mines: inclement weather, silence, and struggle. In the extreme South, the great frozen expanses, ranging from the silence of Patagonia to Cape Horn, crossed so many thousands of times by the flight of the albatross, and then, the glittering Antarctic.

The painter Nemesio Antúnez belongs to that part of our country that lies between these two extremes. Let us say the area between Tarapacá and Aysén comprises the Antúnez longitude. Not as dry as the land of mineral deposits, or as cold as the continent of snow. The islands, floral profusion, single-minded fecundity, lie in the central belt that produces both the sugar-laden grape and the salt of shellfish and fish, the fruit of the coast. Antúnez is as transparent as a lake, his world is the fecund world of dawn, the trembling moment of birth in which pollen, fruit, birds, and volcanoes coexist beneath life-giving light.

There is no disorder in this organic creation, nor the severe lines of poverty. Antúnez's color has been born of intensity and then set aflame in a zenith transformed by the seasons, bound to the changes of nature. His stasis is merely a mask for his watery depths: a mysterious circulatory pulsation created this transparency.

Antúnez's territory is not empty space. In this continuum, men and objects are tenderly integrated, vibrant and expressive, with an ineradicable aroma of their own.

When I met him, Nemesio Antúnez was green, and gridded like graph paper. We became great friends while he was blue. When he was yellow, I left on a trip. He was violet when I returned and we greeted each other near Mapocho Station in Santiago. There a small river flows from the Andes; colossal boulders line the roads toward the cordillera; chill birds warble in the noonday of winter. Suddenly there is the smoke of burning forests, the sun is a scarlet king, a choleric cheese; there are thistles, moss, deafening waters; and Nemesio Antúnez of Chile is saturated in all these things, within and without; his soul is pervaded with subtleties, with his crystalline land. His objects are depicted with delicacy, because in Chile one weaves a fine cloth, sings a fine song, works a fine soil, and, all the while, the land is sprinkled with the pollen and the snow of a spring torrent, an Andean dawn.

September 1959

To a Young Gallant

THE young gallant I met in 1934, dressed in an electric-blue shirt and poppy-red tie, is today celebrating his seventieth birthday. He has not aged, though he has done everything one does to become an old man: he never turned away from a fight, from discipline, from labor, from joy, from any excess.

He has been generous with his poetry and with his life. Defeat could not rout him, nor exile, and his heart did not wither when like a bard of old he bore all the weight of a people, his people, in their exodus.

He has been magnanimous toward the unjust and the envious, and kept himself apart, a bee buzzing in the golden, earthly vibration of his poetry.

When the true history of Spain is written, his medallion-sharp profile will gleam brightly. And it will be known how that golden countenance liberated Spanish poetry: like a flowing spring of light, he added the classical and popular dimension of his joy.

In the absence of the towns of Puerto de Santa María, Jerez, Madrid—of all of Spain—the village of Reggio Emilia honors him. His Italian friends do well to crown with the laurel of Italy the birthday of Rafael Alberti.

Isla Negra, December 1972

NOTEBOOK IV

Sailing in Smoke

Comportment and Poetry

WHEN time is devouring us with the resolute regularity of its lightning flash, when fundamental attitudes, confidence, blind faith, hurtle by, pell-mell; when the stature of the poet plummets like dispirited, nacred spit, we wonder: has the hour come when we must vilify ourselves? the painful hour when we see how man hangs on by tooth and nail, by desire alone? and how, tooth and nail and limbs, the savage tree of hatred invades the house of poetry? In our time it is power, or perhaps inertia, that shrivels the fruit upon the very threshold of the heart, or it may be that his "artistry" overpowers the poet and, instead of the salubrious song that sallies from the ocean waves, we see each day a wretched being who defends the wretched treasure of his favored status.

Ah, time is ashes, it advances on air and water! The stone eroded by ooze and anguish suddenly flowers, roaring like the sea, and the tiny rose retreats to its delicate corolla tomb.

Time cleans and reveals, classifies and continues.

And then, what is left of the filthy villains, the mean little conspiracies of silence, the nasty chills of hostility? Nothing, and in the house of poetry all that endures is what was written in blood to be heard by the blood.

The four prose poems on pages 125–29 appeared in Neruda's magazine *Caballo Verde para la Poesía*, Spain, 1935

Themes

Toward the path of the nocturne stretch the fingers of the grave iron statue whose stature is implacable. Disregarded songs, revelations of the heart, scurry anxiously to its domain: the powerful polar star, the terrestrial gillyflower, long shadows invade the blue. Space and diminished magnitude approach a confrontation, unattended by the wretched children of intellect and inopportune time. While the timeless firefly dissolves its phosphorescent tail into glowing dust, the students of the earth, secure geographers, impresarios, decide to sleep. Lawyers, receivers.

Lonely, alone, a hunter overtaken by night in the deep forest, overwhelmed by the luminous aluminum of the sky, startled by raging stars, solemnly raises his gloved hand and strikes the site of his heart.

The site of the heart is ours. Lonely, alone, only from the heart, with the aid of black night and deserted autumn, emerge our songs, the songs of the heart, as the hand strikes the breast.

Like lava or shadow, like bestial trembling, like bells tolling without purpose, poetry dips its hand into fear, into anguish, into the ills of the heart. The imperious ornaments imposed by solitude and oblivion—stars, trees—are eternally external. The poet in mourning black writes with trembling hand, very much alone.

Gustavo Adolfo Bécquer
1836–1936

Somewhere rain is falling,
the sound of eternity

A hand of blazing honeysuckle inundates the dusk with rain-drenched smoke, with rain-drenched snow, with rain-kissed flowers.

Noble voice, gentle, wounded heart!

What tendrils unfurl, what celestial mourning doves ascend from your brow? What dewy bees distill their honey in your ultimate essences?

Golden angel, ashen asphodel.

Your time-worn curtains are bloody shreds, your throbbing harps have been stilled in the long darkness. The pain of love buries its phalanges of choler and hatred in your heart. But your tears have not dried. Beneath names, beneath events, flows a salty river of blood.

Melancholy clothing, flowering bell.

And beneath it all, the deteriorating, ornate fabric of your statue, washed by many rains and many tears, your phantasmal statue, its eyes plucked out by seabirds, your statue of jasmine blossoms blighted by lightning.

Ill-starred sun. Lord of the rain.

Some Thoughts on Impure Poetry

I_T is worth one's while, at certain hours of the day or night, to scrutinize useful objects in repose: wheels that have rolled across long, dusty distances with their enormous loads of crops or ore, charcoal sacks, barrels, baskets, the hafts and handles of carpenters' tools. The contact these objects have had with man and earth may serve as a valuable lesson to a tortured lyric poet. Worn surfaces, the wear inflicted by human hands, the sometimes tragic, always pathetic, emanations from these objects give reality a magnetism that should not be scorned.

Man's nebulous impurity can be perceived in them: the affinity for groups, the use and obsolescence of materials, the mark of a hand or a foot, the constancy of the human presence that permeates every surface.

This is the poetry we are seeking, corroded, as if by acid, by the labors of man's hand, pervaded by sweat and smoke, reeking of urine and of lilies soiled by diverse professions in and outside the law.

A poetry as impure as a suit or a body, a poetry stained by food and shame, a poetry with wrinkles, observations, dreams, waking, prophecies, declarations of love and hatred, beasts, blows, idylls, manifestos, denials, doubts, affirmations, taxes.

The sacred law of the madrigal and the decrees of touch, smell, taste, sight, and hearing, the desire for justice and sexual desire, the sound of the ocean, nothing deliberately excluded, a plunge into unplumbed depths in an access of ungovernable love. And the poetic product will be stamped with digital doves, with the scars of teeth and ice, a poetry slightly consumed by sweat and war. Until one achieves a surface worn as smooth as a constantly played instrument, the hard softness of rubbed wood, or arrogant iron. Flowers, wheat, and water also have that special consistency, the same tactile majesty.

But we must not overlook melancholy, the sentimentalism of another age, the perfect impure fruit whose marvels have been cast aside by the mania for pedantry: moonlight, the swan at dusk, "my beloved," are, beyond question, the elemental and essential matter of poetry. He who would flee from bad taste is riding for a fall.

I Refuse to Chew Theories

My editor and friend Enio Silveira tells me that I must add a few introductory words to this book of my poetry, so generously translated by three brother poets in Brazil.

On this occasion, as when one is forced to rise and offer a toast at a long dinner table, I don't know what to say or where to begin. I am fifty-three years old, and I have never known what poetry is, or how to define what I do not know. I have never been able to advise anyone about this dark yet dazzling subject.

As a child and as an adult I have devoted more attention to rivers and birds than to libraries and writers.

I have assumed the poet's time-honored obligation to defend the people, the poor and the exploited.

Is this important? I think these are obsessions shared by everyone who has ever written, who writes, or ever will write poetry. Love, it is clear, is concerned with all this and must lay its fiery cards on the table.

I have often begun to read disquisitions on poetry, but I never manage to finish them. A number of overly learned persons take it upon themselves to obscure the light, to turn bread into coal, a word into a screw. In order to isolate the poor poet from his brothers, from his companions on this earth, they tell him all manner of fascinating lies. "You are a magus," they reiterate. "You are a god of obscurity." Sometimes we poets believe these things and repeat them as if we'd been gifted with a kingdom. The truth is, these adulators want to confiscate that threatening kingdom, the communication of song

---

Preface to the Portuguese edition of Neruda's works published in April 1957

among all human beings. This mystifying and mythologizing of poetry produces a profusion of treatises I not only don't read but actually detest. They recall the dietary customs of some Eskimo tribes in which some members chew the food so that others can devour it. Well, I refuse to chew theories; instead, I invite anyone to walk with me into one of the red-oak forests of southern Chile where I fell in love with the earth, or into a stocking factory, or a manganese mine (the workers there know me), or anywhere a man can get some fried fish.

I don't know whether it's necessary to separate men into categories of natural and artificial, realist and illusionist: for me, it's enough to put on one side men who are men and on the other those who are not. The latter have nothing to do with poetry, or, at least, nothing to do with my poems.

I see, standing at the end of this long Brazilian table where I was asked to say a few words, that I have spoken too much and said too little. Overcoming my reservations about prologues and dedications, I did not refuse, because of my strong attraction to Brazil, poetic, earthy, intense country that I love.

I grew up in the south of America, beneath the cold rains that for thirteen months of the year (as we Chileans of the South say) fall upon towns, mountains, and roads, until they drench the archipelagos spilling out into the Pacific, sweep across the solitudes of Patagonia, and freeze in the purity of Antarctica.

This is one of the reasons why this luminous country, an eternal green butterfly opening and closing its wings on the map of America, electrified and mesmerized me, leaving me to search out the source of its mysterious magnetism. And then, when I discovered its gentle people, the fraternal and powerful people of this indelible land, my heart was made complete.

To this land and to these people I lovingly dedicate these poems.

This Adolescent Book

THIS book (if I remember correctly) was written thirty-six years ago, and though far removed from it, I am still captive to the springtime by the sea that inspired it, to the air and the stars of those days and nights. The women's eyes that open in this book have been closed by time; the hands that blaze in this book, the lips interrupted by fire, the wheat-colored bodies that stretch across these pages, all that life, that truth, that water, has flowed into the great, pulsing, subterranean river of life that springs from other, from all, lives.

But the fog, the coast, the tumultuous sea of the South of Chile, all the things that in this adolescent book blazed a trail toward the nucleus of my poetry, still bore into my memory, scourging it with the authority of its foaming sea, its menacing geography. I grew up, I loved, in that fluvial and oceanic landscape, with the wild abandonment of youth.

Yet, there on the cold shore of those austral seas, in Puerto Saavedra, in Bajo Imperial, something awaited me.

One midsummer, still a youth, dressed in black, I came upon a patio where all the poppies in the world were growing in wild profusion. I had scarcely noticed poppies before, blood and rubies scattered in the wheat fields. But here, by the thousands, they swayed on long slender stems, like perpendicular serpents. Some were white, nuptial, and foamy, anemones in a sea that bellowed for them like a black bull, some had a purple rim around their corollas, an encircling wound, others were purplish, violet, yellow, coral, coppery, and some I had

---

Preface to the French edition of *Veinte poemas de amor y una canción desesperada*, 1960

never seen before, black poppies, preternatural phantoms in that solitary patio at the edge of an Antarctica that reserved to its own domain the ultimate, icy poppy: the South Pole.

The port was redolent with the milky, poisonous fragrance of the million poppies that awaited me in that secret garden.

The Pachecos' garden. They'd been fishermen, the Pachecos . . . The abandoned boat . . .

Because the great storms of those frigid seas vent their fury there. Years ago, the community had made a living from shipwrecks, and at the back of the Pachecos' garden, amid an infinity of poppies, was a lifeboat from some sunken ship. There, gazing toward a sky whose blue was tempered by steely winds, I often lay daydreaming: a pinpoint in the center of a blue spiral, weighed down by the naked truth of the sky, I pondered mighty questions as the waves of the sea swirled about me.

These poems were written with air, sea, heads of wheat, stars, and love, oh yes, love . . . Since that time they've gone their own way, wandering and singing . . . Time has stripped them of their swaddling clothes: one of the cataclysms that like a fiery sword hover above Chile fell upon Puerto Saavedra and obliterated my memories. The sea that resounds in this book rushed in and a groundswell swept away the houses and the pines. All that remained were broken, twisted docks. A huge wave flailed the poppies. As of this year 1960, nothing survives.

Nothing . . . May my poetry treasure in its goblet that long-ago spring, now dead.

Paris, November 1960

A Summing Up

THIS is my first step backward toward my own past, toward my childhood. It is my first return through the forest toward the source of life, my life. The road has been obliterated, we leave no trail to retrace, and if the leaves trembled then as we passed by, they do not tremble now, and we are deaf to the oracular lightning that flashed down to destroy us. To walk back toward memory when memories have turned to smoke is like sailing through smoke. In 1962, in Valparaiso, after many years of roaming, all I can see of my childhood is rain and dense smoke. Those who love me can seek after it there: its only key is love.

Surely, the wild winds born in the volcanic shadow of still unnamed cordilleras, rivers, and archipelagos have not changed, but leave in their path the storm-swept reeds and hostile ridges of my origins. This is the patrimony of Americans. Our birth and our growth are conditioned by a nature that both nurtured and castigated us. It is difficult to rid ourselves of the traces of this death struggle, when the light smote us with its scimitar, the forest beckoned only to disorient us, and night wounded us with its starry cold. We had no one to turn to. No one before us had lived in those regions, no one before us built buildings, or abandoned bones in cemeteries that only later came to be: our dead were the first dead. The advantage is that we could dream in a pure air no one had breathed before, and so our dreams were the first dreams of that land.

Now I bring these blossoms of Antarctic shadow to be transmuted

---

Preface to Neruda's *Sumario: Libro donde nace la lluvia,* published by A. Tallone, Alpignano, Italy, 1963

134

into beautiful typography. I surrender their roughness to Tallone, rector of supreme clarity, of communication.

I never dreamed, in the solitudes that gave me birth, that I would achieve such honor, and as I deliver these imperfect pages to the rectitude of such a great printer I feel as I did when as a child I found and broke open a wild honeycomb in the mountains. I learned then that the wild honey that diffused its aroma from the tormented tree was housed in precisely arranged cells, and thus the secret sweetness was preserved and revealed in a fragile but firm geometry.

Birds, Little Birds...

ROM snows to sands, over volcanoes, beaches, pastures, rivers, rocks, thatched roofs, roads, waves, everywhere, the birds. Birds, little birds, gigantic birds, birdy birds, wordy birds! Not all flying, some spying; some singing, some winging; flashing like a golden beam, blending into ash and night. And their flight! Flight in the wide freedom of the air, fleet as arrows or slow as ships. Different styles of flight, some cleaving the sky, some piercing it with knives; and sometimes, with the overflowing multitudes of migration, flooding the universe with liquid birddom. As a boy I often paused beside the Araucan river: water and birdsong caught me in their web. Like a sponge my blood soaked up songs and roots. Later the forests burned, leaf by leaf, burnt branches throbbed for the last time, ashes, but unbowed, and the heat and the smell of fire pulsed like waves of fury through my bloodstream. But soon again fledgling woodpeckers fed in the bosky light and the ponderous stork thundered among the cinnamon trees. All was restored to its original profound aroma.

Emerging from the Straits of Magellan, sailing through archipelagos of stone and ice, I was followed by the great albatross whose wingspread almost spans the width of Chile as it hovers, dancing, in the air. The ocean expanse was slick as oil, drizzling rain pocked the spuming salt, mountains were buried beneath ashen death; the only signs of life were the greatest wings on the planet, performing rituals of order in the midst of a dying world. Save us, albatross, with your life-giving ferocity, with your will for flight! Save us from the desolate wastelands, from invading dusk, from cosmic assault.

Preface to Neruda's *Pájaros*, January 1963

And finally, an honest but idle man—and would that it continue so—I have been visited by the tiniest of songsters, by finches and linnets, larks, wrens, and crown sparrows. Their profession is to dart after grain, a worm, or water, bursting into song, happiness, delirium. Often I held them in my hand; they pecked me, scratched me, they looked askance at my foreign flesh, my unknown bone, and I freed them, let them sigh, fly away, turbulent, bold-eyed, leaving in my hand a whisper of fluttering wings and a waft of clay and pollen.

Loicas have flashed their military ID's at me, exposing their purple hearts along the roadways.

Though birds, those skim-birds, skitter-birds, sky-birds, professed all before me, I never learned to fly, or sing. I learned to love them indiscriminately, heedless in the familiarity of my ignorance, studying them from crest to toe, content with my stupid stability, while they laughed, fluttering overhead. So, to humble them, I invented a few birds to represent me, to fly among the true birds.

And so I have fulfilled the mission that caused me to be born in Chile, my native land. This small book is part of my last will and testament. And if, as is only natural, more wings and better songs are needed, the birds will come to my defense.

Poets of the People

SOUTH America has always been a land of potters. A continent of clay pitchers. These singing pitchers have always come from the people. They made them with clay and with their hands. They made them with fine white clay and with their hands. They made them with stone and with their hands. They made them with silver and with their hands.

I have always wanted the hands of the people to be seen in poetry. I have always preferred a poetry where the fingerprints show. A poetry of loam, where water can sing. A poetry of bread, where everyone may eat.

Only the poetry of the people sustains this memory of hands.

As poets closeted themselves in their laboratories, the people continued to sing with their clay, their earth, their rivers, their ores. They produced extraordinary flowers, and remarkable epics; they told stories of adventures and tales of catastrophes. They celebrated their heroes, they defended their rights, they crowned their saints, they wept for their dead.

And they did all this by their hands alone. These hands were clumsy, but they were wise. They were blind, but they broke stone. They were small, but they took fish from the sea. They were dark, but they sought the light.

This poetry has the magic of all things that have been created naturally. This poetry of the people has the seal of all the things that are exposed to nature, to rain, sun, snow, and wind. It is poetry that

---

Preface to *La lira popular* (*The Lyre of the People*), an anthology published in Santiago, March 6, 1966

must be passed from hand to hand. It is poetry that must ripple in the air like a flag. Poetry that has been pounded, poetry that lacks the Grecian symmetry of perfect faces. There are scars on its happy, bitter face.

I am not offering a laurel wreath to these poets of the people. It is they who bestow on me the strength and innocence that must animate all poetry. It is through them that I touch its nobility, its surface of leather, of green leaves, of joy.

It is they, the people's poets, the obscure poets, who show me the light.

A Chilean "Outlaw"

I have a strong aversion to replying when I am asked what book I'm working on or what my future projects are. Experience has taught me that when you talk a lot about something before doing it, the odds are good that it will never get done.

When I was a very young poet (only sixteen), I thought of a brilliant, beautiful title for a long poem that I announced to everyone who would listen. The title was wildly applauded by my young fellow poets. Soon the poem was taken for a fact. Then they congratulated me on my great success. And I grew accustomed to their praise. So what need was there to write the poem? And that's where the matter rested for forty-six years: a solitary title without a single verse beneath it.

I bring this up only to tell you that I can now speak about what I've been doing these summer months on the coast of Chile. I can talk about it because it's done. It is a long poem. This time I have all the verses but what's lacking is the title.

This poem recounts a long, romantic story flooded with brilliant color, though everything ends in the black of mourning.

It so happened that when the news of the discovery of gold in California spread through the world, a large number of Chileans went north to seek their fortunes. They set out from Valparaiso, then the most important port along the southern coast. These men were miners, farmers, fishermen, and adventurers, drawn by the lure of glitter-

---

This article and the one that follows, both dealing with Neruda's play, *Fulgor y muerte de Joaquín Murieta*, were written in 1966

ing adventure. In Chile they'd learned how to get along in a poor and rugged land.

The curious thing is that these Chileans arrived in the gold fields before the North Americans. It seems strange, but the Yankees had to cross the continent in slow wagons, while the Chileans, with their sailing ships, arrived much more quickly.

Among them was the famous Joaquín Murieta, the most notorious of Chilean outlaws. But was he simply an outlaw, a renegade?

This is the theme of my poem.

Murieta was lucky. He found gold, he married a Chilean girl, but as he continued his dogged search for fresh lodes, he was overtaken by a tragedy that changed his life.

Mexicans, Chileans, Central Americans, all lived in the poor barrios of the towns that sprang up like mushrooms around San Francisco. There, every night, you could hear the throbbing of guitars and the songs of the brown-skinned continent.

Soon this profusion of foreigners, gold, song, and happiness incited violence. The North Americans formed bands of white vigilantes that raided these settlements by night—burning, razing, and killing.

There seems little doubt that the idea for the Ku Klux Klan was born there. The same frenzied racism that typifies the Klan even today motivated those crusading Yankees who wanted to clean out all the Latin Americans from California, and, it follows, to get their hands on the Latins' strikes. In one of these raids, the wife of Joaquín Murieta was murdered.

Murieta was away, but when he returned he swore vengeance.

From that moment on, no humiliation, no assault by racists went unpunished.

By night, the band of avengers rode out in search of the North Americans, who fell like flies whenever they encountered Murieta and his men.

For more than a year these guerrillas lived in hiding and fought as they could. Following the tradition of Robin Hood, they stole from the rich to give to the poor; that is, they returned to the plundered what they had taken from the plunderers.

Joaquín Murieta died as he lived. He fell in an ambush, his body riddled with bullets. His severed head was exhibited at the San Francisco Fair, and the impresarios who charged for the privilege of viewing that dismal trophy became wealthy men.

But Murieta, or rather, Murieta's head, took on new life. He became a legend that a hundred years later still lives in the memory of Spanish-speaking peoples. Many books, many songs, many ballads keep his memory alive. North Americans called him an outlaw. But the word "outlaw" was ennobled in the memory of the people, and, when it referred to Murieta, it was uttered with reverence.

Murieta's birthplace is disputed by Mexico and Chile. The debate persists in the mist of fable and legend, but, for me, Murieta was Chilean.

His story intrigued me because of the racial conflict and the extent of the greed and blood surrounding the man—real or legendary.

And that is why I happily devoted many hours this summer to chronicling this strange life and singing these long-ago adventures.

Why Joaquín Murieta?

I wrote a big book of poetry, I called it *La barcarola*, and it was a kind of ballad; I dabbled a little in all the materials I like to use, sometimes water or wheat, sometimes simple sand, an occasional hard and precise crag or quarry, and always the sea with its silence and its thunder, eternities at my disposal right outside my window and within reach of my paper, and in this book there are some episodes that not only sing but tell a story, because long ago that's how it was, poetry sang and told a story, and that's the way I am, too, old-fashioned, there's no getting around it, well, one day I was pecking away at the past when pouf! dust whirled as if an earthquake had struck, bullets flew, and an episode appeared complete with a horse and rider, and this rider began to gallop through my verses, which by now were as wide as a path, or a trail, and I sped along behind my verses and discovered gold, California gold, Chileans panning for gold, crowded ships from Valparaiso, greed, turbulence, new beginnings, and this vengeful and avenging Chilean, rash and resounding, and then my wife Matilde Urrutia said to me: But this is theater. Theater? I replied. I didn't know it, but there it is, in my book and on the stage Murieta returns, we're told of his rebellion and of the deeds of rustic Chileans who like hounds on the scent rushed after gold, Chileans who tightened their belts and worked at any old job they could find, only to be paid in the gringos' coin: the rope, the bullet, or at the least, a kick in the head; but they don't suffer too much because there's love as well, with verses that rhyme just as in my old days, a little of everything, folk dances, and music by Sergio Ortega; and then Pedro Orthous, the famous director, put in his oar and cut a little here and lopped off a lot there, and if I protested, I was told that the same thing had happened to Lope de Vega and Shakespeare, they were cut, too, modified for you, the audience, and there I was, a mere apprentice in the theater, and I accepted, so that Murieta would ride again, I wanted Murieta to fly high, spurring on his horse and waving a Chilean flag, Viva Chile, my beauty! I wanted him, horse and all, to streak like a meteor returning to its homeland because I summoned him, I sought him, there beside the clamoring sea, day after day I dug into my work and suddenly out jumped this brigand and his mount striking sparks in the California night, and I said to him, Come on out, come on, and I made him ride the highway of my book, galloping to relive his life and his drama, his splendor and his death, like a cruel dream, and so that's how it was, that's my story and my song.

Once Again in Temuco

Once again I find myself in Temuco. The city has changed so much that it is as if the Temuco I knew had disappeared. Winter-colored wooden houses have been transformed into large houses of dreary cement. There are more people in the streets, fewer horses and carriages are lined up before the blacksmith shops. This was the only city in Chile where one saw Araucan Indians in the streets. I am pleased that it is still so. Indian women in their large purple shawls. Indian men in the black ponchos on which a strange white fret is repeated like a lightning flash. Before, they came only to buy and sell their sparse wares: weaving, eggs, hens. Recently they came for a different purpose. I will tell you the surprising thing that happened.

All the people came to the stadium to hear my poetry. It was a Sunday morning and the crowded amphitheater reverberated to the cries and laughter of the children. Children are the great interrupters, and no poetry in the world can survive the howls of a child announcing its breakfast time. As I climbed onto the wooden platform to the public's applause, I felt that affinity with Herod that can beset the most paternal being. Then the crowd grew still and in the ensuing silence I heard the strangest, the most primordial, the most ancient, the harshest music on this planet. It came from a group at the rear of the audience.

The Araucan Indians were playing their native instruments for me, and singing their sorrowful songs. Never in history had such a thing occurred, my reticent compatriots contributing their ritual art to a cultural and political gathering. It was something I'd never expected to see, and, moreover, their act of communication was directed toward me. I was deeply moved. Tears came to my eyes as ancient

145

hide drums and gigantic flutes resounded in tones that predated music, muted and acute, monotonous and heartbreaking. It was the voice of wind-driven rain, the moan of a prehistoric animal martyred beneath the earth.

So this is to tell you that the Araucan people, or what remains of them, are stirring, emerging from their immemorial dream and expressing a desire to participate in a world which until now has been denied them.

The Cup of Blood

When I am returning from remote regions, captive to the extraordinary fatalism of trains, like our ancestors on horseback, I doze and daydream, and think my private thoughts. I look back across the blackness of the years, and woven through them like a snow-covered vine, I see a sense of patriotism, a savage tricolor wind, present from my earliest years. I am part of a piece of poor southern soil close to Araucania; my actions have been determined by faraway clocks, as if that wooded and perpetually rain-soaked land held a secret I do not know, a secret I do not know but must know, a secret I seek desperately, blindly, exploring long rivers, fantastic vegetation, thickly wooded mountains, the seas of the South, sinking into flora and rain, never reaching that prized foam the waves deposit, then scatter, never arriving at the meter of special earth, never touching the sands that are rightfully mine. Then, while the nocturnal train shudders violently at wood or coal stops as if being pounded against invisible coral reefs in a night sea, I shrink and grow small, I am a pupil with my schoolmates on the outskirts of our town, a child again in the frozen South, holding close to my heart the great damp forests of that southern world. Dressed all in black, wearing my poet's tie, I walk into a patio; my aunts and uncles are gathered there, they are enormous; guitars and knives lie under a tree, song soon mingles with the harsh wine. To the sound of gunfire and music they slit the throat of a quivering lamb, and hold to my lips a burning cup of blood. I feel I am dying, like the lamb, but I want to become a centaur like the men, and pale and indecisive, alone in the middle of my childhood desert, I raise and drink the cup of blood.

My father died recently, a strictly secular event, and yet something
religiously solemn happened in his tomb, and this is the moment to
reveal it. Some weeks later, my mother, to use the prosaic but terrifying words, also passed away, and so that they could lie side by side we
removed my father's body from its niche. We, my brother, some
of my father's railroad friends, and I, went at noon to open the sealed
and cemented niche. We removed the already moldy receptacle containing my father's remains, and on it, the palm leaf and black, shriv-
eled flowers. The dampness of the mausoleum had split open the
coffin, and as we lowered it from its resting place, before our unbe-
lieving eyes, a veritable torrent of water flowed out of it, a seemingly
inexhaustible liquid streamed from it, from its substance.

But there was an explanation: this tragic water was rain, the rain,
perhaps, of a single day, even a single hour, of our southern winter,
and this rain had run through roofs and balustrades, bricks and other
materials, even other corpses, to reach my father's tomb. So this
awesome water, this water flowing from an unfathomable impossibil-
ity, an extraordinary hiding place, to reveal to me its secret torrents,
this elementary and awesome water and its mystifying spilling, reminded me once again of my inescapable connection with a prede-
termined life, region, and death.

1943

The Odors of Homecoming

MY house nestles among many trees. After a long absence, I like to lose myself in hidden nooks to savor my homecoming. Mysterious, fragrant thickets have appeared that are new to me. The poplar I planted in the back of the garden, so slim it could barely be seen, is now an adult tree. Its bark is patterned with wrinkles of wisdom that rise toward the sky to express themselves in a constant tremor of new leaves in the treetop.

The chestnut trees were the last to recognize me. When I arrived, their naked, dry branches, towering and unseeing, seemed imperious and hostile, though the pervading spring of Chile was germinating amid their trunks. Every day I went to call on them, for I understood that they demanded my homage, and in the cold of morning stood motionless beneath the leafless branches, until one day a timid green bud, high overhead, came out to look at me, and others followed. So my reappearance was communicated to the wary, hidden leaves of the tallest chestnut tree, which now greets me with condescension, tolerating my return.

In the trees the birds renew their age-old trills, as if nothing ever happened beneath the leaves.

A pervasive odor of winter and years lingers in the library. Of all places, this was the most suffused with absence.

There is something of mortality about the smell of musty books; it assaults the nostrils and strikes the rugged terrain of the soul, because it is the odor of oblivion, of buried memory.

Standing beside the weathered window, staring at the blue and

Published in *Novedades*, Mexico, 1952

white Andean sky, I sense that behind my back the aroma of spring is pitting its strength against the books. They resist being rooted out of their long neglect, and still exude sighs of oblivion. Spring enters every room, clad in a new dress and the odor of honeysuckle.

The books have been unruly in my absence. None is missing, but none is in its place. Beside an austere volume of Bacon, a rare seventeenth-century edition, I find Salgari's *The Captain of Yucatan*, and in spite of everything, they've got along rather well together. On the other hand, as I pick up a solitary Byron, its cover drops off like the dark wing of an albatross. Laboriously, I stitch spine and cover, but not before a puff of cold Romanticism clouds my eyes.

The shells are the most silent occupants of my house. They endured the years of the ocean, solidifying their silence. Now, to those years have been added time and dust. Their cold, glinting mother-of-pearl, their concentric Gothic ellipses, their open valves, remind me of distant coasts, long-ago events. This incomparable lance of rosy light is the *Rostellaria*, which the Cuban malacologist Carlos de la Torre, a magus of the deep, once conferred upon me like an underseas decoration. And here, slightly more faded and dusty, is the black "olive" of the California seas, and, of the same provenance, the oyster of red spines and the oyster of black pearls. We almost drowned in that treasure-laden sea.

There are new occupants, books and objects liberated from boxes long sealed. The pine boxes come from France. The boards smell of sunny noon in the Midi, and as I pry them open, they creak and sing, and the golden light falls on the red bindings of Victor Hugo. *Les Misérables*, in an early edition, arrives to crowd the walls of my house with its multitude of heartrending lives.

Then, from a large box resembling a coffin, comes the sweet face of a woman, firm wooden breasts that once cleaved the wind, hands saturated with music and brine. It is the figure of a woman, a figurehead. I baptize her María Celeste, because she has all the mystery of a lost ship. I discovered her radiant beauty in a Paris *bric-à-brac*, buried beneath used hardware, disfigured by neglect, hidden beneath the sepulchral rags and tatters of the slums. Now, aloft, she sails again, alive and new. Every morning her cheeks will be covered by mysterious dew or saltwater tears.

All at once the roses are in bloom. Once I was an enemy of the rose, of its interminable literary associations, of its arrogance. But as I watched them grow, having endured the winter with nothing to wear and nothing to cover their heads, and then as snowy breasts or glowing fires peered from among hard and thorny stems, little by little I was filled with tenderness, with admiration for their ox-like health, for the daring, secret wave of perfume and light they implacably extract from the black earth at just the right moment, as if duty were a miracle, as if they thrived on precise maneuvers in harsh weather. And now roses grow everywhere, with a moving solemnity I share—remote, both they and I, from pomp and frivolity, each absorbed in creating its individual flash of lightning.

Now every wave of air bears a soft, trembling movement, a flowery palpitation that pierces the heart. Forgotten names, forgotten springs, hands that touched briefly, haughty eyes of yellow stone, tresses lost in time: youth, insistently throbbing with memories and ecstatic aromas.

It is the perfume of the honeysuckle, the first kisses of spring.

Let's Go to Paraguay

I am living behind Notre Dame, beside the Seine. Sand barges, tugboats, laden convoys as slow as freshwater whales, pass before my window.

The cathedral is an even larger ship raising its arrow of chiseled stone like a mast. Every morning I look out to see whether it is still there beside the river, the cathedral ship, whether, while shadows covered the world, the sailors carved in ancient granite have given the order to weigh anchor, to set sail across the seas. I want to go with her. I would like to go up the Amazon River on this gigantic ship, to explore the estuaries, travel the tributaries, and at some place in my beloved America suddenly drop anchor until wild lianas weave a new mantle of green over the ancient cathedral and blue birds invest it with a new splendor of stained glass.

Or perhaps anchor her on the endless sands of the southern coast near Antofagasta, near the guano islands, where the excrement of cormorants has whitened the hills—as the snow denuded the figure-heads of the Gothic ship. How imposing and natural this church would be, another boulder among the reticent rocks splattered by the ocean's furious foam, solemn and solitary amid interminable sands.

I am not of these lands, these boulevards. I do not belong to these plants, these waters. These birds do not speak my language.

I want to sail up the river Dulce, sail all day through arching branches, startle herons into sudden snowy flashes of lightning. Right

Published in *Pro Arte*, Santiago, November 30, 1950

this moment I want to ride horseback, whistling, toward Puerto Natales in Patagonia. On my left passes a river of sheep, hectares of curly wool advancing slowly toward death; to my right, burnt posts, meadows, the smell of wild grasses.

Where is Santocristo? Venezuela calls me, Venezuela is a flame, Venezuela is blazing. I do not see the mists of this autumn, I do not see the changing leaves. Beyond Paris, like the beacon of a lighthouse, light intensified, Venezuela blazes. No one sees that light in these streets; they see buildings, harbors, and windows, hurrying people, blinding gazes. They are submerged in the autumn. Not I.

Beyond all this I see Venezuela, as if an enormous butterfly of fiery strength were beating against my window. Where will you carry me? I want to be a part of the tapestry of Mexico's markets, a nameless market, the thousandth market. I want to be that burnt color, I want to be woven and unraveled, I want my poetry to be strung like banners from the trees in small villages, I want my verse to have the weight of cloth, to protect a mother's flanks, to cover a farmer's mane.

I do not know Paraguay. As a man may shiver with pleasure when he thinks about an unread book by Dumas or Kafka or Balzac or Laforgue—because he knows that someday he will hold it in his hands, that one by one he will turn its pages, and from them will emerge the freshness or fatigue, the sadness or sweetness, he sought— so, too, I consider with delight that I do not know Paraguay, that for me life still holds Paraguay in store, a haven, an incomparable cupola, a new immersion in humanity.

When Paraguay is free, when our America is free, when its people speak to and hold out their hands to one another through the walls of air that now imprison us, then let's go to Paraguay. I want to see where my people, and others, suffered and conquered. There the earth is scarred, wild brambles in the luxuriant greenery keep watch over a soldier's tattered uniform. There, prisons have groaned with martyrdom. That land has seen a school of heroism, seen its earth sprinkled with harsh blood. I want to touch the walls where perhaps my brother wrote my name; with new eyes I want to read my name as if for the first time, learn it anew, because those who called me then called in vain. I could not come.

I am rich in my native land, in the earth, in the people I love who love me. I am not an embittered patriot, I do not know exile. Every day my flag sends me starry kisses. I am not exiled, because I am the earth, part of my own earth, indivisible, and vast.

When I close my eyes, so that dreams may course through me like a river, trains and forests pass, deserts, comrades, villages. America passes. It passes inside me as if I were passing through a tunnel, or as if this river of worlds and things suddenly narrowed its channel and poured all its waters into my heart.

My heart holds earth, and in this earth there are trees, and in the trees, a lasting fragrance. At times it is the cold odor of the southern laurel, which as it falls from its forty-meter tower in the forest strikes like thunder, freeing a hundred casks of invisible perfume. Or it may be the odor of mahogany, the red fragrance of Guatemala that permeates every house, awaits you in offices and kitchens, in parks and forests. Or others as sweet.

"Unforgettable perfume. Where will you take me? Don't you know the ocean?"

"Yes, I know the ocean. But I am your flowing hair, I am your plumed crest, I follow you and encircle you, I am your comet's tail, I am the only ring of your only marriage; I am your life."

Yes, you are my life, you are my race, you are my star. You are the great conch of blood and mother-of-pearl that sounds and resounds in my ear. He who has heard your sea will hear no other; he who was born beside your rivers will be born anew in them every day of his life; he who knew the araucaria forests of Lonquimay is born with a responsibility: he will sing in the storm.

And so it is, gentlemen, as I awake and see the ship of Notre Dame de Paris, bone and ash, rising above the Seine, assailed and lashed by the ocean of time, august, grave in her ancient seat of power, I can think of nothing, I can dream of nothing but

to reach your shores, oh, America, on this ship, or on another,
to live among your people, who are my people, among your leaves,
to struggle beside each one of my brothers, to conquer,
so that my victory may be vast, and yours, as vast as our broad earth,
suffused with peace and perfume,

and there, someday, on a new riverboat, on a machine, in a library,
  on a tractor
(because our cathedrals will be those, our victories will be those
  broad victories),
I, too, after struggling and conquering, will be earth, only earth, only
  earth, only your earth.

Keep Your Lamp Burning, *America*

O<small>F</small> all the lands where man lives, dreams, suffers, triumphs, and sings, your country has always meant something special to me. Peru, to me, was the womb of America, a hallowed land encircled by tall, mysterious stones, by foam-nibbled shores, by rivers, and metals deep beneath the earth. The Incas left more than a small crown of fire and martyrdom in the amazed hands of history; they left a vast, expansive ambience chiseled by the most delicate fingers, by hands that could coax melancholy and reverence from sound, and raise colossal stones to last throughout infinity.

As eternal as the equinox, they left imprinted on the face of America a pensive tenderness, a delicate and moving presence that from their vessels, jewels, statues, weavings, and hand-carved silence has illuminated the road of all that is profound in America. The enriching waves of Inca civilization washed over my country, bringing to the rough shadows of the land of the Araucans the texture of liturgy and cloth; the psychic vibrations of the guardian forests of the South came into contact with sacred turquoise and vessels bursting with spirituality: we will never know to what degree these essential waters from Peru permeated my country's awakening, submerging it in a telluric harmony of which my own poetry is but one simple expression.

Later, the ancient conqueror was to build his glittering storehouses containing the greatest splendor of the legend of America. In Peru, earth, gold, and steel are layered one upon the other like geological strata: earth converted into forms as diaphanous and vital as the essential seeds whose fruit will fill the pitchers that quench man's thirst;

Written in 1943, while traveling through Peru

gold whose power from the secret repository of its buried statue will attract, across time and oceans, men of different continents and different tongues; and steel whose brilliance will slowly forge sorrows and a new people.

There is something cosmic about your Peru, something so powerful and refulgent that no custom or fashion has been able to efface it, as if an enormous, recumbent statue, mineral and phosphorescent, monolithic and organic, still lay beneath your earth, covered by cloths and treasures, by epochs and sands, as if its vitality were to appear on the heights of abandoned stones, on the deserted soil it is our duty to discover. America is your Peru, your primitive, eighteenth-century Peru, your mysterious, arrogant, and ancient land, and in none of the states of America would we find the same concretions which, like gold and corn, spill into your cup to offer us such boundless perspectives of America.

Americans of Peru, if with my Chilean hands I have touched your rind and split open the sacred fruit of your fraternity, do not think that I leave you without declaring my love for your present life and your present magnificence. You must forgive a man who is American to the bone if he places his hand on your silence.

For many years, from a silent America, two countries that are the watchtowers and leavening of freedom in America have been watching you. These two countries are Chile and Mexico.

Geography placed them at the harsh extremes of the continent. It was Mexico's fate to be the bastion of our lifeblood when the survival of America demanded she gallantly reassert the fundamental tenets of our America, opposing the great materialist country to her north. And it was also Mexico which raised the first banners when the liberty of our continent was threatened, and was defended by our valiant northern brothers.

As Simón Bolívar predicted, Chile has known liberty. Through the sacrifice imposed by its harsh land, through exposure to insuperable obstacles, my country, with the same burning and delicate hands that survived the cruelest tasks and the cruelest climate of our latitudes, succeeded in touching the heart of man, raising it toward liberty like a radiant cup. My country's history advanced toward the dawn through hardship and travail, and we Chileans today are dedicated to dispersing such shadows.

From these two points—one Antarctic, the other musical and explosive—we look toward Peru in the hope that your steps will lead you toward the responsibility imposed by the name American. If the difficult historical destiny of America entrusts to your hands a lamp of freedom that tomorrow's wind could extinguish forever, it is your duty, not only to your own country but to the rest of our vast America as well, to keep, to make burn more brightly, to defend, this essential light. If in the light of dawn we study the map of America, with its beautiful rivers and splendid volcanic altars, you will see that there are areas where frozen tears form an icy enclosure around tyranny; you will note that in the most prosperous, the richest, the most powerful of our American states, new tyrants have just arisen. And these new tyrants are identical to those we suffered in the past; epauletted, they wield the whip and the sword. We see the tigers and crocodiles of our fearsome New World fauna lying in ambush to attack the smallest shred of freedom. So, Peruvians, Chileans, Colombians, all those who breathe the air of liberty bequeathed by the giants of old, beware, be on your guard. We must be on guard against the ancient, apoplectic fauna we thought was safely calcified in museums, its enormous defensive bone structure, its decorations, its bloody claws. The thirst for power and the willingness to torture still live in the world; our executioners lie in wait, day and night. And you must also be on guard against false liberators, against those who, not understanding the spirit of the age, attempt to fashion from violence a bouquet of flowers to place on the altar of man's freedoms.

The sons of American liberty—Sucre, Bolívar, O'Higgins, Morelos, Artigas, San Martín, Mariátegui—are despised both by caveman reactionism and by sterile demagoguery. Liberty in America will be the child of our deeds and our thoughts.

Ramón López Velarde

At almost the precise time in 1921 that I was arriving in Santiago de Chile from my home town, Ramón López Velarde, the quintessential, the supreme, poet of our far-flung Americas, was dying in Mexico. Of course, I wasn't aware that he had died, or even that he had existed. Then, as now, we filled our heads with the latest word from across the Atlantic; much of what we read evaporated like smoke or steam before our voracious appetites; a few revelations not only dazzled us but solidified with time. But it never occurred to us to consider anything going on in Mexico. Only that the gunfire of its revolutions still echoed in our ears. We knew nothing of the unique flowering in that bloody land.

Many years later, I rented the López Velardes's old villa in Coyoacán, on the edge of the Federal District of Mexico City. Some of my friends will remember that enormous house: every room was invaded by scorpions, beams were falling under the onslaught of efficient insects, and the floorboards sank under one's feet as if one were trekking through humid jungle. I managed to get two or three rooms into shape, and in them I began to absorb the atmosphere of López Velarde, and to steep myself in his poetry.

That phantasmagorical estate still bore traces of a decaying park, gigantic palm trees and evergreen ahuehuetes, a baroque pool so cracked it held no "water" but moonlight, and everywhere statues of vintage-1910 naiads. Wandering through the garden, one came upon them in unexpected places, peering from within a vine-covered gazebo, or simply walking with elegance toward the crumbled, empty pool, to take the sun on imitation rocks.

I regretted deeply having lived too late to have known the poet. It seemed to me, I don't know why, that I might have helped him live a little longer—how much, I don't know, perhaps only a few verses more. I felt, as I have seldom before felt, the friendship of the spirit that still pervaded the ahuehuetes. I was studying his work, the scanty pages he wrote during his brief lifetime, which to this day shine like few others.

There is no poetry more carefully distilled than his. It dripped from coil to coil, extracting the perfect drop of orange-blossom alcohol; it aged in minute phials until it reached fragrant perfection. Its autonomy is such that it lay dormant, as if in a pharmacist's blue flask, enclosed in tranquillity and oblivion. But at the least touch we know that across the years this electric energy has remained unchanged. And we feel as if the unerring aim of an arrow that carries with it the scent of jasmine has pierced the bull's-eye of our hearts.

It must be established also that this poetry is edible, like nougat or marzipan, or delights to crunch between our greedy teeth, village cakes prepared by mysterious beauties. No poetry before or since has been so sweet, no cakes were ever mixed from such celestial flour.

But beneath this fragility lie water and eternal stone. Make no mistake. Do not misread this elaboration and exquisite precision. Few poets who have written so little have said so much, and so eternally, about their country. For López Velarde also records history.

At the time Ramón López Velarde was singing, at the time of his death, his ancient land was shuddering. Centaurs thundered across the land, fighting for bread for the hungry. Petroleum was attracting the cold freebooters from the North. Mexico was being robbed and besieged. But it was not conquered.

Our poet left this testimony. We find it in his work, veins seen through the transparency of skin: no bold lines, but the lines are there. They are the protest of the patriot who wished nothing more than to sing. But this civilized, almost secret, poet, with his two or three piano notes, with his two or three authentic tears, with the purity of his patriotism, was the consummate singer.

He is also the most provincial of poets, and even in the last of his unfinished verses one notes the silence, the shimmer of the hidden gardens of the houses whose white-stuccoed walls reveal only pointed treetops. Thence, too, the liquid eroticism of his poetry, circulating through his work like an underground stream, enveloped in endless summer, in chastity soon to become sin, in lazy, abandoned hours in high-ceilinged bedchambers where some insect's rasping wings interrupt the dreamer's siesta.

I learned somewhere that ten centuries ago, between wars, the custodians of the Royal Crown of a now defunct monarchy dropped the Precious Object and the antique cross on the Crown was irreparably bent. Very wisely, the ancient kings did not remove the twisted cross on the Crown radiant with precious stones. Not only did the Crown survive, but the twisted cross became a part of escutcheons and ensigns: that is, it became the mode.

In some manner, that episode from the past reminds me of the poetic mode of López Velarde. As if at some time he had observed a scene from the corner of his eye, and had faithfully reproduced the oblique vision, the twisted light, that gives all his creations such unexpected clarity.

Ramón López Velarde is the last master in the great trilogy of Modernism, the one who put the period to the movement. A murmurous era ended. His great brothers, the opulent Rubén Darío and the lunar Herrera y Reissig, opened the doors of an antiquated America, let in fresh air, filled municipal parks with swans and young ladies' albums with impatient wisdom, sadness, remorse, madness, and intelligence albums whose dangerous contents later exploded in the salons.

But this revolution cannot be complete if we do not give thought to its last archangel, who gave to American poetry a savor and a fragrance that will be everlasting. His concise pages, in some subtle way, achieve the eternity of poetry.

Isla Negra, August 1963

Shakespeare, Prince of Light

GONERIL, Regan, Hamlet, Angus, Duncan, Glansdale, Mortimer, Ariel, Leontes . . .

These names from Shakespeare were part of our childhood; they crystallized and became the substance of our dreams. Even when we could scarcely read, we knew that behind the names lay a continent with rivers and kings, clans and castles and archipelagos, that someday we would explore. The names of these somber, or radiant, protagonists revealed to us the texture of poetry, the first peal of a great bell. Later, much later, come the days and years when we discover the lines and lives of these names. We discover suffering and remorse, martyrdom and cruelty, beings of blood, creatures of air, voices illuminated for a magic feast, banquets attended by bloodstained ghosts. All that action, all those souls, all those passions—all that life.

In every epoch, one bard assumes responsibility for the dreams and the wisdom of the age: he expresses the growth, the expansion, of that world. His name is Alighieri, Victor Hugo, Lope de Vega, Walt Whitman.

Above all, his name is Shakespeare.

These bards amass leaves, and among the leaves one hears birdcalls; beneath these leaves roots grow. They are the leaves of great trees.

They are leaves, and eyes. They multiply and gaze down on us, insignificant men, through all the passing ages, they gaze on us and help us discover ourselves: they reveal to us our labyrinths.

Written in 1964, the year of the four hundredth anniversary of Shakespeare's birth, and the year in which Neruda translated *Romeo and Juliet*

In the case of Shakespeare, there is a third revelation, as there will be others: that of the sorcery of his distilled poetry. Few poets are so compact and secret, so secure in the heart of their diamond.

The sonnets were carved from the opal of tears, from the ruby of love, from the emerald of jealousy, from the amethyst of mourning.

They were carved from fire, made from air, sculpted from crystal.

The sonnets were uprooted from nature so whole that, from first to last, one hears how water flows, how the wind dances, and how, golden or flowering, the cycles of the seasons and fruits follow one after the other.

The sonnets hold an infinity of keys, of magic formulas: static majesty, speeding arrows.

The sonnets are banners that one by one rise to flutter from the castle tower. And though exposed to weather and to time, they conserve the magenta of their stars, the turquoise of their half-moons, the splendor of their blazing hearts.

I have read Shakespeare's poetry for many years; the poems, unlike the plays, do not tell of lives, of battles, of derring-do.

There is the stark whiteness of the page, the purity of the road of poetry. Along that road glide endless rows of images, like tiny ships laden with honey.

Amid this excess of riches in which the driving power of creativity moves in time with intelligence, we see, we can almost feel, an unwavering and flourishing Shakespeare, and note that the most striking aspect of his poems is not their abundant power but their exacting form.

My name is written in my copy of the *Sonnets*, along with the day and the month in 1930 when I bought the book on the island of Java.

It has been with me, then, for thirty-four years.

There, on that far-off island, it was my model, the purest of fountains, deep forests, a fabulous multitude of hitherto unknown myths; it was crystalline law. Because Shakespeare's poetry, like that of Góngora and Mallarmé, plays with the light of reason, imposes a strict, if secret, code. In a word, during those lost years of my life, Shakespeare's poetry kept open a line of communication with Western culture. By Western, naturally, I mean Pushkin and Karl Marx, Bach and Hölderlin, Lord Tennyson and Mayakovsky.

Of course, poetry recurs throughout the plays as well, in the towers of Elsinore, in the castle of Macbeth, on Prospero's ship, among the perfume of pomegranates in Verona.

A phantasmagorical wind blows through the tunnel of each play. The oldest sound in the world, the sound of the human heart, is the matter from which these unforgettable words are formed. Fantasy and humanity appear in all the plays, along with the parlance of the common man, the signs of the marketplace, the vulgar voices of parasites and buffoons, all accompanied by the steely ring of suits of armor locked in crazed combat.

But what I like best is to follow the extravagant flow of Shakespeare's poetry, a harmony painted on the wall of time in blue, enamel, and magic seafoam, an amalgam imprinted on our eternity.

As an example, in the pastoral idyll *Venus and Adonis*, published in 1593, there is the flickering of cool shadows on flowing waters, the insinuating green of singing groves, cascades of rippling poetry, and myth fleeing into the greenery.

Then suddenly a steed appears, dissipating fantasy with its pounding hoofs, as "His eye, which scornfully glisters like fire, shows his hot courage and his high desire."

Yes, if a painter were to paint that horse: "His art with nature's workmanship at strife, as if the dead the living should exceed." There is no description that can equal that of this amorous, furious horse galloping with real hoofs through marvelous sextets.

And I mention it, though Shakespeare's bestiary contained traces of many beasts, and his herbarium retains the color and scent of many flowers, because that pawing steed is the theme of his ode, the generative force of nature captured by a great synthesizer of dreams.

This autumn I was given the task of translating *Romeo and Juliet*.

I accepted the request with humility. With humility, and with a sense of duty, because in fact I did not feel capable of decanting that passionate love story into Spanish. But I had to do it, since this is the anniversary of Shakespeare's birth, the year of universal veneration of the poet who opened new universes to man.

Translating with pleasure, and with honor, the tragedy of those star-crossed lovers, I made a discovery.

I realized that underlying the plot of undying love and inescapable death there was a second drama, a second subject, a second principal theme.

Romeo and Juliet is a great plea for peace among men. It is a condemnation of pointless hatred, a denunciation of the barbarity of war, and the solemn consecration of peace.

When Prince Escalus, in moving and exemplary language, reproaches the feudal clans who are staining the streets of Verona with blood, we realize that the Prince is the incarnation of enlightenment, of dignity, and of peace.

When Benvolio reproaches Tybalt for his warlike temperament, saying: "I do but keep the peace; put up thy sword," the fierce swordsman replies: "What! drawn, and talk of peace? I hate the word . . ."

So, peace was despised by some in Elizabethan Europe. Centuries later, Gabriela Mistral—persecuted and insulted for her defense of peace, dismissed from the Chilean newspaper that had published her articles for thirty years—wrote her famous phrase: "Peace, that accursed word." One sees that the world and the press continued to be governed by Tybalts, by swordsmen.

One reason more, then, to love William Shakespeare, the greatest of all human beings. There will always be time and space to explore in Shakespeare, to lose ourselves, or begin the long journey around his statue, like the Lilliputians around Gulliver. And though we may go a long way without reaching the end, we always return with hands filled with fragrance and blood, with flowers and sorrows, with mortal treasures.

At this solemn moment, it is my pleasure to open the door of tributes, raising the curtain so the dazzling, pensive figure of the Bard may appear. And across four centuries I would say to him: "Greetings, Prince of Light! Good health, sir itinerant actor! We are the heirs to your great dreams; we dream them still. Your words do honor to the entire world."

And, more quietly, I would whisper into his ear: "My friend, I thank you."

Unreality and Miracle

A black sun rose above the mountains of Chuquicamata and cast shadows, scars, triangles, and wounds across the great stretching sands of Chile.

Then it created islands, gods, blizzards, violet-colored beasts, buildings, fishermen of river and sea, and beetles.

By the time the solitary sailor Max Ernst discovered Easter Island at dawn, and announced his discovery in the first collages of those times, the American continent had long been in timeless convulsion; its rivers flowed covered with runaway hats subjected to the volleys of hunters who stalked the procession of hats from East to West. Not only did such strange things happen quite routinely, but various political events in our republics—like the strange death of the Paraguayan dictator Dr. Francia as he was studying the symmetry of the starry skies through his telescope—demonstrate the obvious influence of the Comte de Lautréamont, Uruguayan by birth, on these mysterious occurrences. (I must add that the mortal remains of the terrible tyrant—who was, at the same time, a learned man—lay for weeks beneath mounds of oranges, thwarting all investigations into his disappearance.)

At this date, it is too early to know whether the wind that vitiated the old myths, causing them to assume the new forms and the vitality they exercise to the present, blew from America or from Paris. I leave this task to historians and to the explorers of this and other shores.

Meanwhile, let us celebrate unreality and miracle: man proves his existence by entering and exiting through doors of darkness.

Written for a Surrealist exhibition in Paris, May 1972

NOTEBOOK V

*Reflections
from Isla Negra*

Answering a Query

YOU may ask, where will poetry be in the year 2000? This is a loaded question. If I ran into that question in a dark alley, it would scare the pants off me.

Because, what do I know about the year 2000? And even more to the point, what do I know about poetry?

What I do know is that poetry's funeral rites will not take place in the next century.

Poetry has been given up for dead in every age, but it has shown that it is centrifugal and enduring; it has proved its vitality, exhibiting every sign of a healthy recovery; it seems to have eternal life. It seemed to have ended with Dante. But shortly thereafter Jorge Manrique launched a spark, a kind of sputnik, that kept twinkling in the shadows. Later, Victor Hugo seemed to have swept the boards clean, leaving nothing for anyone who followed. But soon a dapper young dandy named Charles Baudelaire appeared on the scene, followed by a young vagabond named Arthur Rimbaud, and poetry got a fresh start. After Walt Whitman, who could hope to write poetry? He had sown all the leaves of grass: no one could walk on the green. Nevertheless, Mayakovsky came along and built a house of poetry that echoed with toots and shots, sighs and sobs, the roar of trains and armored cars. And the story goes on.

It is clear that the enemies of poetry have always sought to put out its eye, or choke it to death. They have gone about it in many

The thirty-three articles in "Reflections from Isla Negra" appeared in *Ercilla*, Santiago, between March 1968 and January 1970

ways—individualistic field marshals, enemies of light, bureaucratic regiments marching in goose step against the poets. They succeeded in discouraging a few, in deceiving others, even, sadly, in causing the retreat of the least of them. But poetry kept spraying like a fountain and flowing like a wound, kept building hammer and tong, singing in the desert, rising tall like a tree, overflowing like a river, scattering stars like night on a high Bolivian plateau.

Poetry stood beside the dying, stanching their pain; it was in the vanguard of victories, accompanied the solitary, burned like fire, was light and cool like snow; it had hands and fingers and fists; it had buds like spring; it had eyes like the city of Granada; it was swifter than guided missiles; it was stronger than fortresses. It sank its roots into the heart of man.

It is not likely that at the beginning of the new century poets will be leading a revolution to promulgate poetry. Poetry will spread only as the result of human progress, of the development of the human race, and of the accessibility of books and culture. It is not probable that poets will come to dictate or govern, though some of them do that now—some very badly, others less so. But poets will always be good counselors, and woe to him who does not listen. Often, governments have public communication with their people. Poetry has a secret communication with man's suffering. Poets must be heard. This is the lesson of history.

It is entirely possible that in the year 2000 the latest poet, the one most in vogue everywhere, will be a Greek poet no one reads today: his name is Homer.

I believe this, and so I am beginning to read him again. I am going to seek his influence, sweet and heroic, his curses and his prophecies, the marble of his mythology, his blindman's staff.

As the new century approaches, I will try to emulate Homer in my writing. It won't look too bad on me, that style immersed in fable and the renowned sea.

I will carry the banners of Ulysses, King of Ithaca, through the streets. And since, by then, the Greeks will have emerged from their prisons, they will accompany me, to set the norms for the new style of the twenty-first century.

My Name Is Crusoe

C HILE attracts strange happenings. Our dry, hirsute, sandy, humid, vine-tangled land exudes a magnetic phosphorescence. Recently, seismologists came here to draw a map—of necessity, superficial—of the secrets of our earth. Our country, long before any other, knew what it was to be shaken by atomic blasts. We are sheltered, and threatened, by a belt of volcanoes whose craters are as little known as the fire of distant planets.

The fact is that our iron-laden soil attracts unusual events. The mutiny of Cambiaso, in the icy nights of Punta Arenas, offered us a vision of a red-and-gold-uniformed emperor riding a white horse and carrying a skull-emblazoned pennon that rippled in the breeze.

These outbursts of carnage do not happen everywhere.

I have often wondered why it was that Robinson Crusoe came to a Chilean island to specialize in solitude.

Well, I'll tell you why.

Because he had already been here. It wasn't his first visit. And I'm not sure he didn't come back later.

Because on January 10, 1709, Alexander Selkirk (a year after having been rescued from his sojourn in the Juan Fernández Islands) was named chief petty officer of the *Bachelor*, a frigate that pirated our seas. Selkirk–Crusoe knew what he was doing; he was, in fact, drawn by the magnet of the island.

We need to examine why *Robinson Crusoe*, one book among many, has fascinated half a world.

Man does not want to live alone. Solitude is contrary to nature. A human being has an insatiable curiosity about other human beings.

Animals seldom look at or notice other animals. Only dogs, men, and ants display that compelling curiosity about their own kind; only they look at, touch, and sniff at one another.

The unbearable solitude of the Scots sailor, who set himself the task of building a solitary world, still provokes our imagination, is still our enigma.

In the journal of his voyages, Captain Woodes Rogers recounts the liberation of Alexander Selkirk. It is good journalism, and the captain treats the event as an exceptional news report. Let us imagine that Robinson Crusoe had been found and rescued only yesterday, and that we read the news in *El Mercurio* or in *El Siglo*. Captain Rogers writes:

Immediately our pinnace return'd from the shore, and brought abundance of craw-fish with a man cloth'd in goat-skins, who look'd wilder than the first owner's of them. He had been on the island four years and four months, being left there by Captain Stradling in the ship *Cinque-Ports*. His name was Alexander Selkirk, a Scotchman, who had been master of the *Cinque-Ports* . . .

Had they been French, he would have submitted, but chose to risque dying alone in the Iland, rather than fall into the hands of the Spaniards in these parts, lest they murder, or make a slave of him in the mines; for he fear'd they would spare no stranger that might be capable of discovering the South Sea. . . . When left, he had with him his clothes and bedding, with a firelock, some powder, bullets, and tobacco, a hatchet, a knife, a kettle, a Bible, some practical pieces, and his mathematical instruments and books.

He diverted and provided for himself as well as he could; but for the first eight months had much ado to bear up against melancholy, and the terror of being alone in such a desolate place. . . . After he conquer'd his melancholy he diverted himself sometimes by cutting his name on the trees, and the time of his being left and continuance there. He was at first much pester'd with cats and rats, that bred in great numbers from some of each species which had got ashore from ships that put in there to wood and water. The rats knaw'd his feet and clothes while asleep, which obliged him to cherish the cats with goats flesh; by which many of them became so tame that they would lie about him in hundreds, and soon deliver'd him from the rats.

He likewise tam'd some kids, and to divert himself would now and then sing and dance with them and his cats; so that by the care of Providence, and vigour of his youth, being now about 30 years old, he came at last to conquer all the inconveniences of his solitude and to be very easy.

When the castaway created his little empire, he didn't realize that he was fulfilling an ageless human aspiration, that of controlling nature, conquering it by the sheer force of intelligence. The motto for his solitude had to be: "Reason, reason, always reason"—the same that Unamuno proposed to the Chileans. The sailor who became Robinson and who taught cats and goats to dance was a new Adam—without an Eve, but powerful, nevertheless. His solitary song was like a hymn to a new creation.

A strange destiny, one that astonishes us to this day. And when Selkirk returns to his beloved Scotland, telling the story of his deeds from tavern to tavern, he begins to feel a nostalgia for his great cloister of sky and sea. The Pacific Ocean, unreal, incomparably abundant and vast, called him still, with its most persistent chorus. It continued to change him and finally transformed him completely.

An incomparable writer, Daniel Defoe, hears about the solitary sailor, the far-off land, the magnetism of the Chilean islands.

Alexander Selkirk died. But on a ship of print—one that sails still today—a new sailor returned to the Juan Fernández Islands.

"Who are you?" he was asked.

"My name is Robinson Crusoe," was the reply.

Far-ranging Beetleology

TO A BEETLE

One day, I approached a beetle,
questioned him about his life-style:
what were his autumnal habits?
who forged his segmented armor?

I searched him out in hidden waters,
southern lakes in my dark woodlands,
found him hidden in the ashes
strewn by rancorous volcanoes,
sometimes slowly creeping upward
from deep roots toward his own darkness.

That solid suit, are you the tailor?
Zinc-hard eyes, they're your creation?
How about the metal trousers,
slashing scissors, tie, and pincers?
Not to forget your saw of gold.
Was it resin used to ripen
all your species' iridescence?

(I wish I'd been born a beetle,
burrowed, with a beetle's heart,
deep in dark and compact matter,
scrawled my name in hidden patterns
in the agony of the wood.)
(Thus my name some distant morning
would once again see light of day,
emerging from nocturnal channels,

threading through dim twisting tunnels,
on glistening wings be borne away.)
"Nothing's more beautiful than you,
mute, unfathomable beetle,
sorcerer (or sorceress),
wee rhinoceros in the dew,"
I said to him, but with no reply.

I questioned him, and he said nothing.

Well, what else would a beetle do?

Punta del Este, 1968

WHEN I was a child in Temuco I wrote a little elegy, "To a Small Scarab I Inadvertently Crushed beneath My Foot." It exists today because my sister Laura has an album bulging with my execrable early poems. And every so often, someone discovers them and publishes a few, giving me a retrospective stab in the back.

But recently, in Punta del Este, as I was writing a different poem—not at all elegiac; rather, electric—I spied another beetle among the roots of some pine trees. It belonged to a different family and had an upturned horn like a tiny beast from some remote zoological age. I could not identify it. Nothing strange in that, however, as entomologists believe the order Coleoptera numbers some three hundred thousand species. There is room for error, for there will always be one more coleoptera. They are so hard, so enigmatic, and so beautiful that the world would be incomplete without their legions. Though Leonov didn't tell me this specifically when he visited me at Isla Negra, I'm sure that from afar he saw the earth as a great blue coleoptera on the wing.

In those forests of the South, which have patiently and methodically been murdered under the watchful eye of our governors, I was always enchanted to observe the silent insect world beneath big stones or fallen tree trunks: insects, if not on horses, settled on a corolla or skittering on the surface of the swamp.

There I learned to venerate and to fear the golden carabuses, or *peorros*. Svelte and ovoid, dressed in the most elegant suits in the forest, some wear aureate crimson; others affect a golden emerald; still others, yellowy sapphire. But whenever I would try to pick one up for my schoolboy collector's box, every last one of them drove me back several meters, squirting a stink at me that was pestilential perfection.

The "snake mothers" (*Ancistrotus cumingi*), seven or eight centimeters in length, affixed with an iron grip to the primeval trees, provided me the satisfaction of being easily collectible, in spite of their imposing size. The problem was keeping them alive in a perforated box, feeding them crushed leaves and wood chips. Eventually, I had a small flock of them. I may be the only man to have shepherded coleoptera.

But the most vivid memory of my life on the frontier is of our wonderful stag beetle (*Chaisognathus granti Steph.*). This bizarre creature sheathed in hard jade astounds us with its green antlers and burnished brilliance. The jewel of the forest, its radiant beauty has disappeared—or will—with the desecration of the forest.

The upshot of all this is that after fifty years I have written a few lines on that subject from the past, a poem that this time has not fallen prey to my sister's album.

Just as I finished writing, my working vacation in Punta del Este was interrupted. The newspapers had discovered me. When I looked up, pleased with my lines on the small and unusual beetle, I saw moving toward me a human being, staring at me from the place where his head should have been. His eyes were two strange protuberances formed by the thick lens of his telemechanism. He frightened me. He looked like a beetle. This invader's antennae clicked picture after picture, as many of the subject of my poem—who defended himself with waving feet—as of me, the defenseless protector and minstrel of beetles.

A Lady of Clay

MAY Marta Colvin forgive me, but the best piece of Chilean sculpture I know is a clay "Pretty Woman with Guitar," one of the many sculptures to emerge from the universal umbilicus of ceramics: Quinchamalí. This lady with the guitar is taller and broader than most pieces. The potters and artisans told me that it is very difficult to execute such a large piece. This one was made by a little ten-year-old country girl who died some time ago. It was so beautiful that it was sent to be exhibited at the New York World's Fair. Now it is gazing at me from the most important table in my house. I consult her constantly. I call her the Earth Mother. She has the roundness of hills, of shadows cast by summer clouds on fallow land, and in spite of the fact that she traveled across the seas, she has the renowned odor of clay, of Chilean clay.

The potters told me that in their work they must mix the clay with grass, and that they burn cow manure to get the pure and opaque black of Quinchamalí earthenware. Then they complained to me about the outrageous prices the local landowner was charging for cow manure. I never achieved enough influence to roll back the price of cow dung for the sculptors of Quinchamalí. And though this petition to the powers that be is extremely humble, I hope the Agrarian Reform will provide this product for these miracle-working women as easily and simply as would the cow. The truth is that these ceramics are our most illustrious art form. The only gift I ever gave Picasso was a small black piggy bank, a toy, with the odor of Chile and clay, the creation of the celebrated potter Práxedes Caro.

With spurs and ponchos, with bracelets from Panimávida, sirens from Florida, little pitchers from Pomaire, our flagging pride is revived. Like water, they appear without fanfare; they are distinguished and utilitarian art; they have a fine bouquet, and are without ego; they survive one doesn't know how, come from one doesn't know where, but they reflect our humility, our depths, our fragrance.

That's why I think that of the many dreary museums of Santiago, the single delight is the one that displays its treasures on Santa Lucía Hill. It was founded by the writer Tomás Lago many years ago, in an act of love that has continued to proliferate in various beautiful collections. In Mexico, I myself scoured the countryside with the genial Rodolfo Ayala, that madman Ayala, searching through churches and markets, palaces and secondhand shops, for a stunning collection that today enriches this charming museum.

I am deeply moved by such anonymous creations, and sometimes, in regard to my poetry, I call myself a potter, a baker, a carpenter. Man has no style, man has no life, except by the labor of his hands. I have always thought of my poetry as a handicraft, anti-literary, because even dreams are born of our hands. This popular art, which has been housed and exhibited with pride and love in our best museum, reveals, more than any museum of history, that the greatest truth lies in the living, and that the works of the people are eternal, burning no less brightly than the works of heroes.

Our native land is being methodically destroyed. The destroyers are ourselves. We feed on fire and devastation. The forests have been burned; the marvelous Chilean woodland is but a tear stain in my heart. The most beautiful rocks in the world are being dynamited to splinters along our shore. Oysters, mussels, partridges, sea urchins, are pursued like enemies, all the more quickly to eradicate them, to erase them from the planet. The ignorant say of our depredations: "Indian blood will out." A lie. The Araucan named the cinnamon tree king of the earth. He fought no one but those who invaded his land. We Chileans wage war against everything that is ours, and, to our misfortune, against everything that is good. Never have I been so ashamed as when I saw in a book on ornithology, where it indicated the habitat of each species, this description of the Chilean wild parrot:

"*Tricahue. An almost extinct species.*" I will not reveal here the place where the few remaining specimens of this magnificent bird may be found—in order to avoid its extermination.

And now I'm told that a spark from our "cultural revolution" has drifted as far as the Museum of Popular Art and may be about to destroy it.

May the Araucan cinnamon, god of the forest, protect us all.

A Novel

Aᴍᴏɴɢ my possessions, I treasure the yellowed, parchment-like pages of a book I have always admired for its madness and its truth. It is the story of the amorous adventures of Don Henrique de Castro, written by Don Francisco de Lamarca, whose real name was Loubays-sin de La Marque, a French gentleman about whom we know very little but who, it seems, was a Gascon who wrote in Spanish.

The book is about well-known, full-blown loves of the type con-sumed by the chivalric fires of Amadis of Gaul, so that the narrative thread of the novel weaves among several continents: from the Duchy of Milan to the Kingdom of Naples—even to the Moluccas—among Infantas, soirées, balls and banquets, amid Turks, shepherds, chamber-lains, princes, and warriors.

But the marvelous thing about this book is that it begins in the middle of the Araucan war, in my country. And throughout the profuse rhetorical gallantry, the land of Chile lends a solemnity that would have been lacking had the book been nothing more than an account of the love affairs of Don Henrique, Sicandro, Leonora, Don Esteban, Don Diego, and Doña Elvira.

This is how the *Historia tragicómica* begins:

> In the region of the Antarctic there is a province called Chile, which is bounded on the west by the Ocean Sea, and on its eastern border by a great and high range of mountains.

Later, in describing the Indian Lautaro, the author says: "Valdivia had a page, the son of a cacique, whom he doted on and loved as if one of his sons." When this young warrior abandons Valdivia to become the leader of the Araucans, thereby changing the course of the war, La Marque's description ennobles him:

> Has greater proof of a man's valor ever existed? Is there any example, either in an ancient or a modern book, of a man who, being one of the victorious, goes over to the side of the vanquished? For only the bravery and strength of this young barbarian could have snatched from the hands of a nation as martial as the Spanish such a great and illustrious victory.

No less stirring is the description of the death of Pedro de Valdivia, defeated by Lautaro at the climactic moment of Valdivia's endeavor:

> As he uttered these last words, Valdivia died beneath the hoofs of the horses, and none of his party was present to comfort or aid him in his plight.

For taking the life of the Conquistador, the author rebukes death with these grave words:

> Why are you of this strange disposition, that you never give except to take away? Witness this poor Captain Valdivia, who called upon you a thousand times when, sweating under the weight of arms and tormented by hunger, he marched, carrying a banner as a poor soldier (without money or clothing, often wounded). But now, when he is at the height of his glory, now that he knows power, riches, and contentment, now you pronounce your harsh sentence.

I was deeply moved to find scattered through the 880 pages of this forgotten novel the landscape and the fragrant names of the South of Chile: Penco, Concepción, Imperial, the Valley of Tucapel, the Araucan rivers—"the land of Chile, with more fires than Etna."

The book ends with the adventures of Don Lorenzo de Castro, who, along with the Pizarros and Almagros and Atabalipas or Atahualpas, was one of the invading legions. Though there are as well, it goes without saying, fabled hermits and the incense that enslaves the amorous.

So, then, someone should investigate, and scholars verify, whether this is the first Chilean novel written by a man who had not known the land but had seen its splendor through the diamantine verses of *La*

Araucana. Notwithstanding, the most salient fact is that its many idylls and episodes are woven and unraveled amid the gunfire of the Chilean wars and the smell of blood and rain in this southern land.

For the record: this book was published in Paris under the imprint of Adrian Tisseno on January 19, 1617.

The Hunter after Roots

EHRENBURG, who read and translated my verses, used to chide me: Too much *root*, too many *roots* in your poetry. Why so many?

It's true. And I'd been told this long before the fourth volume of my *Memorial de Isla Negra* broke through the soil. It was entitled *El cazador de raíces (The Hunter after Roots)*.

The lands of the frontier put down their roots in my poetry, and have been entangled there ever since. My life is one long, winding pilgrimage that always comes full circle to the forests of the South, to lost woodlands.

There great trees were sometimes felled by the mighty weight of their own seven hundred years, or uprooted by storms, or blighted by snow, or destroyed by fire. I have heard titanic trees fall in the depths of the forest: an oak toppling with a sound of mute catastrophe, as if a colossal hand were knocking at earth's door, seeking a tomb.

But the roots themselves remain in plain view, exposed to the treachery of time, to humidity, to lichens, to inevitable annihilation.

Nothing is more beautiful than those great open hands, wounded and blasted, that lying across a forest path tell us the secret of the buried tree, the enigma of the foliage, the deeply rooted muscles of organic power. Tragic capillaries, they reveal to us a new beauty; they are subterranean sculptures, the hidden masterworks of nature.

I have been thinking all this because Mrs. Julia Rogers, a forest spirit, has sent me the roots of a five-hundred-year-old oak, weighing a hundred kilos. The moment I received her gift, I knew that these were the roots of some distant ancestor, some organic father who somehow had materialized in my house. At one time I may have listened to his counsel, to his multitudinous murmuring, to his green words on the mountainside. And perhaps now, after so many years, these words had come into my life to communicate their silence.

Another hunter after roots!

Imagine her on the scent through humid humus, amid the trenchant fragrance of the *tricuspidarias* and the *labrinias*, there where the *araucaria imbricata*, the *cupressaceae*, the *libocendrus*, and the *drimys winteri* stand lordly as towers. Riding horseback through needle-sharp rain; feet sinking in wet clay; listening to the guttural cries of wild parrots; breaking fingernails, digging for the next, always more impressive, always more tangled, always more Laocoön-like root.

Mrs. Rogers writes me that sometimes tree roots have withstood a hundred years of wind, storm, and winter cold. This gives to the masterworks she collects their spidery tracery, their ashen-silver color, the majestic and heartrending beauty formed by the feet of trees.

As if war had been declared against it, the great forest of the South is being totally eradicated, leveled, burned. The landscape becomes increasingly monotonous, stripped to feed the paper mills. The natural forests are disappearing, replaced by pine groves with endless rows of impenetrable green. Perhaps these Chilean roots the huntress gave into our keeping will be relics someday, like the jawbones of megatheres.

But it is not just for this that I applaud her enthusiasm, but also because she reveals to us a complicated world of secret forms, one more lesson in aesthetics from the earth.

Years ago, as I walked with Rafael Alberti past waterfalls, through the thickets and forests near Osorno, Rafael pointed out how every branch was different from the next, how the leaves seemed to compete in that infinite variety. "Why, they look as if they'd been chosen by a landscape gardener for a marvelous park," he said.

Sometime later, in Rome, Rafael recalled our walk, and the natural opulence of our forests.

It was once so. But no longer. I become melancholy when I remember my wanderings as a boy and youth between Boroa and Carahue, or around Toltén in the low hills along the coast. What discoveries! The grace of the cinnamon tree, its fragrance following a rain; the lichens, whose winter beards hung from the countless faces of the forest.

I would turn over the fallen faces, looking for the lightning flash of some coleoptera: the golden carabuses, dressed as sunflowers for a miniature ballet beneath the roots.

Later in my life, crossing the cordillera on horseback toward Argentina, beneath green arches of gigantic trees, we encountered an obstacle: a tree root taller than our mounts, blocking our passage. By dint of muscle and ax we made our way past it. Those roots were like an overturned cathedral: that magnitude revealed filled us with awe.

These thoughts are prompted by the existence of a zealous new hunter after roots. An important task, like collecting volcanoes or sunsets.

One thing is certain: the roots that have always appeared in my poetry are once again growing in my house, as if beneath the earth they had pursued me and finally caught up with me.

A Letter for Víctor Bianchi

THE coast was shaken by the groundswells of July. The sea swept away many homes along the shore. Fences were scattered like matchsticks from a box crushed beneath the feet of the milling crowd. It was amazing to see boats washed up on a street in Algarrobo.

The great crag of Punta de Tralca bore the brunt of the pounding seas. It looked like a white-maned lion. The huge, crashing waves washed over it completely. Long stretches of coast were as if snow-covered, and crackling with the cold fire of mounds of foam. At Trueno de Tralca the sea was an army firing interminable rounds of artillery, massing ranks of cosmic cavalry. The great ocean continued its assault throughout the night and the following, gloriously blue day.

I was mesmerized, anxious, overwhelmed, yearning, before the spectacle of nature's terrorism.

It seemed perfectly natural, Víctor, that suddenly you were beside me. I'd been expecting you.

Because, Víctor Bianchi, you were always an active spectator at the scene of great events and disasters, unusual occurrences, mysterious upheavals, places where stars fell.

You were among the dead and the survivors of the havoc of the heavens on the very crown of Aconcagua that terrible day. Our broad tropical rivers have seen you skim their waters in a light canoe. And oh, the unknown islands you intrepidly explored, descending, small as you were, into uncharted chasms. Another day it was volcanic fissures in the desert. Or geometric mines of jewel-like salt. Or hidden waterfalls of Colombian quicksilver.

I seem to remember you, driven by your uncontrollable curiosity, disguised as an emperor penguin among millions of penguins in Antarctic reaches, where you learned secrets and languages unknown to anyone but you.

You and your adventurous guitar. Not Jorge Bellet, none of the companions in our journey, was startled when, to cross the Andes with me, all you strapped to your mount were a bedroll and a guitar. What a boon that melodious box proved to be, how disarming your songs, how charming, in San Martín de los Andes, where we landed like meteorites from Chile, covered with the dust of the Andes, like stardust.

But you were always clearheaded, and meticulous: energy controlled by knowledge. At daybreak, or before, you would go ahead to scout the path my exile was to follow. You would mark a trail through desolate forests, crags and thickets, abysses and waterfalls: the route we were to follow several hours later. You always rose early to trace the map of the road in your mind. You joined us in this unparalleled adventure, without our summons. You always arrived in time, bringing your wisdom, where, even without knowing, those who needed you awaited your coming. That was your gift. And you were so prodigal with it, so expert and so generous, that one day at dawn, perhaps never knowing, you made the leap from the highway to another planet, your guitar in your hand.

So, when the salt and snow of the high seas crashed over the rock of Trueno and shook the coast in the full light of day, when sky and ocean conspired in the blue catastrophe, I heard a small sound by my side, and you were there.

Only natural. When you heard the surf, you must have thought: "I'm needed. There are things to be done. I must help."

I turned, and you were there with your guitar.

Dynamic and sonorous—serving and singing were the poles of your destiny. And when they told me that on a road in Antofagasta, in the dawn mists of the pampa, a truck had hurtled you into the other world, I thought to myself: "That's Víctor Bianchi for you. My stalwart companion with another surprise for us. Once again, he's set off with his music toward new horizons."

My Evening with the Sculptors

I am going to explain why, though my attendance was obligatory, I did not attend a gala function one night at the Gran Teatro of Viareggio. It was a ceremony honoring prize-winners, of whom I was one. As mine was the international prize, it was perhaps only just that they expected me to be there. The box where Matilde was seated was draped with garlands illuminated by television spotlights. This was in 1967. My sin still haunts me.

Marino Marini had invited me to dinner that night. This sculptor of magic horses and the painter Morandi, the Beatified Angel of bottles, constitute the supreme duo of Italian art. Matilde went in one direction, and I, accompanied by my publisher, went in another to Marini's house; I planned to join Matilde later among the garlands of Viareggio. It did not work out that way, I'm afraid.

Marini had invited only a few friends; the women all in long gowns.

With the obligatory drinks in hand, we sat facing the garden. Far away, at the back of the garden, a long row of trees stretched into darkness. Marino Marini seemed to me more urbane and witty, more cosmopolitan than I had imagined. With a stranger, the name is the man. And with so much of the maritime in his name, I had imagined Marino Marini to be closer to the sea, closer to nature. His slight and graceful build, his subtle courtesy, the smiling flash of his intelligence, continued to surprise me through the meal, which was taken beneath the trees. Everything was good and beautiful: eating and listening, watching and drinking. The most beautiful of the Florentine women was seated beside me; she had wide golden eyes perfectly matched to the Arabian garment that covered her from chin to ankle.

"Imagine," I said to my neighbor, "though Marino Marini has my unbounded admiration, I should at this minute be dining with a different sculptor, due to certain obligations I have as a Chilean."

"Why is that?" the dazzling Florentine asked. So I told her that there was a city named Valdivia in a faraway country named Chile, and in that city almost a hundred and fifty years ago a Byron of the sea named Lord Cochrane had performed such feats that we Chileans had never forgotten him. That was the beginning of the freedom of our seas. And now we wanted to raise a monument to his memory in Valdivia. And as this seaman had been a native of Great Britain, we had thought that another Englishman, Henry Moore, should be the chosen sculptor.

"So you would like to see Henry Moore?" asked the golden-eyed enchantress.

"That isn't possible; he lives in England," I replied. "For tonight, it is enough for my archives to be among all of you, and with Marino Marini. If I survive, I'll look for my Englishman."

The lady got up from the table, leaving behind a reverberating vacuum. We were having coffee by now. She returned quickly, and whispered into my ear. "I'll be waiting for you in my car. You can see Henry Moore. Just say goodbye, don't say where we're going."

I followed in the wake of her splendor. Then came a trip through an unfamiliar, flowering night. We passed through villages, strips of luminous light, forest darkness, again villages, traveled paved roads and dirt roads. Onward! Lord Cochrane awaited. Or rather, Lord Cochrane's sculptor.

We came to a country estate that struck me as both mythical and patriarchal, a kind of domain of Le Gran Meaulnes. The golden fairy opened the portals. Ten persons stepped aside, leaving me alone in the circle with Henry Moore and my doleful presentiments. What was happening in Viareggio? And Matilde, the television, and the garlands?

Now, Henry Moore did look like a sailor. Short, stout, genial, and strong. Naturally, he'd never heard of Valdivia. Not naturally, he'd never heard of Lord Cochrane. He agreed to my proposal. Valdivia, the City of Water, would pay him for the monument. Absolute freedom. Perhaps something suggesting a mast? Maybe a wave?

I was eloquent. I believe he liked the idea.

I like carrying out commissions. With the job, the artist assumes responsibility and precision. Clearly, one never would ask a great sculptor for polemical sculptures, or the modest poet of thirty-five books for polemical chronicles.

I don't know how we became sidetracked into such a strange conversation. It's something I never talk about. But for the half hour I spent with Henry Moore, all we talked about, and heaven knows why, was Death. Moore reflected on the subject with great simplicity. I had the sensation of being with a great stonecutter who knew the extremes of hardness—that is, infinite stone. I seem to remember that the idea of death did not perturb him, that he would never be overwhelmed at the thought. In that degree of maturity, we were in accord. A full life makes acceptance of the inevitable less rending.

The night was filled with sounds: dogs, and frogs, distant horns: I realized that we were alone. Our conversation was fascinating, but it seemed never to end. I searched for the phosphorescent eyes of my friend from Florence. The eyes carried me back through stars and vineyards, dark roads, silence filled with music, to the gala night of Viareggio.

When we arrived, she murmured: "Now are you happy with your Mata Hari?"

Although she'd raced through the countryside like an astronaut, it was too late when we arrived at the Gran Teatro. The mayor and his committee had retired.

I doubt that anyone in the audience would have recognized me, but as a precautionary measure, I waited in the shadow until everyone had left.

Once the place was deserted, I went to look for Matilde.

She is angry still.

Rocking Caracas

Venezuela observes its elections with a kind of savage passion. They've suffered so many eclipses in their tortured history that now everything is bright with paper and fireworks, airplanes, and an unholy din of infernal noises.

Caracas becomes a carnival of color hung with millions of posters and portraits, smothered in green and white and blue and red leaflets. Vote for the Anchor, or the Key, or the Horse. Vote for Yellow, vote Green, vote White. Vote for Burelli, for Prieto, for Caldera, for Gonzalo. And for Arturo, Gustavo, Wolfgang, for Miguel Otero.

Radio, television, newspapers, telephones blare with deafening good cheer. Hitler, Bolívar, Fidel Castro, Frei, all come out to do a turn.

We went to the beach with Inocente Palacios, the great old man of the arts, Miguel Otero Silva, who was celebrating his sixtieth birthday, and their friends.

Matilde waded into the shallow warm waves with the Venezuelans. I stayed behind in the beautiful, gleaming wood house to write. When she returned, I asked: "How was it? Did they swim?"

"I swam," she replied. "The others talked politics between waves."

A visit in the Venezuelan night with the painter Alejandro Otero turned out to be a blazing miracle, almost impossible to describe. Colossal structures, stairways to the skies, sparkling towers, starry spheres, occupy a site in Caracas that communicates a new thrill, a planetary shudder.

What is phenomenal is that this painter of geometrical purity, this master of a style that seemed lost in individual obscurity, should be reborn in this totally fascinating popular art. His enormous constructs, resembling space missiles, captivated us from the first moment we saw them.

The Vibrating Tower, more than twenty meters high, transmits movement and light as if through a mysterious circulatory system: millions of fireflies and silvery bees working in a vertical hive. *The Bride of the Wind* oscillates in a rotation of astronomical purity, moving to a remote rhythm, to the night's respiration. *Rotor* and *Integral*, seemingly animate, brilliant and oscillating independently, reverberate and lazily rotate like carefully constructed spacecraft landed in the heart of Caracas.

The revelations of this optic and classic art, in some way derived from Venezuelan light, have given me the same pleasure I enjoy from a huge and precise game. The joy derives from the intelligent surprise that leaves no room for fraud. Such clear art needs no theory: it is truth at the end of the labyrinth.

But one must understand that if the resplendent works of Le Parc or Soto, responding to the allure of money, run to hide in collections or museums, they must be liberated. Darkness is intolerable for such active objects, for such a luminous conscience.

So this is the great adventure: Alejandro Otero's initiation in space.

In Brasília, in Philadelphia, in Santiago de Chile and Santiago de Cuba, in Red Square in Moscow, in the parks of France, before the passing parade, I can see these stalagmites constructed with the passion that through joyous creation establishes faith in the destiny of man.

In Brazil

In Rio I visited Burle Marx, the Conquistador of flowers, the Liberator of gardens, the Green Hero of Brazil, who with Niemayer and Lucio Costa form the procreative trilogy of splendid cities. He takes me for walks beneath enormous leaves, he shows me thorny roots that defend themselves beneath the earth, tree trunks with skin rash, astonishing *quermelias marmoratas*, mysterious *ilairinas*, and, especially, the treasure of the bromeliads, collected from the heart of Brazil, or discovered in Sumatra. We walk through kilometers of magnificence, flowering scarlet, yellow, violet, returning home with a perfect water lily quivering like a flash of blue lightning in Matilde's hand.

But Jorge Amado calls from Salvador and we fly to the market capital of Bahia to eat *vatapá* and drink beer in that magic seashell city. As I had done in Rio, I again read my poetry to an audience of young students, dashing off hundreds of the autographs that are so exhausting.

With Jorge I wander through the twisting clefts of Salvador, beneath a paralyzing sun. We climb into the plane, saturated with the citrus aroma of Bahia, with emanations from the sea, with the fervor of the students. We leave below, in the airport, the Amados: robust Jorge, ever-sweet Celia, Paloma and João: my Brazilian family.

Up into the sky! To the broad heavens! High above the earth: the white city, the Venus city: BRASÍLIA!

Representative Marcio opens every door to me. But Brasília has no doors: it is bright space, an extension of the mind, radiance become architecture. The public areas throb with children, the palaces lend implicit dignity to their institutions. The architect Italo, a friend of Niemayer's, has been ten years in Brasília, and takes us on a tour of the new Itamaraty, the Congress, the still-unfinished theater, and the Cathedral, a rose of iron whose great petals open toward infinity.

Brasília, isolated in its human miracle, in the midst of Brazilian space, is testimony to man's supreme creative will. From this city one would feel worthy of flying to the stars. Niemayer is the terminus of a parabola that begins with Leonardo: the utility of constructive thought; creation as social obligation; spatial satisfaction of intelligence.

Travel Diary

From Ipanema, with its blue ocean, its islands and peninsulas, its humpbacked mountains, and its rumbling earth tremors, Vinícius de Moraes drives me to Belo Horizonte (an enormous Antofagasta on a plateau), then to Ouro Prêto, colonial and calcareous, with the clearest air in South America, and a basilica on each of the ten hills rising like fingers of the hands that hold the compact masses of its people. Elizabeth Bishop lives here—the great North American poet I met several years ago on the summit of a pyramid in Chichén Itzá. She wasn't in Brazil, so I wrote her a little poem in English. It had a few errors, which is only as it should be.

The liberator of slaves and advocate of independence, Tiradentes, gazes on the churches from a tall column in the center of the plaza where he was drawn and quartered. Tiradentes—Toothpuller, so called because he was a dentist—led a revolution that was defeated in the very bosom of the church-dominated, slavery-supporting monarchy. So now, a miniature atop a ridiculous column, they have elevated him to glory, instead of placing him among the crowds of blacks and whites passing through the plaza of Ouro Prêto.

In Congonhas, where we went to see the sculpture of Aleijadinho, we suddenly found ourselves in a crowd of pilgrims chanting the canticles that bronze-voiced priests usually direct from the temple; women, children, street vendors—in short, the whole motley crowd —were singing or eating fried tidbits, and the smallest children were perched on the stone prophets sculpted by our American Michelangelo.

Slicing through the crowds of the poor the way a knife cuts through cheese, we made our way to the statues, where Matilde took my picture with Isaiah, Daniel, and Ezekiel. I didn't feel too bad beside them, except that they were better poets than I; now portrayed in stone, they look powerful or pensive, wrathful or sleepy. There's a small fish beside Jonah; we barely caught a glimpse of the tail above the black and white faces of the pilgrims. I press closer to see whether it's a siren (how beautiful it would be to see a prophet in the net of a daughter of the sea), but no. It's only a whale, his whale; a smiling Aleijadinho placed it at Jonah's waist, so he wouldn't leave it behind on the heavenly railroad.

Later, in the early evening, we drove through jungles, across great rivers, down roads where a morpho butterfly suddenly flitted before us, sending cold shivers up and down our spines. The trees along the road are covered with scarlet fire; fruit like air-grown watermelons hang from the branches. We see giant termite mounds built by the insects that invented the skyscraper; and later, that night, exhausted by so much splendor, we sleep in Petrópolis, in the cool city of Brazil where Gabriela Mistral may have lived her happiest and her most desperate hours. Sleep well, Gabriela!

Emerald-Green Colombia

A restaurant on the forty-sixth floor in São Paulo, where one lunches almost in the clouds: then a jet, or a four-seater mosquito, shuddered, lifted off, and deposited me in Manizales.

It's been twenty-five years since I visited Colombia.

From above I recognize the spine of her high mountains, the hatchwork of mountain and river, valley and mist: a geography of wet emeralds that rise and fall against the sky.

I am to preside over the jury of a contest of Latin American university theater.

The toy plane drops down to a four-meter-wide runway between two gorges: the blade of an Andean knife.

Manizales was unrecognizable: much larger, modern, and clean like no other city.

I immersed myself in the daily scene, with new theater every day from Peru, Brazil, Venezuela, Argentina, Ecuador, and Colombia. Theater that is lyric or waggish, experimental or satanic, popular or intellectual. In every case, lively and vital, well-wrought and commendable. I spent a week in that dark hall, living with strange characters—harlequins and bums, schizophrenics and sugar daddies.

The play I liked best was a Brazilian piece inspired by the traveling puppet theaters of Brazil. In this three-act play, the actors re-create the movements of marionettes; the female vampire, the wise little black, and the enamored plantation owner arrive in heaven suspended from nonexistent strings.

Freshness and popular roots are combined in this harmonious theatrical work that was unanimously awarded first prize.

(After I left for Bogotá, the Golden Mask, through a palace intrigue, was awarded to a nauseatingly obscene North American play.)

My life in Manizales consisted of the street by day and the theater by night. Pursued by droves of autograph hunters, I went to get a haircut in the local barbershop. The patient barber parted my hair, snipping while I signed books and scraps of paper, surrounded by some fifty onlookers.

In Bogotá the greatest poets of Colombia—Rojas, Zalamea, Carranza, de Greiff, Camacho, and Castro-Saavedra—formed a bodyguard to stave off curiosity seekers and their autograph books.

I decide not to go on to Mexico, in spite of the love I have for the country and of all the things that await me there. Student blood runs in the streets, and for me the Olympic torch is extinguished.

During those same days a solitary guerrilla is killed in the mountains of Colombia: his name is Ciro. According to police records, he is an outlaw. But for many he is a hero. Surrounded by an entire battalion of soldiers, the boy died shooting. Great sadness amidst the friendship and the radiance of Colombian poetry.

When I do not wish to be decorated by Señor Lleras Restrepo, there is no shortage of people who are offended.

My reply: Nothing can stand between me and the green heart of Colombia. One medal more or less means little to me. My poetry will always celebrate you, my Emerald.

Then the Museum of pre-Columbian gold, with its gleaming masks, necklaces, shells, butterflies, and frogs. Here our buried America is alive, pointing its finger at crucifying Christians. The miraculous goldwork has no voice: it is a silent flash of gold. There should be a great golden bowl at the exit of the museum to hold the tears.

Tomorrow we fly to Venezuela.

Farewell to Tallone

From Alpignano, near Turin, Bianca writes me: "Our Alberto did not get to read your letter, or print your new book. Two months ago he left us forever." Alberto Tallone, a printer, was preparing to print Leonardo da Vinci's prose and was traveling through Leonardo's province to immerse himself in his presence. There, on the outskirts of a village, he saw Bianca pass by, and in that instant found her so Leonardoesque that he followed her to immediately declare his love. A few days later they were married in that very place.

I have spent many happy days in that Italian house with the printers Alberto and Bianca.

Their press was in their home, broad and shining; like Gutenberg's, hand-operated to produce the epitome of fine typography.

I was honored, my work dignified, because some of my books were printed by the man I consider the modern master of typography. And because, perhaps by caprice, he chose my poetry: he made few exceptions for contemporary writers. But in his editions of the classics he designed a new and spacious garden, severe and pure. Tallone's type, which he himself cast, flowered on Magnani de Pescia paper. The Garamond letters triumph over even the splendor of watermarked Rives or Hosho from Japan.

Severity reigns in the immaculate beauty of his editions. He had as directive the words of Charles Péguy: "The true beauty of a book should spring from the written work itself, the absence of illustrations, the beauty of the typography, the beauty of the actual printing, the absence of polychrome, the beauty of the paper."

We ourselves are the impetus for books that come to the eyes and hands of many people. May they be spread through millions of cities, countrysides, workshops, mines, and fisheries. But we poets have the obligation to defend the perfection of the book, its luminous body. Some sectarians have used abusive language about my own books, because they demonstrate that Chilean printers can compete in excellence with others more famous. These bitter recriminations don't bother me; my books have also been issued in popular editions, at the lowest possible prices. I encourage both, for different reasons. The rest is up to the publishers.

Besides printing the most beautiful books of our age, Tallone had the simplicity, the poetic nature, and the roguishness of the ancient artisans to whose illustrious family he belonged. He was a fascinating conversationalist. Instead of an ordinary dining room, in his house he had a trattoria, with a counter and small tables, like a small restaurant. He explained that his father, who'd been a court portrait painter, was famous for his bohemianism. He painted portraits of the king's children, but it took him so long that the princes were noticeably older by the time he finished. He used the money to buy large pieces of lavish furniture, but then, accompanied by a happy crew of friends, the painter would disappear and the authorities would carry away all the furniture. That's why Alberto ate so seldom in the family dining room. During the times of dismantlement his mother took her children to a nearby restaurant, where they were served on credit. So, when a grown man and already a famous printer, he'd set up his own trattoria; and many were the happy meals we ate there.

Tallone was mad about locomotives; he collected them. Matilde and I didn't know this, and once had a bad fright when we entered his garden and walked onto the railroad tracks where a large locomotive was puffing quantities of black smoke. We thought we must have lost our way and somehow ended up at the local railroad station. But here came a smiling Bianca and Alberto Tallone: the smoke was in our honor. I have the Petrarch, Dante's verse, Ronsard's loves, Shakespeare's sonnets, Cino da Pistoia's poetry, Pythagoras, Anaxagoras, Zeno of Elea, Diogenes, Empedocles, all printed by his magical hands.

My most recent manuscripts arrived too late for him to elevate them to the apex of typography. Bianca, heroic and alone, announced that she would print them.

In my copy of Galeazzo di Tarsia (1520–1553), printed by Tallone in 1950, I read these magnificent lines:

> *Donna, che viva gia portavi i giorni*
> *Chiari negli occhi ed or le notti apporti . . .*

Farewell, Alberto Tallone, great printer, good friend. Your eyes were bright with day, now they are dark with night. But in your books—man's small castles—beauty and clarity will live: through those windows, night will never enter.

The Esmeralda in Leningrad

THE *Esmeralda*'s in! The *Esmeralda*'s in!

Faces peer from kitchen windows, shipwrights look up from their repairs, children run as if it were the first day of spring, bearded old men in striped trousers, cane in hand, pause for a moment. All eyes turn toward one point. All the secret inhabitants, all the invisible people, come out of their dens; the fifty hills of the port gaze toward a single point. Every eye in Valparaiso, even those that haven't taken time to look at the flowers and the stars, observe at the same moment a white dot gradually growing larger, a dove with spreading wings, a sailing ship as beautiful as a white rose. It is the *Esmeralda*.

To understand my country, you must know the *Esmeralda*.

Chile is a land of lofty mountains: high peaks and vertiginous abysses. Copper and iron ore juts from the mountainsides. Higher lies white snow. Chile is a titanic, narrow balcony. The cordillera turns us back. We Chileans stand in a long row, looking at our sea, its wrathful expanse, its ocean waves. And in these harsh reaches the *Esmeralda* is our luxury, the moonstone jewel in our marine ring.

Other ships before have borne this name. Some were heroic, some short-lived. The name will live forever, not only in memory: the most beautiful of our ships will carry it always, because it is a word for the color green.

But the most recent ship is the most beautiful, the best.

When the prodigious Scotsman Lord Cochrane, with Chilean crews, liberated the seas off our coast, Chileans saw a great highway open before them: the highway of the sea. The Spanish Empire had padlocked all the ocean ports: the bolts were blasted open in the battles of Callao and Valdivia. Trade flew the flags of peace, and all the ships of the world called at Valparaiso.

The Pacific! The pride of the planet! Immense mystery!

We have wanted the sea to be an infinity of sea lanes, wanted, between hellos and goodbyes, to exchange flowers for ore, songs for machinery, hopes for grains. Quickly forgotten, the cannons of war, the naval battles, disappeared beneath swelling waves. Atomic blasts were scars on our conscience, but the ocean itself submerged them. The fact is that this ocean is prophetic and communicative, it wants to close distances, it demands new ships, civilizations, revolutions, ideas, and languages that will communicate and multiply.

At this moment, our small white ship skims the sea, its sails swelled by lusty Baltic winds. She is approaching Leningrad, the most beautiful city of the North, with the statue of Peter the Great in its center, and the image of Lenin in its hearts and factories.

Amid the shadows of Dostoevsky and Pushkin, our boys will walk toward the Nevsky Prospekt. In the Hermitage they will see the most beautiful paintings in the world and the jewels of emperors. They will board a ship whose cannons helped change the course of world history—a ship smaller than the *Esmeralda*. Her name is the *Aurora*, and when I visited her many years ago I felt very proud that her captain knew my poetry.

I celebrate the arrival of the *Esmeralda* in Soviet ports.

Some people will stop in the street—old people who endured the hunger and cold of their unforgettable siege, children who breathe the far-spreading air of emerging mankind. They will look, and they will think of my faraway country situated between the highest mountains and the deepest chasms of the sea. They will see that all roads meet, and that the flowering month of May in Russia has been communicated to us through our vernal ship. And when the *Esmeralda* returns and all the eyes of Valparaiso strain to catch sight of the white rose returning from the seas, we will see on her prow and on her great white petals a new dimension in friendship and understanding between peoples.

Two Portraits of One Face

C HANCE placed side by side on a wall of my house the portraits of two youths born in different times and different countries. Their destinies and their languages were divergent. Nevertheless, the two portraits arouse the same amazement in everyone who sees them hanging there together. You would think they are one and the same person. Both have a certain indomitable quality in their gaze. Both have a heavy head of hair. The same eyebrows, the same nose, the same youthful, defiant face.

One is a photograph of Rimbaud taken by Carjat when the French poet was seventeen; the other is a likeness of Mayakovsky made in 1909 when the young Soviet poet was studying in the Stroganoff School of Applied Arts.

These two youthful images share the characteristic that worked to such disadvantage in their early lives, an obstinate and disdainful scowl: theirs are the faces of two rebellious angels.

Perhaps they are united by a secret sign that in some way reveals the essence of the innovators.

For both are innovators. Rimbaud reorganizes poetry; in him it reaches its most violent beauty. Mayakovsky, sovereign architect of poetry, creates an indestructible alliance between revolution and tenderness. And these two faces of young innovators were joined by chance on a wall of my house, both gazing at me with eyes that explored the world, and the heart of man.

Mayakovsky would have been seventy-five. Had we been able to meet and talk, we might have been friends.

This possibility has a strange effect on me, almost as if someone told me I could have known Walt Whitman. The glory and the legend of the Soviet poet have grown so large that it is difficult for me to imagine him walking into the Aragby Restaurant in Moscow, or even to imagine his tall figure on the stage, reciting the echeloned verses so like regiments assaulting enemy positions, crackling with the rhythm of successive waves of gunpowder and passion.

His image and his poetry are held like a bouquet of bronze flowers in the hands of the Revolution and the new state. There is no doubt that they are indestructible, well constructed, steely, and strong, but no less fertile for that. Borne on the winds of change, Mayakovsky's poems had a role in the change, and this is the grandeur of his fate.

It is a privileged position: the involvement of a true poet in his country's most important historical era. In this, Mayakovsky's poetry is eternally separated from that of Rimbaud: Rimbaud is splendid, but vanquished—the most glorious of the *maudits*. Mayakovsky, in spite of his tragic death, is a sonorous and sensitive component in one of the greatest victories of man. In this respect, he is closer to Whitman than to Rimbaud. Whitman and Mayakovsky were part of the struggle, they lived their great eras. Whitman is not merely a decorative element in Lincoln's War of Emancipation: his poetry develops in the light and shadow of battle. Mayakovsky continues to sing in the urban landscape of his nation's factories, laboratories, schools, and agricultural products. His poetry has the dynamism of massive space missiles.

Vladimir Mayakovsky would have been seventy-five. What a loss that he is not with us!

Houses from the Past

I am frightened by houses I have lived in; the arms of their compasses are opened wide, waiting: they want to swallow you and bury you in their rooms, in their memories. I was widowed by many houses in my lifetime, and I remember each of them with fondness. I couldn't enumerate them, and I couldn't go back to live in them, because I don't like resurrections. Space, time, life, and oblivion not only invade a house to spin cobwebs in all the corners; they also store a record of everything that happened in certain rooms: the love, illness, misery, and happiness that will not be relegated to the past but want to live on.

There are no phantoms more terrifying than those of old gardens. Verlaine wrote a melancholy poem that begins: *"Dans le vieux parc solitaire et glacé . . ."* Two spirits have been condemned to return to their gardens, and the resurrected past pursues them to kill them once again.

And I don't like to see trees that have known me. Some years they grew along with me, but after I left they grew alone, because no man is indispensable to a tree. All a tree needs are earth, water, clouds, and the moon. A human being is superfluous, his atmosphere is alien to the rings of a tree's morphology, to its vital space of leaves and roots.

Nonetheless, those roots and branches hope to grow on in one's soul. That's why all is lost for the person who returns to an old, abandoned garden.

Only once have I wanted to return to a house I lived in. This happened in Ceylon, after many years had passed.

I couldn't find the house. I knew the name of the neighborhood, Wellawatte, a suburb between the city of Colombo and Mount Lavinia. I had rented a modest bungalow right on the reverberating shore. Before me, the coral reefs erupted into starry, marine phosphorescence. The ships knew the lanes and channels they must follow to cross safely the white, flowering reefs. Foam burst on the blue horizon nearby.

It may be that in that house, which was more solitary than any I have ever known, I had more time to get to know myself. I greeted myself as soon as I arose, and all through the day posed endless questions to myself. I felt secure in my own companionship, a state I have seldom achieved. I was aided in my understanding by the epic movements of the torrid ocean, the lashing typhoons that rained down coconuts from the palms in a clamorous green bombardment. And knowledge, self-knowledge, this long self-examination, along with wind and fruit and sea, are contained in my little book *Residencia en la tierra*, a tormented gazetteer of my self-exploration.

The fact is that I lived there in the most advanced stages of poverty: the poverty of a consul trying to exist on U.S. $166.66 that he never received.

A hungry consul is not very fashionable. Among men in dinner jackets, you can't say, "A sandwich, please, I'm fainting." That's why I smile when in biographical descriptions they refer to me as a diplomat. In some—for example, in *Esquire*—I was even called an ambassador. Ambassadors, in my understanding, can count on their food, and a little something besides. I was merely a consul drowning in poverty.

I found the street. It had no name, only an unromantic number: 42nd Lane. That may be why I'd forgotten it. With Matilde I walked down the narrow street, the same that forty years before led me every day to the city of Colombo.

Strange: all the houses were alike, small one- or two-story buildings with the suburban garden of the tropics that blushes in shame for its smallness in comparison to the color and splendor of gardens in general.

Stranger still: the very next day they were going to demolish the house, my house.

Well, then, those rooms had continued to direct my life without my knowing. They had set an appointment, and quite unaware, I had arrived punctually, on the last day of its life.

I went in: the tiny little living room, and then the narrow bedroom that had contained nothing but a cot for so many years of my residence on earth. Then, at the back, perhaps the ghost of Brampy, my servant, and of Kiria, my mongoose.

I fled from memory toward the sun, toward life.

It was a fateful experience. I'd fallen into the trap the house I lived in had set for me, the house that wanted to die. Why had it sent for me?

These are matters that will remain a mystery so long as houses and men exist.

Days in Capri

O<small>NE</small> of the best times for working were those days we spent in Capri. The island has two shining and clearly defined faces. Summer in Capri is "touristential," overcrowded, and crammed with hell-holes I, unfortunately, never knew. They were within my reach, but not my pocket's.

Capri saves its better side for winter, the poorer face of hospitable and ingenuous working people. Moreover, in winter, the heights of Anacapri are tinged with evening purple. Bushes, weeds, and grasses spring up everywhere to greet the faithful friend who remained through winter, to live with the other island, the real island: simple stone surrounded by Tyrrhenian foam. That's where I wrote a large part of one of my least-known books: *Las uvas y el viento.*

The country woman who cooked and cleaned for us arrived very early. Dressed in gray, small and quick, she could have been any age at all. I baptized her Olivito, because she looked like a little olive tree, sweeping through the rooms as if blown by an invisible wind from the Marina Maggiore.

She cleaned the house, and shortly after noon she was ready to leave in her olive-gray clothes.

"Why do you leave so early?" Matilde asked one day.

"I'm building my house, *signora,*" she replied, adding that a woman without property was no one: "*Una donna senza proprietà no vale niente.*"

With her own hands, both fragile and formidable, she was building a *casetta* of stone. She invited us once to come see her construction. This was no "little house." This was a two-story stone building with arches and balconies. When we arrived, she had just completed the pool. She greeted us happily, her hands covered with clay and cement.

I was writing every morning, page piling upon page. The theme was "*El viento en el Asia*" ("The Wind in Asia"), a long poem about China, about the Revolution, about Mao, who at that time seemed heroic to me. There were also long sections on the crickets the Chinese sell in tiny cages that stack to form skyscrapers.

Well, one day I noticed that my *lavoro* had disappeared. Beside the table was my wastebasket, and occasionally pages from my manuscript dropped into it. Olivito's efficiency could not be expected to reach the point of divination: the papers on the table were *lavoro*, the papers in the wastebasket were trash.

I cried to high heaven. With Olivito and a Municipal Inspector, especially designated to grub through refuse, we went to the garbage dumps of Capri. Horror! The dumps were not just hills, they were mountain ranges. The official waved a vague hand toward one mountain where my ardent verses might be buried. But the volcano remained dormant. No internal combustion revealed the existence of verses, good or bad.

So I had to reconstruct the long poem the wastebasket had swallowed. Was it worthwhile? I've often asked myself since, but not for reasons of poetry.

The fiery, eloquent, and energetic Mario Alicatta and his wife, Sarah, came from Naples to visit me in Capri.

Alicatta listened to my enthusiastic perorations about the onion, an enthusiasm he shared. As I pontificated on its different preparations, tastes, and odors, Alicatta's bushy eyebrows wagged more and more violently, until he could no longer contain himself, and interrupted me with a cascade of eloquence.

"How dare you—you, a newcomer to the use and cultivation of the onion—how dare you give me a lesson on this foundation of Mediterranean cuisine? We, Phoenicians, Etruscans, Levantines, Romans, elaborated a thousand preparations for the *cipolla* before you were ever discovered, centuries before you understood what an onion is."

I replied, with no less brio: "It isn't always a matter of who invented what. The New World gave size, multiplicity, and vigor to the onion. We made it more powerful and more widespread, we directed it to unexplored kingdoms. In gratitude, the onion became more juicy, more transparent, more essential than anywhere else in the world. We Americans cannot live without it, nor it without us."

So the challenge was issued: alternately, in my house and his, in the presence of implacable judges, we would settle this all-important controversy: each presenting his onion menu.

Alicatta arrived punctually, accompanied by judges. Matilde and I had prepared onions in a marinade of red wine, salad with feathery sliced onions, fried meat pies smothered with onion, and a Capri shrimp cocktail in a lemon sauce loaded with red onion.

Before finishing the "onionthon," Mario, eyes bulging and hands waving above his head, erupted: "Enough, enough! My meal is unnecessary. I declare you the winner. It's humiliating to confess, but you Americans know more than the Phoenicians. And you can teach Romans to eat onion."

But truly, the winner was Matilde. She had shed her good tears in the battle of the onion.

From Capri, too, came *Los versos del capitán*, my secret book that Paolo Ricci, the Neapolitan painter, a close friend and Judge of the Onion, published anonymously in a beautiful edition of fifty copies.

The first purchaser was the great Togliatti. For many years, the book's progenitor remained unknown. It struggled on its own until it became a man. I acknowledged its parentage after it had gone through many editions. It was old enough to come out of the dark and be born again.

Those days in Capri were fruitful, amorous, and perfumed by the sweetness of the Mediterranean onion.

A Leg for Fernand Léger

THE Mexican General Santa Anna was a lucky warrior, a soldier of the people.

It was his destiny to wage war in the interminable skirmishes, mounted sorties, uprisings, and knife fights that stud the history of Mexico. The clashes in the dry and thorny borderlands fell to the general's lot. Many of his actions are miracle, blood, and legend, because Mexico sheds such glamour on its history that magicians and minotaurs sprout like volcanoes metamorphosing into medallions of the finest metals.

Santa Anna fought in the wars between the Mexicans and the gringos, in which invader and invaded had won a more or less equal number of victories. But finally a gluttonous North America gobbled up large chunks of beautiful and savage Mexican territory.

Well, a cannonball—one of those ancient balls they fired with a prayer—tore off the General's knee at the height of a battle. The military surgeon prepared to amputate the leg. Try to imagine a battlefield in the last century, in that devastating climate, a feverish General by the light of oil lamps, his leg being sawed off, a night of translucent stars streaked by phosphorescent fireflies, and an insect chorus dominated by exuberant grasshoppers.

General Santa Anna, by the strength of his strength and the luck of his luck, was at the peak of his career. And on that Promethean peak, fate nipped him in the bud. He had been made dictator because of his military power, and the adulators that sprang up like mushrooms under the ahuehuetes in Chapultepec Park conferred on him the title of Most Serene Highness. I have seen photographs from that time, pictures memorable for his Christ-like beard and piercing eyes black as crows. No doubt, he gave off that majestic light that scheming cultists confer in every era on the most rapacious among them. So then, at that crossroads, at the foot of cruel mountains, amid the smell of recently spilled blood and burnt gunpowder, and at the hands of his surgeons, His Most Serene Highness was being separated from a gangrened leg. Almost certainly, that stupendous soldier endured and survived the amputation without anesthesia. But after the threat of death had been averted, an unexpected and unusual battle ensued.

The surgeon was about to toss the severed limb into the garbage pail when someone, some politico, stayed him, saying, "Are you going to throw away this portion of His Highness's body?" Probably the doctor replied: "Well, what do you think I'm going to do with it?" "This deserves some thought," the disciples chorused. "This leg performed countless feats, it invaded enemy territory, and gathered as many laurels as the rest of the General's body. You must be more respectful."

As the argument between the scientific-minded and the court followers stretched into the night, the surgeon could see no end to it, so he placed the leg in a large bottle of alcohol, hoping that with the light of the new day the debaters would reach an agreement.

Instead, matters grew more complicated.

The news spread with amazing alacrity and created obvious division among the citizenry. Two parties were formed: the Leg Party, and the more sensible but less enthusiastic Anti-Leg Party. Newspaper editorials in Chihuahua and Tehuantepec called on patriots to prevent this blasphemy. The "extremity" was holy, as holy as the Dictator's beard, or his military cunning. The Anti-Legs, for their part, had lost faith in beards from the moment the General outfitted his Palace Guards in the medieval uniform of the Vatican Swiss Guards. As these new Swiss Guards tended to be beardless Indians, large quantities of beards were imported along with the uniforms. Possibly, those beards afforded new occasion for ridicule and mistrust among the iconoclasts. In fact, the Anti-Leg Party seemed to gain ground in a few provinces.

In the end, however, orthodoxy prevailed, science was defeated, and plans were laid for the first funeral monument to a leg.

The best artisans portrayed in ceramic the history and feats of the General's limb—a mosaic that covered the pyramidal monument. And when the day and hour of burial arrived, an imposing cortege filed through the city's streets.

Seven bands with trombones and trumpets led the cortege. White-mounted dragoons followed, and, on a brocade and gold-draped catafalque, the August Leg. Behind, in silence, the carriage of His Most Serene Highness, preceding the ministerial, diplomatic, clerical, mayoral, and financial groups participating, not necessarily voluntarily, in the ceremony.

The Minister of War delivered the eulogy to the leg. Then the Dean of the Diplomatic Corps, the British Ambassador, spoke a few words—without referring to the anatomical specimen being immortalized. He was an exemplar of solemnity.

A twenty-one-gun salute with cannon, and military marches by the bands, climaxed the unique burial. The people, dark-eyed, without voice or vote, dispersed without participating in rejoicing, mourning, or ceremony. Everything returned to its normal abnormality.

Time passed, and the people with the dark eyes regained control of the vital energy of Mexico. Their wrathful flame was ignited and a revolution like an overflowing river once again inundated Mexico. Exhausted by tyranny, poverty, and farce, the people erupted violently in every section of the country. Shots rang out in the capital and in the provinces. Horsemen slung on their cartridge belts and galloped off.

But where? Unfortunately, the masses, so often misguided in the past, were misguided once again. A great avalanche rolled toward the ancient cemetery, where they knocked down and destroyed the unique and marvelous monument executed in Aztec mosaic to the honor and glory of a leg.

Meanwhile, His Most Serene Highness had time to escape, probably to Miami, where he lived long and happy years without another battle, but with only one leg.

Fernand Léger loved this story. Everywhere we went, he would beg me to tell the tale: *"Maintenant raconte-nous cette histoire de la jambe."* He wanted me to write it, so a ballet could be created from it. He proposed that he would design the stage set and costumes for this fantastic story. I never did write it, but now that I have—and my great friend, France's great painter, is dead—I dedicate it to his memory.

Ramón

I am writing in Isla Negra,
I am writing
a letter and singing.
The day was incomplete,
like an ancient statue
of a sea goddess
sucked from her cold bed,
streaming mire and tears,
and with the revealing
movement
of the sea and its sands,
I recalled the labors
of the Poet,
the persistent radiance of his foam,
the new breath of his waves.
And to Ramón
I dedicated
my morning hymns,
the snake
of my calligraphy,
so when
he emerges from his
prolix capybara's tower
he will be greeted by the serene
sweep of a breeze from Chile;
may the magus's Merlin-cone glitter,
spilling all its magic stars.

Fragment from
Navegaciones y regresos, 1959

Spain is a nation of lost discoverers, of unknown inventors. The only place a Spaniard is born is Spain, for reasons that predate his birth: either by will, or because he was rejected by all other lands and had no recourse but to be born there. There are some few Spaniards who were mistakenly born elsewhere—one being the Spanish Christopher Columbus, who never reached the Spanish Levant, where destiny had intended him to be born. Once the place of birth is established, the Spaniard gives himself over to the difficult profession of being Spanish, Spanish to the core, with all the tragic joy that has sustained Spain.

But, you see, this extremely serious country does not take its representatives seriously; they make their voyage through the world, but only after their deaths, and because of outsiders, is their stature recognized inside Spain.

As with Gaudí and Picasso—we need look no further in the history of repentance—we find this true of the invincible genius of Ramón Gómez de la Serna.

We know that there are peculiar birds that lay their eggs in other birds' nests; at times, the currents of culture play the same devilish tricks. From all the tumult of Dadaism, only one great work emerged. The egg that hatched a winging *Ulysses* was cracked open in Dublin, far from Zurich and Paris, and the great bird wet its wing feathers in the antediluvian mists, the twisting, turning alleyways, of Ireland.

So it was, too, that of all the countries involved, the great figure of Surrealism was Ramón. Of course, he is larger than the school, both because he predates and postdates it and because the enormity of his talent won't be contained, even in a school of so many floors.

This Spaniard, who has yet to be taken seriously, is the person who so serenely demolishes the Parnassus of the Spanish Republic, crowded with medallions of distinguished writers.

Ramón's revolution is not a skirmish; it is a full-scale battle that reveals the true value, the treasury, of the language. With robust energy he gave the dark dawn such a drubbing that everything began to glitter, and in my opinion, with Ramón, all that's gold—even all that's not gold—glitters.

His work is its own destruction. But in spite of the appearance of incoherence, his work is tightly knit, unified by the spectral light of cataloguing. Ramón opened the world's chest of drawers, and set about listing all things and all creatures, the most tattered and the most eminent; with his baptismal ink he reinaugurates the world. And this world, which once seemed incommunicable because it was so specifically Spanish, so personal, is now passed down like the inheritance of a great king.

Our language will continue to be dependent on his inventions and the startling metaphors of his *greguerías*; his mournful invocations, the only ones that conjure up the Greek; his athletic gymnastics that oiled the skeleton of grammar, so language could assume the authentic colors of delirium.

Ah, but beware! There is so much truth and reason in Ramón's monumental activity that little by little his truths and reason are being discovered.

As an American poet, a settler of a different land where there are more rivers and trees than persons and characters, I grant to myself the honor of writing about Ramón, in order to stimulate his continuing discovery and to live along with his fabulous gifts.

I don't know why I do it. Perhaps out of impassioned duty.

Lost: One Green Horse

THE Aguilar publishing house in Madrid is preparing an anthology of the work of Julio Herrera y Reissig, decadent poet of Uruguay's highest poetic achievement. They need the issue of my magazine *Caballo Verde* (*Green Horse*) that was devoted to the Uruguayan. But that issue is nowhere to be found. I will tell you what happened, and what didn't happen.

I carried my Herrera y Reissig passion to Madrid, to the others in my generation. It's true that some learned scholar there had written a few words about him. But erudition isn't passion. And nothing is more passionate than the poetry of this essential Uruguayan, this classic of all poetry. So I read his Gothic *décimas*, his ten-line stanzas, to Vicente Aleixandre, and then to Federico, Alberti, Altolaguirre, Cernuda, Miguel Hernández, and a few others. I compared this wild American, the scintillation of his disturbing images, to his fellow Uruguayan Lautréamont, whose delirium continues to inflame world poetry.

With the eruption of his volcanic figures, Herrera y Reissig lifts the vulgarity of an epoch to the sublime. He can be compared only to the architect Gaudí, who explodes the art of 1900 with his systematic paroxysms, as necessary as a marine grotto to the refurbishing of beauty. With cruel premeditation, Lautréamont coldly dissects frogs, reptiles, and resentments. *Les Chants de Maldoror* is the most perfect crime in universal poetry.

I wanted to give priority to honoring Herrera y Reissig because among the Modernists his phosphorescence, his firefly incandescence, is unique. While Rubén Darío is the undisputed king of cold, marbled

Modernism, Julio of Uruguay blazes with subterranean, submarine fire; his verbal mania is without parallel in our language. In Spain, Rubén Darío enjoyed a wealth of disciples and recognition, while the immortal Uruguayan poet passed unperceived; he had no chorus, he was not emulated with the same intensity as Rubén.

Herrera y Reissig is structural and prophetic; like a clockmaker's art, his is a work of precise consequences, a vortex flashing with exactitude. He is so thoroughly imbued with the insuperable irrationality of poetry that he shrinks before nothing; it is difficult to surpass him in the absurd.

> *In the erroneous quadruped*
> *unruliness arched its back . . .*

As I read *La tertulia lunática* (*The Lunatic Assembly*) to my Spanish companions, green sparks flew, sulfurous diamonds, and the faster the amazing equations of Julian *décimas* flowed, the more powerful the poetic communication.

I decided to publish a double issue—numbers 5 and 6—of my magazine *Caballo Verde* and to dedicate it in its entirety to Herrera y Reissig. I recall that Ramón Gómez de la Serna wrote a lavish page and a half, sketching the outlines of the great poet. Vicente Aleixandre delivered his homage: a poem with a long, flowing mane. Miguel Hernández and others wrote magnificent dithyrambs. Federico wrote with more understanding than any of them, since, when he was in Buenos Aires, we had discovered our mutual admiration for Herrera y Reissig and had decided to carry a funeral wreath to his tomb in Uruguay. I wrote my poem *"El hombre enterrado en la pampa"* ("The Man Buried in the Pampa").

Manuel Altolaguirre printed the double number of the journal in the great Bodoni typeface that gives special brilliance to poetry. Everything was ready; the pages were to be sewn the following day. But the following day the Civil War began. It came from Africa; Spain was overrun with rifles. There was no time for books. The first bombings began. Disaster followed.

And everywhere, the death of poets: Federico in Granada, Machado on the French frontier, Miguel Hernández in prison.

So it goes. War blasts men and windows, walls and women, and leaves tombs and wounds. And in its bloody gusts it also whirls away books, leaves of paper, that will never return.

This may have happened, this must have happened, to my *Caballo Verde*.

Collectors write me from Chicago, from the Philippines. They want to read this last number honoring Julio.

The press was operated in Altolaguirre's house. We put ourselves into those verses, invading the shop, the kitchen, the privacy, of my admirable friend. We left, crushed by the war, exiled, wounded in spirit.

Altolaguirre turned to cinematography. He came back to Spain to show his first film. Leaving Burgos, the car he was driving was involved in an accident, and he was killed.

The mystery of *Caballo Verde*, of its last issue, still haunts Viriato Street in Madrid, a city I haven't visited since the war.

Is my best issue lying somewhere, in some cellar, lifeless and yellowed? No one has ever found out. It isn't only the collectors who write me who know it can't be found. I, too, feel its ghostly presence, clad in phantasmal pages, wandering through long nights of war and peace.

There Are Typos, and Then There Are Howlers

MY next book enters and leaves the printers' without ever showing me its face. It found itself a pawn in the age-old battle of errata. This is the bloody battlefield where poets first suffer the pain of their books of poetry. Errata are the caries in the lines, and pain shoots down to your toes when the poems hit the cold air of publication.

When it comes to errata, there are typos, and then there are howlers. Typos crouch in a copse of consonants and vowels, clad in green or gray; they are as difficult to discover as the stingers of insects or reptiles concealed in the lawn of typography. Howlers, on the other hand, make no effort to disguise their rabid rodents' teeth.

In the book I referred to, one howler drew blood. Where I had said "The green water of the language [*idioma*]," the machine went into a decline and printed "The green water of the idiot [*idiota*]." I felt the teeth marks in my soul. Because, for me, language, the Spanish language, is a stream bubbling with inexhaustible drops and syllables, it is an undammable current descending from the cordillera of Góngora to the popular language of a blind man singing on a street-corner. But that "*idiota*" that took the place of "*idioma*" was like a discarded shoe floating down the middle of the river.

The novel can ignore the mischievous typos committed by composition and linotype. But poetry is sensitive, and feels the prickle of every obstacle. Poetry resents the clatter of a coffee spoon, the steps of people coming and going, the inopportune giggle. The novel has a more mountainous and subterranean terrain where prehistoric costumes and mechanical blunders may hide.

My great friend Manuel Altolaguirre—that gentle Spanish poet who printed my poetry review in Madrid—was a glorious printer. With his own hands, he set the type, marvelous Bodoni. Manolito honored poetry with his own poetry, and with his hands, the hands of a diligent archangel. He translated and printed with singular beauty Shelley's "Adonais," his elegy on the death of the young Keats. What splendor radiated from the golden, enameled strophes of the poem in the majestic typography that highlighted each word as if it were being reborn in a crucible.

Even so, Altolaguirre was capable of typos and howlers. Some even appeared on a title page, where they were noticed only after the books were distributed to the booksellers. To him, to my very dear Manuel Altolaguirre, belongs this stunner among errata. I will tell you about it because it happened to a magniloquent and mellifluous Cuban rhyme maker, as carefree as a man could be, for whom my friend was printing a typographical masterpiece in a very limited edition.

"Any errors?" the poet inquired.

"None, of course," Altolaguirre replied.

But upon opening this most elegant book, one discovered that where the poet had written, "I feel a savage [*atroz*] fire devouring me," the printer had set his howler: "I feel a fire behind [*atrás*] devouring me."

The happy-go-lucky author and the culpable printer went out in a boat and dumped all the copies in the middle of Havana Bay.

I was unable to do the same when in my *Crepusculario*, in place of "kisses, bed [*lecho*], and bread," the printer substituted "kisses, milk [*leche*], and bread." I have seen that horrendous howler translated many times into other languages and have shed many tears over that spilt *milk*. But as the edition in Spanish where it originally appeared was pirated, I never caught up with the editor; I was denied the pleasure of throwing the howler in the bay.

Certain typos from the past bring a nostalgia for streets and roads that no longer exist. I am thinking of those that still appear in the reprints of my *Tentativa del hombre infinito*.

In those days, just as they are beginning to do again, we had abolished all punctuation marks. We wanted our poetry to achieve an immaculate purity, the closest approximation to naked thought, to the intimate labor of the soul.

So, when I held in my hand the first proofs of that little book published by Don Carlos Nascimento, I noticed with pleasure a shoal of errors darting among my lines. Instead of correcting them, I returned the proofs intact to an astonished Don Carlos, who said: "No errors?"

I proudly replied: "There are, and I leave them so."

My first editor was inured to my effrontery, which had little or no effect on him. With his cynical smile, he stuffed into his pockets poems and errata alike. When I was young, I thought I found in every fatal error a spontaneous fountain that added to my creation, making it more enigmatic. I even considered publishing a book in which every word was a typo or a howler.

I am far removed from that romanticism now, and I pursue errata with pruning shears, insecticide, and shotgun.

But always I spy the ears of some erratum camouflaged in my strophes as if in a thicket.

Let us as writers recognize that the sudden shock of another's error leads us to a truth we hadn't fathomed: to the guts of the press, to its iron viscera, its membranes, its black digestive system. Errata lead us straight to the work of a human hand. We must descend from our castle of words and recognize the infinite labor hidden behind each line: the movement of eyes and hands, the anonymous associates of our thought—the workers who from the time of Gutenberg have been part of the army that fights by our side.

Universal Night

Mᴏʀᴇ than thirty years ago I happened to arrive in Saigon in an automobile—a black limousine—of supreme elegance, lacquered like a coffin. I was driven by an impeccable French chauffeur attired in an imposing uniform.

Once in the center of the city, I asked him: "What's the best hotel in the city?"

"The Grand Hotel," he replied.

"And what's the worst?" He looked at me, surprised.

"A hotel I know in the Chinese district," he said. "It has every discomfort you could want."

"Take me to that one," I directed.

Vexed, he changed direction and drove toward the Chinese quarter. He deposited my dusty suitcase at the door, dumping it upside down, thus indicating his disdain. Mistakenly, he had taken me for a gentleman.

The room, though shabby, was spacious and pleasant. There was a bed covered with mosquito netting, and a night table. At the opposite end of the room was a wooden platform with a porcelain pillow.

"What's that for?" I asked the Chinese bellboy.

"For smoking opium. Shall I bring you a pipe?"

"Not right now," I replied, giving him some expectation of increasing his clientele.

So I was right in the heart of Saigon's China. The cities of the East—from Calcutta to Singapore, from Penang to Batavia—consist of the vaguely official European establishments of the colonizers, surrounded by enormous rings of Chinese banking, working, and residential districts.

It is a sacred principle with me that in every new city I immediately go out into the streets, through markets, up and down through sun and shadow, into the splendor of life. But that night, too exhausted, I lay down beneath the protective gauze of the netting and fell asleep.

It had been a difficult journey; the lurching bus had rattled my bones the length of the peninsula of Indochina. Finally, the rickety vehicle could go no farther; it had stopped, paralyzed, in the middle of the jungle, and there, wide awake in the darkness of a foreign land, I'd been picked up by a passing automobile. It turned out to be the car of the French governor himself. Which explains my glorious and majestic entrance into Saigon.

In that Chinese bed I slipped into infinity, peering through the windows of dream at the rivers of the South of Chile, the rain of Boroa, my sparse obsessions. Suddenly I was awakened by cannon fire. The odor of gunpowder drifted through the netting. Another cannon blast, and another—ten thousand detonations. Bugles, jingling bells, horns, tolling bells, fanfare, howls. A revolution? The end of the world?

It was something much simpler: the Chinese New Year.

Tons of deafening, blinding gunpowder. I went out to the street. Fireworks, rockets, and Roman candles scattered blue, yellow, and amaranth stars. What truly amazed me was a tower shooting cascades of multicolor fire; as the shower cleared, you could see an acrobat dancing in the middle of a fiery, spherical cage. The contortionist was dancing amid burning sparks, thirty-five meters in the air.

One New Year's Eve years later, I experienced danger as I walked through the streets of Naples. Fireworks, rockets, Roman candles, erupted from every window of every Neapolitan house. An unprecedented contest in phosphorescent madness! What seriously affected me, a passerby lost in those streets, was that in the ensuing silence, after the explosions of light had subsided, all manner of indescribable objects began to fall about my head: wobbly tables, large books and bottles, sprung sofas, peeling picture frames containing mustachioed photographs, battered pots and pans. The Neapolitans throw from their balconies their year's odds and ends. Joyfully, they shed their useless junk, and with the birth of each new year assume the duty of uncompromising cleanliness.

But when it comes to enjoying a New Year's Eve, there's no place like Valparaiso. It is a luminous seaport spectacle. Among the fire-bedecked ships, the tiny *Esmeralda* is the jewel of sailing ships: her masts are crosses of diamonds that blend with the celestial necklace of the festival night. On that night, the ships not only radiate fire, they speak in their secret voices: all the foghorns of Neptune, ordinarily reserved for the dangers of the sea, fill that night with hoarse joy.

Yet the marvel is the hills, which blink on and off in the encircling illumination, reflecting in light and shadow the fervor of marine brilliance. It is a moving sight to see these twinkling hills, every eye winking in response to the ships' greetings.

A New Year's Eve embrace in Valparaiso is unforgettable. There, too, in a way, we burn the remnants of the year and in the flashing of light and fire await, cleansed, the days ahead.

Book of Seven Colors

I have received two books from Elsa Triolet, almost simultaneously. One is a novel, *Le Rossignol se tait a l'aube*. The other is *La Mise en mots*.

I don't know how to translate the second title. The arrangement, the presentation, of words? This book is more than that. It is the intimate process, the ordering, of written thought. It is the drama of the writer, the happiness of the writer. It is the drama and happiness of Elsa Triolet, bilingual author, flesh-and-bone author, with her soul divided between two languages and two countries, Russia and France. "To be bilingual is to be a bigamist," Elsa Triolet confesses. The magnificent Elsa: clairvoyant, with those incomparable eyes that came from the East and opened more widely in the illumination of France.

But the book about words, published by Skira, is not only textually astonishing, it is publishing magic. It is white, white as a white dove; it is smooth, like a body of marble; it flies, like a butterfly of seven colors. It flies with the words of Elsa Triolet, flies counter to time, on strong, immaculate, enduring wings.

"You understand, I've often deceived myself in my life. Or, more accurately, not so much deceived myself as been deceived by others. Blinded by the sun of faith, I saw only fire and sun. But that was never part of my writing. There I was guided by what I could touch. I've walked with my hands extended before me like a blind woman, groping to find my way."

This book is interwoven with Elsa's vital concerns—a self-examination, scrupulously honorable, that leads to the paintings of Francis Bacon and Paul Klee. Suddenly a sky by Nicholas de Staël, with the bluest of blues, transports a luminous Brazil to her pages; a touch of Piero di Cosimo or El Greco brings the magic whisper of their ages.

I envy beautiful books, and this is one I wish was my own, so my fingers could touch my own poetry.

Through the highways and the byways of our America, books like this beautiful big work by Elsa Triolet don't become known as they should. This is not entirely the fault of the publisher: the reproach is aimed at the silence of our journals, which have space only for passing fads. From *Bon soir, Thérèse* through *Le Cheval blanc, Le Cheval roux, Rose à credit, Luna-Park,* and *Le Rendez-vous des étrangers,* Elsa Triolet is a streaking comet's tail of reflection and emotion; in the sky of France, a Milky Way of scintillating stars. It is our loss if we do not know her.

She defended Mayakovsky's life, and she also defended his bequest: his loves and his truth, as well as his poetry. No one more than she has revealed the intimate turbulence of this great poet of the Revolution, and no one has been more incisive in response to the slanderers who still, even today, attempt to wound the woman Mayakovsky held most dear. One would have thought that the thrust of Mayakovsky, his shattering poetic integrity, would have been sufficient to silence the envious for all time. But envy acquires superhuman strength. We are indebted to Elsa for defending what is just.

But Elsa Triolet is still more. Aragon maintains that Elsa, who is his wife, made it possible for him to free himself from his chimeras, from the obstacles that burdened him, from the negative forces that pursued him. "She," says Aragon, "gave me back the courage to be, and, even more, the strength to become."

Many were the times I spent observing or sharing life with the Aragons. It is only natural that we learn from creative intelligence, from subtlety and happiness, passion and truth. These qualities make me recognize my own infuriating limitations.

But what I most admired in this industrious pair was their work. Constant, passionate, uninterrupted, fruitful, unlimited, inexhaustible work, as if they drew strength from their own labor. Work as the greatest duty of love and conscience.

Shortly before he died, the great poet Reverdy, describing the early days of another illustrious pair of writers, Sartre and Simone de Beauvoir, told me how he'd watched them, then unknown, enter the Deux Magots. Each carried a roll of white paper. A few hours later, each went out carrying a roll of paper black with ink.

Both Aragon and Elsa Triolet have given us paper black with dazzling poetry; hope in the most hostile days; faith in the destiny of man.

Elsa Triolet laments in this book that she cannot say more than it is possible to say with words. Yet she has charged words with infinite expression. This bilingual woman has spoken for all latitudes, for all beings.

With Cortázar and with Arguedas

I<small>T</small> would be imprudent to allow exasperation to take the place of careful thought in the confrontation that has arisen between Cortázar and Arguedas. This is a debate as profound as it is endless, and it is difficult to concede, or refuse to concede, the argument to either of our eminent opponents.

It has always been my position that a writer in our forgotten countries should live in those lands and defend them. The formidable books from the Pacific coast that denounce the martyrdom of the Indians might never have been written in exile, without the inescapable daily contact with the sorry plight of those peoples. That may be why my life has been one long departing and returning, an exodus to make possible a homecoming. I could have stayed in many places. I stayed here.

In the books of Cortázar, Vargas Llosa, Fuentes, and García Márquez, there is a constant thematic preoccupation with America, a vigor rooted in our truths, an ambience that is uniquely our own, that they re-create, not infrequently, with greatness. This is what we must remember. From afar, exiled or no, they are more American than many of their compatriots who live on this side of the ocean.

I deeply mistrusted an earlier, elitist generation that once in Europe easily forgot our cradle of clay. Those writers packed their suitcases, set out to conquer Paris, and almost immediately, with or without difficulty, began writing in French. Bitterly and dogmatically, I assailed this cultural dualism. Yet to this day I am moved by many of Huidobro's poems written in French, to say nothing of the marvelous and forgotten Ecuadorian poet Gangotena, who vanished in the flower of his youth and who always wrote in that language.

On the other hand, it behooves us to affirm the existence of those of our writers who endured the harshness, penury, envy, and insults that constitute the daily bread of every one of our provincial countries. I've often felt an itch in my soul, a desire to set off for some distant shore. The literary skirmishes in Latin America are a part of the air we breathe, and professional backbiters sharpen their teeth on them. Throughout my professional life I have been saddled with entire literary families, from fathers to nephews, who devoted themselves to attacking me.

Yet envy is self-generating, endemic, and undying in semi-colonial literary countries. It has such powers of revival that it springs up in different configurations—never, of course, taking the form of a sprig of wheat or a loaf of bread. It is eminently bitter and destructive; no nourishment can be derived from it.

Novelists such as Arguedas, Ciro Alegría, Icaza, and others who endured in this harsh land were obviously great men, but it is significant that a new sense of America is emerging from writers who represent us from afar, with the luminous truth or worldly fantasy of a García Márquez. I can say the same of others I know, like the magical Cortázar, or the extraordinary Vargas Llosa.

What matters are essences. And these writers have made an *essential* contribution: that's what counts. This is why the debate can and must be continued, while at the same time, I scarcely need add, minimizing the personal aspects. Those involved are too dignified to allow a debate to degenerate into the literary squabbles so typical of our continent's cultists.

The matter has profound implications.

"The temptation of the world," Ehrenburg called my inclination toward the universal, as opposed to the work of a folkloric Cuban poet.

That temptation of the world that draws us toward the active integration of classicism and the experimental can also lead to cosmopolitanism. It can divert us into an unenduring superficiality. This is a danger.

But how shall we free ourselves from an imperious and tantalizing Europe? Why should we cut the bonds of elegance that bind us to her?

Moreover, it is easy for the American, and no less the native American, to immerse himself not in our ocean but in a mud puddle, and to so limit himself in form as to embrace the past. This is a different danger.

This danger will not sever our roots. It so happens that the more we sink into ourselves, the more we renew ourselves, and the more local we become, the more likely our universality. I know a great book that concerned itself with only a small region of Spain called La Mancha. And it became the most spacious novel ever written.

Everyone is right. And from these "rights" will be born other new arguments. Present and past humanism has strengthened and proliferated through dispute, when the debate has been dignified and profound.

I am sure that the confrontation between Cortázar and Arguedas will result not only in great new books but in great new roads as well.

Destruction in Cantalao

I have shared many years of my life with the sea. I haven't been a sailor but a stationary observer of the ocean's many faces. I have been fascinated by waves themselves; the seaquakes and sea swells of the Chilean ocean have terrified and mesmerized me. I became an expert in cetaceans, seashells, tides, zoophytes, medusas, in all the fish of the marine kingdom. I admired the *tridacna*, the devouring giant clam, and in California collected the Gothic, snowy *spondylus*, the earshell that captures the rainbow in its mother-of-pearl shell. I lived a long time beside the sea in Ceylon, and with the fishermen removed strange phosphorescent creatures from their nets. Finally, I came to live on the coast of Chile, facing the crashing surf of Isla Negra. Here winters are an infinity of iron-gray sea and lowering clouds.

The sea has seemed cleaner to me than the earth. We don't witness there the diabolical crimes of the great cities, or imminent genocide. No malignant smog hovers over the sea, nor the ashes of smoked cigarettes. The world is oxygenated beside the hygienic blue waves.

But because I profited so much from repose and work in the marine solitude, I was nagged by a vague remorse. And my fellows? Other friendly or unfriendly writers? Did they have the same creative luxury of working and resting by the seashore?

That is why, when some coastal property near Isla Negra was offered for sale, I reserved what was probably the most beautiful site to found a colony of writers. I made payments on it from the proceeds of my own work, thinking in this way to repay a part of my debt to the great outdoors.

I called this literary property Cantalao, as this was the name of an imaginary town in one of my first books. And in this year of 1970 I made the last payment, but not before I lost some land because of improperly surveyed boundaries. In questions of boundaries, the poet always loses.

Before turning the place over to the writers, I constructed a cabin with the double objective of storing materials—nails, boards, cement —and of using it as a hideaway from time to time. I built it with solid logs and fragile windows, windows from old churches. Some of them had green, red, and blue panes, with stars and crosses. A single room, without water or electricity, this cabin jutted from the cliff. To the north its neighbor was the imposing stony mass of Punta de Tralca, which in the language of the Araucans means Thunder Point. Hundred-meter waves crash there and sing as they are unleashed by the storm.

This morning I went to Cantalao to put into place an anchor I'd recently bought in the port of San Antonio. This was done with considerable difficulty; it needed the aid of a tractor, but finally it was installed on an elevated piece of ground. Nothing is as basic as an anchor. In every project, the anchor should come first. At least on the coast, a construction shouldn't begin with the first stone but with the first anchor.

The tractor and its operators departed, leaving me alone. I opened the door of the cabin; I hadn't been there for two months.

I had written the major part of my new book of poetry at the cabin—a long, stormy poem not yet delivered to the printer. The last time I was there, I discovered with a smile, obviously bitter, that the cabin had been invaded. As there was almost never anything in it, the thieves had found little to take away. A broken hammock, two glasses, and three books—the only ones I kept there—were missing. One was the stories and poems of Melville. Another was a book of English poetry; I'd written a poem on the first page that now only the thieves would read. The third was one of my treasures: a small book I'd bought in Colombo in 1930, an Aldine edition of Shakespeare, published in London in 1897. Farewell, old and faithful companions.

But my visit today was even more distressing. New vandals had taken advantage of badly fastened shutters to shatter the windows.

They'd driven in wedges or awls to break out the noble old church windows. Fragments of blue, green, and red carpeted the floor. Scattered there, they seemed to shout the portrait of the plunderers. Cruel and bloody shards: the eyes of pointless aggression, severed fingers, the mangled faces of evil.

Realize, this is an anonymous cabin, until now without an owner, without occupants, waiting for those who will inhabit it tomorrow with their work and their dreams.

I may never know the poets who will live there.

But maybe someday some sophisticated criminal will say, remembering: "Cantalao . . . Cantalao . . . That name sounds familiar. Isn't that the place where I cut my teeth, stealing books and breaking windows consecrated to the joy of light?"

Black Handkerchiefs for Don Jaime

It wasn't easy for Don Jaime Ferrer to "break into" Isla Negra. There weren't many islanders in those years. They'd come from distant points, from the frontiers of medicine, the latitudes of music, the mountains of poetry. We were terrible. We used paraffin lamps and, by our own sweat, or sometimes with the help of others, drew water from our wells. An *inn* in this sunset paradise? Ridiculous!

We feared the long lines of automobiles, the roulette wheels and poker chips of Viña del Mar. Probably it also meant motorcycles and bikinis, show biz and rumbas, in Isla Negra. All night we'd hear loud-speakers bawling trashy songs, over and over and over.

We were a closed circle, until, gradually, Don Jaime's goodness and seriousness and skill cracked it open.

All my life I have praised those who do things I don't know how to do and that have always seemed better than the things I do. And now that Don Jaime is dead, it falls to me to commemorate his long labor.

The summer people from Santiago, who expect food served at the drop of a hat, wine cooled or breathing, dazzling white tablecloths, and waiters scurrying among restaurant tables, can't get it into their heads how difficult it is to construct, establish, and build up a summer resort on the coast.

For example, from my house we have to drive forty kilometers to buy fish, a hundred and forty to buy a good lock, eighty-five to have a picture framed. And at times the problems caused by a missing screw or a broken windowpane, not to mention a clutch, are still unsolved even after fifty trips to the nearest villages. A leak in the roof is a tragedy in three acts. Rebuilding a fence the sea has torn down is worthy of an epic poem. And for more than half the year not a single soul walks through the doors of the inns.

Shore resorts suffer a long solitude; they wait in the desert. The only thing you can count on in winter, autumn, even spring, is taxes: tax inspectors, tax notices, tax audits.

Don Jaime knew his business backwards and forwards, and his good humor was as persistent as his patience. He built an inn out of nothing, and it came to be the best-known spot on the coast. At any hour during the winter the traveler found a chimney blazing with gigantic logs that seemed to be waiting just for him. The fire, the fragrant odors from the kitchen, the waiters alert as sentinels: this was the impeccable organization he built. And no one will forget the warm rolls snuggling in a white napkin, as if fresh from the nest. Don Jaime, genial and wise, became an institution in Isla Negra; he triumphed over local prejudices and left behind, in virgin territory, the science of a warm welcome.

I asked Camilo, his best disciple, also a hotelier, what Don Jaime Ferrer's secret was—in addition, naturally, to his wisdom and energy.

Curiously, Camilo was at first silent, meditative. Then he told me several things.

"It seems he always bought too much, too much of everything. Too many sheets, too many onions, too much ham, too many fillets and fish. We criticized him at first for being wasteful, but it always turned out that everything was used."

So, one of the secrets of the great hotelier was abundance. What seemed to be excessive was always strictly necessary.

He also told me that one time, in his enthusiasm, Don Jaime had bought an incredible quantity of handkerchiefs. Incredible because, though half were white, the other half were black.

"He was even right about that," Camilo said. "Because now that so many people have been weeping for him, we've made use of the black handkerchiefs, too."

So, then, Don Jaime Ferrer is dead, after succeeding in an honorable and difficult undertaking. Loyal to Isla Negra, he asked to be buried in the tiny cemetery in the nearby hills of Totoral. I didn't arrive in time to bid him farewell, and I have regretted this greatly. His inn, with the smell of burning logs, has always reminded me of the English taverns of the coasts and fields beloved by Robert Louis Stevenson. The family is still there, and the familiar spirit, the welcome, the fire, and the wine. But Don Jaime, the founder, is greatly missed by the islanders of Isla Negra.

65

I have no memory of my life in Parral. It's clear that my parents took me to the frontier almost as soon as I was born.

A North American journalist tells that he searched diligently for the place where I was born, but couldn't find it. Not the house of course, because it was destroyed in an earthquake. He asked everywhere, but no one knew. I don't know either.

The good mayor of Parral, Enrique Astorga, has made me a native, a Parralite, again. The city received me with affection, though not with intimacy, since my life was spent in other parts of the country. But my mother's grave is there, and my prolific family, the Reyes, keeps sprouting up everywhere—though until now there hasn't been a Reyes poet.

My clearest memories are of Temuco, in the South. My poetry is saturated with that landscape. The sea, the mountains, and the rivers of that region are entangled in my soul. It rains in me today as it did sixty years ago in Temuco.

The house of the railroad conductor Reyes, my father, was humble, even shabby. Now that it's July, they'd be slaughtering hogs in the back of the patio. I always ran away, fleeing from the frightful screaming. It didn't bother anyone else, but I thought it was one of the worst atrocities in life.

When I grew old enough, my solitude was altered by school. It seemed to me that there were enough boys—of every color and with strange-sounding names—to populate a city; the teachers with their big mustaches instilled in me a terror I feel today, but manage to keep fairly well hidden.

The arithmetic teacher always singled me out for his sympathy and his disdain. From time to time, as a treat, he gave me a piece of candy during class. He never directed a question to me; it was taken for granted I would never learn anything. Every December, he gave me my three ritual black marks. This seemed to be a performance carried out for six successive Decembers.

What is curious is that I always had the highest esteem for Señor Peña, for that was my teacher's name. It never occurred to me to hate him. It was natural that we should be incompatible.

I have written somewhere that the school had some catacombs, or cellars, where we used to play. My imagination filled those subterranean spaces with ghosts, treasures, and possible infernal surprises. It was pitch-black down there. Sometimes, in our games, we would forget and leave one of the boys tied to a column, to punish him. Frightened ourselves, we had to go back down to free him.

But the place of my dreams was Puerto Saavedra, where I ate with gusto sandy figs I'd never seen before, and where the enormous Cautín River emptied into a terrifying ocean with waves big as mountains. There I set eyes on my first penguins, and the wild swans of beautiful Lake Budi. On the shores of the lake we fished, or hunted, for mullets, using harpoons or spears. It was hypnotizing to watch those motionless stalkers, lances held high, to see the flashing spear and then a thrashing fish. There, too, I often saw the rosy flight of flocks of flamingos across virgin territory.

Puerto Saavedra also had a small, white-bearded wizard, the poet Don Augusto Winter. He had come from the North. His sisters were known for the home canning so typical of the South. Don Augusto was the librarian of the best library I've ever known. It was tiny, but packed with Jules Verne and Salgari. There was a sawdust-burning stove in the center, and I would settle myself there as if sentenced to read in the three summer months all the books written through the long winters of the world.

Puerto Saavedra smelled of salt waves and honeysuckle. Behind every house were gardens with gazebos; climbing vines perfumed the solitude of those transparent days.

There, too, I was suddenly taken by surprise by the black eyes of

María Parodi. We used to exchange tightly folded slips of paper you could hide in your hand. Later I wrote for her number 19 of my *Veinte poemas*. Puerto Saavedra permeates the book with its docks, its pines, the eternal fluttering of gulls.

I realize now that I've been writing about trivial things. Those cellars and books and black eyes are probably gone with the wind.

So why have I been telling these silly things? Maybe because in this month of July I am completing my sixty-fifth year of life in this unique and fleeting world.

In the geography of those memories, between Parral and the frontier, between honeysuckle and river outlet, I was a remote, shy, solitary witness, clinging to the wall like lichen. I suspect that no one heard me and that very few saw me. Not many people knew me in those days.

Now, wherever I go, people I've never met say, "Yes, Don Pablo." I've won something in this life. In sixty-five years I've earned the right to be addressed as *Don*.

Without Gods and
without Idols

A study by Viviane Lerner, *Realidad profana, realidad sagrada en las "Odas elementales,"* published by the University of Strasbourg, searches for religious elements in my poetry.

This is not the first time those bells have tolled. In June, in a Theological Congress in Bogotá, a theologian from the Vatican Institute proposed that I am a theologian, or, at least, theologic. For lack of training, I cannot respond to these investigators, or place their honorable research in the proper perspective.

I do know that all over the world man has sought communication beyond life, and religions have postulated their parallel codes to attempt to understand the unknowable. Always, the need for saints, for heroes, and for gods stimulated their creation even in the most remote lands and in the most recent, scientific, and rational times.

In my years in Asia, I was overwhelmed by the proliferation of divine images in Oriental churches. The erotic idols of Nepal had six, ten, more than forty bronze arms, and women's bodies were clutched in orgasm in their tentacular embraces. Ganesa, god of wisdom, with the head of an elephant, was my favorite because of his rosy trunk and minuscule eyes. The goddess Kali was not an invention of our revered Salgari; with a scarlet tongue three meters long, and wearing a huge necklace of human skulls, she awaited me in Calcutta.

On the other hand, the Spanish crucifixes of my childhood were no less visions of horror. Later I saw them in other respectable places: pustulant in Grünewald, gruesome to the point of nightmare in the Tuscan primitives.

Nor was I ever entranced with the rose-and-blue dolls representing the Madonna. What I did like was the atmosphere in some time-honored cathedrals—though not St. Peter's—and some mosques. In them, I occasionally found the intellectual and natural solemnity I'd known in the forests of Cautín.

Anti-clericalism went out with the Macfarlane and with anarchy. Society changed, times and fashion changed. Factories became gods. Associated gods produced sausages, weapons, and automobiles. The holy wars of this era have been the oil wars. The heretics that did not prostrate themselves before the pagodas of petroleum were exterminated, not by blazing scimitar or nail-studded cross, but by brutal police, by torture and imprisonment.

But this has not prevented man from elevating his small gods— bearded, ridiculous, or mysterious.

A French colonial told me that during the last war a North American vessel landed a jeep with a military observer for one week in Madagascar. The jeep carried the sign of the International Red Cross on its roof; the man in charge of the mission was a black man from Harlem. He climbed hillsides, crossed valleys, reached unexplored mountains. He visited unknown tribes. He was a jovial black with great white teeth and numerous gold bracelets; he had a ringing laugh and a powerful voice. The natives looked on him with adoration. From time to time, from his jeep, he communicated by radio with planes or ships. When he left, he went crowned in flowers. Soon his memory was converted into a great religion that now has more followers than Protestant and Catholic sects. The natives paint enormous red crosses on the highest, most rugged mountains of Madagascar, so he will see them and deign to return from the sky.

Meanwhile, this man, who now must be old and worn, and doesn't know that he's a god, is probably polishing floors in New York.

Once, when I was passing through Kingston, Jamaica, I stopped for a few days, just because I had nothing to do. And there I read a poem by the most important local poet, dedicated to Haile Selassie, which appeared in the *Jamaica Times* on the day of my arrival. I realized that the poet was referring to the Abyssinian emperor not as a monarch but as a god. A new and affluent religion with multitudes of temples and believers has designated the tiny Negus as God. The new cult proposes that his arrival in Jamaica, where his faithful await him, will provoke a cosmic upheaval and the beginning of a new era.

The sun rises—ancestral lion, paternal and central force of our universe. Night plates the oceans with silvery scales. Meteors trail celestial phosphorus. Sun, water, spring, give us our daily bread. A prayer is born. A poem is born.

Religions were the cradle of poetry, and poetry allied itself with them, nourishing their myths, collaborating like incense in the late afternoon of a basilica. The clothing of the divinities was woven of gold and poetry. The staring eyes of the images did not penetrate the mystery; the words of poetry drove back the shadows, seeking, as a shared duty, the exaltation of beauty and communication with the people.

The understanding between science and poetry, between historical time and the poet's song, has been more difficult. Myths were more responsive to language than to the weight of discovery and truth. Poetry still struggles to become independent of its ancient mysterious servitude.

Robert Frost and the Prose of Poets

SOMEONE has sent me a well-translated book, the prose of Robert Frost, an admirable poet.

As I read through it, it renewed in some manner a private dialogue or discussion I've been having with myself for some time.

What always attracted me to the poetry of Frost was its personal truth, the naturalness of its structure. He was the poet of conversation. He told and he sang ballads about people who were never entirely real, never entirely imaginary.

I remember that poem about a man who'd lived a long life, an old man sitting close to his fireplace and close to death, now very near:

> *A light he was to no one but himself*
> *Where now he sat, concerned with he knew what,*
> *A quiet light, and then not even that.*

The lines of "A Leaf Treader," and those of "The Cow in Apple Time," have always stayed in my mind. In short, a poet of country scenes, of "north of Boston," of Vermont, of muddy roads covered with fallen leaves, a poet with the shoes of a wanderer and a translucent gift of song—one of the poets I like best.

But Robert Frost's prose surprised me. It is the book of a rationalist with a perfect library, a humanist. But also of a virtuoso of ideas, those ideas about poetry and metaphor that lead nowhere. I have always believed that a study of poetry by poets is pure ashes. That ashen foam may well be beautiful, but it will be carried away on the wind.

Maybe what I like—maybe—is for a critic to meddle and tinker in what interests him but isn't vital to him. For me the critical spirit, when too refined, becomes intellectual obscenity, bloody insolence. The analytical dagger doesn't reveal the guts of the poet but the insides of the one who wielded the dagger.

The prose of Robert Frost leads one down roads of metaphor, and though to me Frost is a great man, I continue to believe that the revelation that kills what it reveals is indecent, however luminous the words and irreproachable the conduct.

In any case, I want to make clear my loyalty to Frost the poet both in his natural poetry and in his intellectual prose.

As for my own writing, I am a fanatic enemy of my own prose. But what can you do? If we speak in prose, we also have to write it. Juan Ramón Jiménez, that pitiful great poet consumed by envy, said once that I didn't even know how to write a letter. In that I believe he was not mistaken.

I was also surprised by Robert Frost's lukewarm, bourgeois liberalism. In New York, at conventions for social progress, I met his daughter, an anti-war, anti-imperialist young woman. I thought her principles must have come from her illustrious father. But in his book I find that when he speaks of *protest* in poetry, he does it from the point of view of the *establishment*.

> But for me, I don't like grievances. I find I gently let them alone wherever published. What I like is griefs and I like them Robinsonianly profound. I suppose there is no use in asking, but I should think we might be indulged to the extent of having grievances restricted to prose if prose will accept the imposition, and leaving poetry free to go its way in tears.

Frost's words are beautiful, but more appropriate for a Victorian romantic. They wouldn't be bad in Lord Tennyson, the bard of *In Memoriam*, pure poetry and pure tears.

I ask the great poet: "But, Frost, whom shall we honor with our tears? Those who are dying or those who are being born? Isn't that wrapping life and death in the same shroud?"

I am a man of tears and of protest. I can't confine prose to struggle and poetry to suffering. It seems to me they can have the same cataclysmic destiny. At times I believe that the "Marseillaise" is choral poetry, unequaled in beauty. I also think at times that Keats's "Ode to a Nightingale" and his "Ode on a Grecian Urn" belong at the taxidermist's or in the British Museum.

Fortunately, Frost is a bigger man than his prose, broader than his analysis. And in spite of this, or perhaps thanks to it, a venerable nation circulates through his poetry, spacious and free, the United States of long ago, with its beautiful mountains, its inexhaustible rivers, and, what it seems to have lost, its capacity to be sufficient unto itself, without bathing the world in blood.

We Indians

THE man who invented Chile, Don Alonso de Ercilla, did not
merely illuminate an unexplored land with magnificent diamonds; he
also gave to the world the deeds and lives of the Araucan Indians. To
repay him, we Chileans have taken upon ourselves the task of dulling,
even extinguishing, the diamantine radiance of that epic. Epic grandeur, which Ercilla dropped over Chile's shoulders like a royal cape,
is dishonoring itself, is disappearing. We have been robbing our fabulous heroes of their mythological vestments, leaving them with nothing but a threadbare Indian poncho—mended, caked with the clay of
dirt roads, soaked in Antarctic downpours.

Our recent governments have issued the decree that *we are not a
nation of Indians.* This sweet-smelling proclamation has not been leg-
islated, but the fact is that it is the tacit rule among certain of our
national representatives. *La Araucana* is good, it smells good. The
Araucans are bad, they smell bad. They smell like a conquered people. And the usurpers are eager to forget, or be forgotten. The majority of Chileans go along with these seignorial decisions and decrees:
frenzied parvenus, we are ashamed of the Araucans. Some of us contributed to exterminating them; others, to committing them to neglect and oblivion. Among us, we've been obliterating *La Araucana*
obscuring the diamonds of the Spaniard Ercilla.

Racial superiority may have been a unifying martial element among
the Conquistadors, but their superiority was undoubtedly to be found
in the horse. Siqueiros symbolized the Conquest in the figure of a
great centaur. Ercilla depicted the centaur riddled by the arrows of
our native Indians. This Renaissance invader proposed a new category:
that of hero. And he conceded the classification both to the Spanish

and to the Indians, to his people and ours. But his heart was with the dauntless.

When I arrived in Mexico as a brand-new consul general, I founded a review to promote awareness of our country. The first number was printed in impeccable photogravure. Everyone contributed to it, from the President of the Academy to Don Alfonso Reyes, the quintessential master of the language. As the magazine cost my government nothing, I felt very proud of that first miraculous issue, born of the sweat of our pens—mine and Luis Enrique Délano's. But we committed a little error with the title. A whopping little error, to the mind of our government.

I must explain that in Mexico the word *chile* has two or three less than respectable shadings. To call the review *República de Chile* would have been to kill it. So we called it *Araucanía*. And we graced the jacket with the most beautiful smile in the world: a broadly smiling Araucan woman. Spending more than I could afford, I sent to Chile by certified airmail (more expensive then than now) separate copies for the President, the Minister of Culture, and the Consular Director—who at least owed me, I thought, ceremonial congratulations. Weeks passed and there was no reply.

And then came the reply. It was the death knell of the review. It said only: "Change the title or cancel it. We are not a nation of Indians."

"No, sir, there's nothing Indian about us," our ambassador in Mexico (who resembled a resurrected Caupolicán) said to me as he transmitted the supreme message. "Orders of the President of the Republic."

Our President in those days, perhaps the best we've had, Don Pedro Aguirre Cerda, was the living image of Michimalonco.

A photography exhibition entitled "The Face of Chile," the work of the great but modest Antonio Quintana, traveled through Europe, presenting the natural grandeur of our country: the family of Chilean man—his mountains, his cities, his islands, his harvests and seas. But in Paris, thanks to diplomatic effort and grace, the Araucan photographs were suppressed: "Careful! We aren't Indians!"

They persist in bleaching us at any cost, in erasing the words that gave us birth: the pages of Ercilla, the crystal-clear stanzas that brought the epic and humanism to Spain.

It's time to put an end to such vulgarity!

Dr. Rodolfo Oroz, who has in his possession a copy of the *Diccionario Araucano* corrected by the master hand of its author, Don Rodolfo Lenz, tells me that he cannot find a publisher for this work that has been out of print for many years.

To our University of Chile: Publish this classic work!

To our Minister of Culture: Print *La Araucana*! Give it to every child in Chile this Christmas (and me, too).

To our government: Once and for all, establish an Araucan University!

To my brother, Alonso de Ercilla: *La Araucana* is more than a poem: it is a broad highway.

The Winnipeg and
Other Poems

FROM the first time I heard the word "Winnipeg," I liked it. Words have wings, or they don't. Ungraceful words adhere to the paper, the table, the ground. The word "Winnipeg" is winged. I saw it soar for the first time at a steamship pier near Bordeaux. The *Winnipeg* was a beautiful old ship, with that dignity the seven seas bestow over a length of time. She had never carried more than seventy or eighty passengers; the rest was cocoa, copra, sacks of coffee and rice, and ore. Now she was destined for a more important cargo: hope.

Under my eye and my direction, the ship was to be loaded with two thousand men and women. They came from concentration camps, from inhospitable regions, the desert, Africa. They came from anguish and defeat, and this ship was to carry them to the coast of Chile, to my own world, which would welcome them. They were Spanish combatants who had crossed the French frontier into an exile that would last for more than thirty years.

This was the way the Civil—uncivil—War of Spain was ending: people semi-imprisoned, rounded up from everywhere, crowded into fortresses, jammed together to sleep on the sand. The exodus broke the heart of Spain's greatest poet, Don Antonio Machado. No sooner had he crossed the frontier than he died. Still in the remnants of their uniforms, soldiers of the Spanish Republic carried his coffin to the cemetery in Collioure. There lies buried the Andalusian who sang like no other about the fields of Castile.

When I traveled from Chile to France, I hadn't considered the misfortunes, difficulties, and adversities I might encounter in my mission. My country needed qualified and skilled men, men of creative will. We needed specialists. The Chilean sea needed fishermen. The mines asked for engineers. The fields, tractor operators. The first diesel motors charged me to bring back skilled mechanics.

To collect these people scattered across the map, cull them from the most remote camps, and lead them toward that blue day facing the sea of France, to a gently rocking *Winnipeg*, was a major undertaking, a complicated affair; it was a labor of devotion and desperation.

An assistance program was organized, SERE. The assistance came, on the one hand, from the last moneys of the Republic and, on the other, from what for me is still a mysterious institution: the Quakers.

I declare myself abominally ignorant in matters of religion. The battle against sin in which religions specialize drove me as a youth from all creeds, and this superficial attitude, this indifference, has persisted throughout my life. The fact is that these magnificent sectarians appeared at our port of embarcation; they paid half of every Spanish passage to freedom, not discriminating between atheist and believer, between sinner and minister! Since that time, if I read the word "Quaker" anywhere, I make a mental bow.

Trains kept arriving at the docks. Women recognized their husbands through the windows of the cars, couples who had been separated since the end of the war. They met for the first time before the waiting ship. I've never before or since witnessed such dramatic, delirious embraces, such sobs, kisses, hugs, and shouts of laughter.

Then came the documentation, identification, and health checkpoints. My assistants—secretaries, consuls, friends—were seated behind the tables, a sort of tribunal of hell. And, for the first and last time, I must have seemed like Jupiter to the émigrés. Mine was the final *yes* or the final *no*. But as I am more *yes* than *no*, I always said *yes*.

Well, it's true, once I was about to stamp negative, but luckily I understood in time and was spared that *no*.

It happened when a Castilian dressed in a black smock with full sleeves presented himself before me. That smock was a uniform for the countryfolk of La Mancha. Here was a mature man—deep wrinkles in his sunburned face—with his wife and seven children.

After examining the card containing his vital statistics, I asked him, surprised: "You're a cork planter?"

"Yes, señor," he answered gravely.

"There's some mistake here," I replied. "There are no cork trees in Chile. What will you do there?"

"Well, there *will* be trees," the farmer replied.

"Climb aboard," I told him. "You're the kind of man we need."

And with the same pride that had marked his replies to me, and followed by his seven children, he climbed the gangplank of the *Winnipeg*. Later the reasonableness of the indomitable Spaniard was proved: there were cork trees, and, as a result, we now have cork in Chile.

By now, almost all my good nephews and nieces, pilgrims to an unknown land, were on board, and I was ready to rest from my long task, but my tribulations seemed never to end. The government of Chile, harassed and assailed, sent me a message: "NEWS SOURCES CLAIM YOU ARE FACILITATING MASSIVE IMMIGRATION OF SPANIARDS. REQUEST DENY INFORMATION OR CANCEL VOYAGE ÉMIGRÉS."

What should I do?

One solution: Summon the press, show them the ship crammed with two thousand Spaniards, read the telegram in a solemn voice, and immediately fire a shot into my temple.

Another solution: Board the ship with my émigrés and disembark in Chile, for the cause or for poetry.

Before making any decision, I went to the telephone and spoke with my country's Minister of Foreign Relations. In 1939 it was difficult to talk over long distance. But my indignation and my anguish could be heard across oceans and cordilleras, and the Minister gave me his support. After a bloodless crisis in the Cabinet, the *Winnipeg*, laden with two thousand singing, weeping Republicans, hoisted anchor and set sail for Valparaiso.

Let the critics erase all my poetry if they will. This poem I am recalling today will never be erased.

The Baron of Melipilla (I)

THE *Times* of London, in July and August of 1865, carried the following notice:

A substantial reward will be offered to anyone who can give information that will shed light on the fate of Roger Charles Tichborne. He sailed from Rio de Janeiro on the 20th April 1854 on the ship *La Bella* and has not been heard from since. However, there have been rumours that various of the crew and passengers from that ship were picked up by a vessel bound for Australia. We do not know whether Roger Charles Tichborne was among those drowned or those saved. He is at present 32 years of age. He is rather tall, with very light brown hair and blue eyes. Mr. Tichborne is the son of Sir James Tichborne, now deceased, and is his heir.

They were searching for a young baron in order to bestow on him his inheritance in pounds sterling and estates.

It was known that the young man had passed through Valparaiso and Santiago, where he'd been photographed by Helsby, an elegant photographer of the time. But he had spent most of his time in Chile in Melipilla. He lived there a year and a half, and was known by half the town.

At that time he wasn't a missing heir but the second son of the noble family of Tichborne. His father was the tenth Tichborne to hold the title, and the income from his properties exceeded forty thousand pounds a year.

What a strange sensation to look at the daguerreotype of the young Tichborne: a vaguely romantic gaze, a typical Córdoba hat. A rather weak face, in which large, pale eyes seemed to be lost in time, or the sea.

His disappearance led to a legal process so protracted and so turbulent that it shook a stately Victorian society; the attempt to solve the resulting puzzle disturbed the tranquillity of both London and Melipilla.

It is not only poets who are interested in puzzles. All of us live in basic mystery. Science and religion jostle one another in the shadows, throwing in each other's eyes the dust of beauty, probabilities, distant myths, and approximate truth.

I, a collector of puzzles, make no attempt to solve this one. All that connects me to it is my role as occasional visitor to Melipilla. It amuses me to think that in this remote spot, amid farmers, and vineyards of fiery fruit, the first page of an astounding story was hatched.

Why did Roger Charles Tichborne come to Melipilla, to the house of Don Tomás Castro—Roger Charles Tichborne, who never became the eleventh Baron Tichborne?

When after a stay of a year and a half he left that dusty town and, on muleback, crossed our cordillera, Roger did not know he was an heir; and at the time he disappeared in the shipwreck of the *Bella* in the Atlantic, he was still unaware that all the forces of heaven and earth were seeking to rescue him from his nomadic wanderings.

I have seen Lady Tichborne's photograph. It is a portrait of hope. Beneath her mourning bonnet and above her crossed hands, the thin face with its rueful smile has, from waiting, become nothing more than two blurry eyes searching for a son lost at sea, willing his resurrection.

No one in Melipilla—not the British doctor John Halley, or Carla, Jesusa, or Don Raimundo Alcalde, or Don José Toro, or the Señora Hurlano, or Doña Natalia Salmento—knew whether the young Englishman had been swallowed up by the sea or the earth.

Nevertheless, the inheritance, with its astronomical figures, was to disturb the lives of these Melipillans, who would be called upon to voyage to England to take part in a tempestuous battle of interests and passions.

In October of 1865 a man, a butcher by trade, known as Tom or Thomas Castro, and supposedly of Chilean nationality, appeared in

Wagga Wagga, Australia. In conversations there, he repeated many times that Castro was not his name or Chile his country. He claimed he was an Englishman and that he'd been shipwrecked in the Atlantic and picked up by a ship that had brought him to Australia.

Someone who heard these confidences communicated them to the mother of the missing baron. And Tom Castro was summoned before her.

From the beginning, there were many who had grave doubts. In the first place, the man seemed poorly educated, and suffered from a nervous disorder resembling St. Vitus's dance, a disease Roger never had. Furthermore, this man was inordinately obese—but more than ten years had passed, and his physique could have changed. He was uncertain about some of the family facts. But this might be only natural in the case of a man who'd been shipwrecked, transported from one world to another, and then left to his fate in rugged and unknown lands.

Why did he call himself Tom Castro?

He explained: he hadn't wanted his humble profession to tarnish the illustrious Tichborne family name.

Imagine the moment when this extraordinary man, materialized from Wagga Wagga, from Melipilla, and from a shipwreck, crossed the threshold of the baronial home. The occupants of Tichborne and Alresford were all waiting to greet him.

The story was only beginning. We shall see what fate held in store for this man who seemed to have returned from the dead.

The Baron of Melipilla (II)

Was it really Roger Charles Tichborne who entered the castle of the Tichbornes that day, or was it an impostor trying to take his place?

Lady Tichborne descended the stairs to see him. She opened her arms: it was her son. The black butler, who had raised him, also recognized him.

But the Arundell family, which would inherit the Tichborne fortune if it was proved that this man was lying, refused to recognize him, and soon instituted a lawsuit.

When the litigation began, no one could imagine how it might end. The reverberating scandal dragged in its path such people as Richard Burton, the explorer, translator of *A Thousand and One Nights*, and a number of Jesuit priests who openly opposed the pretensions of this bizarre man.

One of the Tichbornes, Everard, had entered the seminary of the Society of Jesus, and the Church was to share in his inheritance. Consequently, the dispute also became a holy war in which Catholic bishops and Protestant dignitaries intervened, both sides trading less-than-Christian blows.

To complicate matters further, the presumed heir gave erroneous or confused answers to the lawyers' questions. For their part, the judges in that long inquisitorial process showed little inclination to side with the defendant. But the Baron of Melipilla never faltered in his assertions; the bewilderment of British society increased. People flocked to the hearings, where sherry and biscuits circulated as if at a fete. The bulky figure of the pretender, his exotic air, the mystery that seemed to envelop him and which had drawn him from distant lands to Australia and from there to this pitched battle, provoked unrestrained curiosity.

Soon the long arms of the accusers reached out to Melipilla and gathered in many witnesses, who made the long voyage from that distant Chilean city to London, all properly escorted and attended, to testify against the pretender.

So, from Chile came Don Pedro Pablo Toro, from Cuncumén; Doña Mercedes Azócar; Doña Lorenza Hurtado, shopkeeper of Melipilla; and Eudocia and Juana, her sisters. Additional travelers were Doña Francisca Ahumada, who had cut a curl from our Baron's head; Doña Teresa Hurtado Toro and Don José María Serrano. Similarly, from Melipilla to London came Doña Manuela González, Don Pedro Castro, the judge Don Vicente Vial, and Don José Agustín Guzmán.

Every one of these Melipillians, with the exception of Don Pedro Castro, testified against the mystery man. How much must it have cost the contesting family to bring these Chileans across the seas in sailing ships, to wine and dine them in London, and then return them to their native Melipilla?

One very serious event occurred during the trial. A man of conscience, one Father Meyrick, a priest who had been Roger Tichborne's teacher, energetically maintained that the enormously obese man was the same who had been his pupil at Stonyhurst. His words, spoken in a clear voice heard throughout the courtroom, resulted in tumult: "I regret very much that I must say it, but nothing can ever remove from my conscience the conviction that the accused is the true Sir Roger."

Several days later, on the eve of being recalled to testify, Father Meyrick was abducted and permanently sequestered in some distant and unknown establishment of the Society of Jesus. Protestant society reacted angrily: "What country is this? Is this the Spanish Inquisition? Where is the Reverend Father Meyrick?"

The court refused to hear these protests, deciding not to intervene. The fate of the aspiring heir was by now decided. He was condemned as an impostor and sentenced to fourteen years in prison, and as the last of the Tichbornes was a Jesuit priest, the descendants of Lord Arundell won the legal battle and inherited the enormous fortune.

The courageous Meyrick died in his prison.

Fourteen years later, the indicted man traveled across England, lecturing on his violated rights and the injustice of his long incarceration. Death overtook him as he was attempting to attract the attention of a public whose interest in his cause was rapidly waning.

But the baffling case of the Baron of Melipilla, a dusty town in Chile, lives on. Did the baron die in the shipwreck of the *Bella*, or was he saved? And was it he, not an unfortunate impostor, who from London lecture platforms futilely demanded his title and his inheritance as eleventh Baron of Tichborne?

I am merely a humble collector of puzzles. It is up to you to solve this one.

The Struggle for Justice

The Crisis of Democracy in Chile Is a Dramatic Warning for Our Continent

I want to inform all my friends on our continent of the disastrous events that have taken place in Chile. I am aware that a large number of persons will be confused and surprised, since the North American news monopolies will no doubt (in this matter as in others) have produced the same result as everywhere else: to falsify truth and distort reality.

In these tragic moments it is my inescapable duty, insofar as it is possible, to clarify the situation in Chile, because in my travels through almost every country in America, I have personally experienced the overwhelming affection felt toward my country by those peoples of democratic convictions in every nation. This affection was based on a profound respect for the rights of man, perhaps more deeply rooted in my country than in any other in America. But this democratic tradition, the basic patrimony of Chile and the pride of the continent, is today being crushed and destroyed by the combined efforts of foreign pressures and the political treachery of a democratically elected President.

This document is included here because of its obvious historic significance. Its publication in the Caracas newspaper *El Nacional* on November 27, 1947, led the President of Chile, Gabriel González Videla, to file a petition before the Supreme Court requesting the impeachment of Senator Pablo Neruda. "I Accuse," the speech Neruda delivered to the Senate of Chile in response to this action on the part of President González Videla, follows on pages 284–307.

1.   FOREIGN PRESSURE

I will briefly outline the facts.

The present champion anti-Communist, President of our nation, appointed three Communist Ministers to his first Cabinet. To force the Communist Party of Chile to name these Ministers, he said that if the Party did not accept this participation in his government he would resign the presidency of the Republic.

The Communists in his government were true crusaders, attempting to fulfill the promises made to the Chilean public. They were characterized by a dynamism never before seen in Chilean political history. They faced innumerable problems, many of which they resolved. They traveled to every region of the country and were in direct contact with the masses. After only a few weeks in the government, marked by public service of unusual magnitude, they were well known throughout the country for their activities: they were moving toward an open politics, a politics of the people. In the public forum they fought plans that would raise the cost of living, plans engineered by forces embedded within the government.

This new kind of activist people's politics deeply displeased the old feudal oligarchy of Chile, which turned its attention to the President, gradually isolating him from the people. In addition, agents of North American imperialism, of such powerful—more accurately, such all-powerful—companies as Guggenheim, the Chile Exploration Corporation, Anaconda Copper, Anglo-Chilean Nitrate, Braden Copper, Bethlehem Steel, and others, were wasting no time. Representatives of these tentacular organizations that own all the mineral deposits in Chile also moved to surround and isolate the newly elected President. The President's attitude toward his Communist Ministers underwent a change; he placed obstacles in their way, pitted them against other parties, in repeated attempts at provincial Machiavellianism. The Communist Ministers bowed before this underhanded opposition, in the hope that their personal sacrifice might contribute to the solution of the nation's most basic problems. But their sacrifice was in vain.

Using the most thinly veiled subterfuges, and amid a flurry of embraces and impassioned letters of thanks to his Communist collaborators, the President dismissed the Ministers from his Cabinet. This was the first step in his capitulation. The true reason for the dismissal of the Communists, whom today he slanders and persecutes politically, was given to the outside world in such categorical terms that this evidence alone would convict him.

On June 18, 1947, Señor González Videla granted an interview to the correspondent of the London *News Chronicle*. This is the report he cabled to his newspaper.

President González Videla believes that war between Russia and the USA will break out within the next three months, and that the present political policy of Chile, both internal and foreign, must be based on this assumption.

The President made this statement during an exclusive interview granted the correspondent of the *News Chronicle*. He indicated that his coming visit to Brazil is in no way connected with North American and Argentine politics, but rather, that his visit will be limited to a discussion of Chilean–Brazilian affairs. These two statements are in contradiction, since it is logical to assume that the position of Chile and the two most powerful South American countries in the case of war would necessarily be discussed in a meeting between the two presidents.

The President indicated that the imminence of war explains his present attitude toward Chilean Communists, against whom he has no personal objections. He emphasized that "Chile must cooperate with her powerful neighbor, the United States of America, and when the war begins Chile will support the United States against Russia."

Shortly before the present events, several messengers from the United States, expressly trained by the State Department, came to whisper into the ears of Chile's fickle President somber messages of alternatives between unconditional capitulation and economic disaster. Félix Nieto del Río, Chile's Ambassador to Washington—a former Nazi supporter and opportunistic diplomat—and General Barrios Tirado, a member of the high-ranking military coterie that defends the monopolistic interests of the Yankees—a man who is excessively entertained in Washington—played a decisive role in these negotiations. For a period of several months, in addition to the messengers of ill omen, great capitalists of North American industry and banking interests poured into Chile in semi-secret trips—the most notable, the World King of copper, Mr. Stannard, accompanied by his experts in financial terrorism, Mr. Higgins and Mr. Hobbins.

The aforementioned magnates, with their South American associates to smooth the way, obtained from Señor González Videla the
delivery of my nation to the designs of North American domination
—based on an immediate attack against Communism, and a severe
cutback in the progress of Chilean unionization, which had been
won through one of the longest, most heroic, and most difficult battles of the continent's working class.

2.   THE TREACHERY OF GONZÁLEZ VIDELA

In this personal letter to millions, I want to say to every friend,
known and unknown, that I am intimately acquainted with the incumbent President of Chile. Our personal relations span a long period
of time, and, in addition, I served at his request as National Publicity
Director in his campaign for President.

This familiarity permitted me to know what little there is to know
about such men, since between their innermost heart and their external appearance there is little but empty space filled with petty
aspirations. The ideal of Señor González Videla's life can be summed
up in one phrase: "I want to be President." In other places in our
America, superficial, fickle politicians of this type resort to intrigue
and coup d'etats to attain power; this is not possible in Chile. The
bedrock of democracy in our nation obliged Señor González Videla,
in pursuit of his objective, to don the garb of a demagogue, capitaliz-
ing on a deeply rooted and well-organized popular movement. This
was the road he chose to follow to attain power. Strongly opposed by
his own party—divided even today as a result of his candidacy—the
incumbent President used his friendship with the Communists as the
foundation stone of his Presidential career. The Communists, however, in accordance with prevailing democratic practices, demanded
before his selection as a candidate the formulation of a platform that
would specify the substantial reforms necessary for progress in Chile.
These reforms were discussed in a widely attended convention of
democratically organized forces, and the 4th of September Platform
—for this is what that fundamental document is called—was sworn to
and attested by Señor González Videla, in one of the most solemn
acts of the nation's political history.

3. THE 4TH OF SEPTEMBER PLATFORM

This document contains no revolutionary changes of any kind. Its principal points are: Agrarian Reform, based on the expropriation of lands not under cultivation, to be distributed among working farmers; the creation of a National Bank; and the equalization of salaries for men and women. To avoid any chance of misinterpretation, I include portions of the platform. You will note the intense nationalism of this plan for the civil and economic organization of the state, and the peaceful procedures for its enactment. Its adoption would have meant a progressive transformation of the country, and a deliverance, which is today significantly more difficult, from economic crisis.

CONSTITUTIONAL REFORM
FOR THE PURPOSE OF INSTITUTING A PARLIAMENTARY REGIME

Adequate civil and political rights for women. Repeal of illegal statutes that violate individual and public rights. Passage of a law on administrative integrity.

International policy of Chile oriented toward maintaining world peace. Creation of a South American Confederation of States.

National census of products in greatest demand. State importation of products such as sugar, tea, coffee, etc. Regulation and reduction of rents.

Nationalization of insurance, petroleum, gas, electricity, etc.

Creation of a National Bank. Implementation of a monetary policy to restore and stabilize the value of our currency. Hospitalization and distribution of medicines through a state agency.

Creation of a modern steel industry. Creation of a copper industry (smelting, rolling, wiredrawing, and manufacture).

Agrarian Reform, consisting of the subdivision of large landholdings and uncultivated lands among agricultural tenants and workers. Mechanization of agricultural development. Increase in land area under cultivation.

National plan for low-cost housing.

Mandatory union shops. Guarantee of rights of unions, and rights won by workers to join their Central Union, the Confederation of Workers of Chile, and of a Central Headquarters. Improvement in present social legislation. The right to be a union officer at eighteen. Immediate enactment of projected laws for compensation for years of service. Immediate repeal of illegal statutes that prohibit the unionization of agricultural workers. A national plan for pensions and Social Security. Immediate policy for the protection of children. Equal opportunity in hiring and promotion for men and women in public administration and treasury services. Enforcement of the Labor Code proposing equal pay for men and women for equal work. Establishment of maternity insurance. State regulation of the work and salaries of minors.

Strengthening of the principle of state responsibility for education as the most adequate means to assure democratic administration of national education. Education of indigent or abandoned children. Elimination of illiteracy and semi-illiteracy. Technical training for the adult population. Reform of the education system, in accordance with the demands of social and economic order. The elevation of the profession of teaching in all its social, political, economic, and professional aspects, guaranteeing especially the broadest possible ideological freedom for the teacher, and the assurance of the normal advancement of his career.

The then-candidate Señor González Videla distributed copies of this platform by the millions, along with the signed oath he had taken at the democratically conducted convention. As a curiosity, I append his oath:

> I swear before you, representatives of the people of Chile, that I will lead you to Victory, and, with the help of the people, that I shall carry out this Platform for public welfare that this great Convention has drafted for the well-being of Chile and the greatness of our Democracy. Santiago: July 21, 1946.

4.   OBSTACLES TO CARRYING OUT THE PROGRAM

Shortly after the election, Señor González Videla's daughter was married to a young lawyer, a member of one of the leading families of Chile's oligarchy. The President made his diplomatic appointments from among a reactionary group that for several years has directed Chile's foreign relations. When the Communist Ministers proposed objective solutions for resolving problems in accordance with the platform, they were criticized, harassed, and "written off" by the President of the Republic. In meetings of the Cabinet, increases in the cost of living were authorized that were tantamount to extortion of salaried workers. Communist Ministers, in keeping with government policy, made public their disapproval of these measures taken by the Cabinet, and voted against them. Meanwhile, a thick blanket of negotiators and agents from the large imperialist companies were using the weight of their influence to an ever greater degree. The Communist Minister of Land Management, the day before a proposed trip to the southern tip of the continent—where he had been summoned at the request of thousands of poor settlers loudly protesting the scandalous concession of enormous tracts of land to foreign companies in exchange for ridiculous sums made in payment to the state —was forced by the President to postpone his trip indefinitely. The public protests made by the Communist Party against this kind of action were later called by Señor González Videla "attempts at political proselytizing."

5.   ABANDONMENT OF THE PLATFORM

With the dismissal of the Communist Ministers, at the demand of the government and the North American monopolies, the enactment of the popular platform to which Señor González Videla had pledged himself was conclusively abandoned. At the present time, under the official censorship the executive exercises over several newspapers in Chile, one of the inviolable restrictions imposed upon them is that they may not mention the 4th of September Platform. Meanwhile, dominant in the decisions of the government is the all-powerful influence of the insatiable Chilean oligarchy formed by retrograde feudal landowners and voracious bankers, and the tentacular rings of North American companies such as ACM, Ch.E., Anglo-Chilean N., Braden Copper, the Chilean Power Company, Chilean Telephone and Telegraph, and others. The politicians connected with these foreign interests are at the present time the only persons who have the ear of our Chief of State.

To make their control complete, Señor González Videla authorized the delivery of the millimetric map of the coastline—that is, our military defense secrets—to the North American Military Staff; and countless new military and police missions of that nation are operating, free of any control by the Chilean government, inside our sovereign territory.

6. THE ECONOMIC SITUATION

Meanwhile, the economic situation of the country is approaching catastrophe. The imperialist companies have secretly been forced to advance money to Señor González Videla to pay public employees—demanding in exchange, as is to be expected, repressive measures against the workers. The strength of our currency is decreasing at an alarming rate, and inflation continues its dizzying ascent. Naturally, the wages and salaries of the middle and working classes daily become more inadequate.

The Communist Party consistently pointed out to the President that the means to modify this situation must come from within, not from outside, the country. A fundamental modification of our economic structure could lead to the increased production that would put the brakes on this serious crisis. In a nation of large landholders, feudal lords are not required to make an accounting of the administration of their properties, leaving all the weight of the law to fall on the small businessman, who *is* forced to keep records of his operations. Enormous expanses of fertile land are left idle, for the purpose of increasing the prices on agricultural products at each harvest, thus providing the profits necessary to maintain the feudal class, at the cost of social tragedy in Chile: hunger, malnutrition, tuberculosis.

The principal federation of unions, CTCH—Confederación de Trabajadores de Chile [Confederation of Chilean Workers]—proposed to the government the creation of a National Council on the Economy, consisting of principal financial institutions and organized workers. In his about-face, Señor González Videla took advantage of this coalition—formed at the request of the workers—to grant greater and greater power to the capitalists—finally, with a simple decree of this body, eliminating the workers altogether. The national CTCH also proposed a sweeping plan to increase production, and the formation in every industry of a committee of workers and management to study and encourage such an increase. None of this was put into practice, or even considered, by Señor González Videla, who found it easier—to appease his new reactionary friends—to blame the working class for a "slowdown," a slanderous invention of North American agents provocateurs, who hoped to use such an accusation as the basis for their own repressive plans.

7. INSOLENCE OF THE OLIGARCHY

Before his election, Señor González Videla presided over numerous democratic anti-Fascist and anti-Franco committees, to the end of gaining popularity among the electorate. Once he had achieved power, far from prosecuting national and international Fascist groups, he has unrelentingly prosecuted the very forces for liberation of which he was once a member; and this monstrous conduct exceeded all bounds when he imprisoned and exiled Spanish refugees who had been personal friends of the President of the Republic and worked under his command when he presided over the Spanish-Chilean Anti-Franco Committee.

It has been futile to solicit from the government of Señor González Videla any action against groups of Fascist provocateurs inside my country. On the contrary, these groups have prospered under his government, and new groups have been formed. The most important, directed by the Nazi agent Arturo Olavarría, under the suggestive name "Acha"—(Acción Chilena Anticomunista [Chilean Anti-Communist Action, "Acha" meaning "Axe"])—maintains an armed militia which, with the *Horst Wessel Lied* as its official hymn, conducts public military exercises every week, with the acquiescence and protection of the former chief of the anti-Fascist activities.

Similar organizations, and periodicals of the same orientation, are backed by the reactionary oligarchy of Chile, the same group that, while exerting its influence over the preceding government, was the last in South America to support the cause of the Axis. Today these Nazi cliques in Chile work closely with North American military agents.

8. A SUBVERSIVE PLAN BY SEÑOR GONZÁLEZ VIDELA

Shortly before the recent events which have heaped shame on the honor of my country, Señor González Videla summoned to the Presidential Palace the central committee of the Communist Party. He proposed to them a subversive plan, which was explained in minute detail by the President of the Republic, and which suggested the creation of a military government without the participation of any established party. Señor González Videla, with the aid of the armed forces, would abolish the Parliament. Later, he told us, he would satisfy a long-standing ambition of Chilean Communists, making possible a Constitutional Assembly. Eventually, the Communists would have a part in governing the Republic. Meanwhile, through my party, the President was soliciting popular support for his coup d'etat. If this aid was refused, he would proceed with his plan, even against the will of the people.

In this interview, the Communist Party of Chile flatly rejected this seditious proposition, and warned him of the inherent dangers to the lawful processes of our Republic. The Communists also pointed out that any attempt of this kind would take place over our strong opposition, that we would lead the nation's democratic resistance to the imposition of a military state.

The President terminated the interview by saying that if this was the case, the Communists would pay the consequences.

9.   THE COAL STRIKE

In this chaotic state of affairs produced by the moral and political irresponsibility of Señor González Videla, a legal strike—that is, a strike conforming to the guidelines set by the National Labor Code— was declared in Chile's mining region of Lota and Coronel. The strike vote, in which nineteen thousand workers participated, resulted, extraordinarily, in only fifteen votes in opposition.

Señor González Videla found in this strike the pretext for his ultimate betrayal, an excuse to provoke a wide-scale international reaction and to unleash a persecution against workers such as had never been seen in my country.

10.   WHAT IS THE SIGNIFICANCE OF LOTA AND CORONEL?

No one outside Chile can realize what life in a coal mine is really like. In the harsh, cold climate of southern Chile, mine tunnels extend as far as eight kilometers beneath the sea. The miners must work in a semi-prone position, constantly threatened by the firedamp that periodically kills them—even more speedily than their work.

It takes the workers four hours to get to the work site, and this is not paid time. Thousands of workers earn less than fifty cents for those twelve hours, and those who earn as much as two dollars a day are very few. Then, when they emerge from their caverns, they encounter a new tragedy, that of housing and food. Official statistics show the horrifying figure of six workers for every bed. At the site called Puchoco Rojas they operate on a "warm-bed" system. This system—which reveals the terrible tragedy of the Chilean people— consists of a regular turn to use a bed, with the result that for years on end a bed never grows cold. Food, with such miserable salaries, is far below the norm. According to the North American expert, Señor Bloomfield, each man daily consumes two thousand calories fewer than he needs for subsistence. Ancylostomiasis, a terrible disease, pro- duces a high percentage of deaths, added to those caused by endemic tuberculosis and by accidents.

It is only natural that such terrible conditions have generated heroic movements of workers' resistance, which have succeeded in bettering to a barely discernible degree these abysmal conditions. Nevertheless, now and for the first time, a President elected by these very same workers—who hoped that at least once someone would hear the voices rising from their hell—has declared in public that the strike is not due to the frightful conditions existing in the coal regions but to an international plot. And on the basis of this falsehood he has treated the strikers with a cruelty and savagery found only in Nazi systems of slavery and oppression. Señor González Videla refused to settle the strike in spite of the pleas of the union and of the companies affected, declaring cynically to the capitalist representatives: "You don't understand; you shouldn't try to settle the strike; this is the first act of a new world war." And having chosen to classify a drama of exploitation and sorrow in this manner, he called in massive numbers of the armed forces, including air, marine, infantry, and cavalry, to put down a legal strike. As the next step, the agents of Señor Gon- zález Videla, with the cooperation of North American enforcement officers, falsified and forged documents blaming the remote govern- ment of Yugoslavia for the appeals for better working conditions, the same appeals Señor González Videla had found entirely justifiable the preceding year when he was candidate for President. On that occa- sion he wept before ten thousand miners, when he saw the fervor with which they acclaimed the man who might realize their hopes.

11.   CREATING A CLIMATE OF REPRESSION

Shortly before the strike, the President of the Republic had obtained from the most reactionary sectors of the Congress the passage of a Law of Extraordinary Powers, which gave him practically dictatorial powers.

Señor González Videla is using those powers to the fullest, carrying them beyond the limits the law intended.

The coal miners have been barbarously abused. Two hours before the strike was declared, the army surrounded the area of the mines as if it were enemy territory. No members of parliament, no newspapermen, were admitted from that time. A deathlike silence fell over a working population of the greatest importance. All union leaders were arrested and held on ships of war or on desolate islands; some were transported to sites near the Pole. The doors of the union halls, which had been respected by every previous administration, even rightist governments, were chopped down while military bands played marches to make the spectacle more palatable. By night, the occupying army went from house to house searching out miners, who were taken forcibly to the mines without being allowed to dress —if they hadn't already escaped into the woods. By day, the leaders' wives were paraded in handcuffs, some with their heads shaved. They placed pistols to children's breasts to make them tell where their fathers were hiding. They filled trains—like the trains of the Nazi condemned—with families and workers who had lived as long as forty years in that area. Often, the trains served as jails for many days, and no one was permitted to go to the aid of the victims, who were kept isolated and without food. Children and adults died as a result of this treatment. Corpses of miners appeared in the hills, and no one could investigate, as no one was allowed to enter the zone.

And while the UN is debating the crime of genocide—and the delegate from Chile surely will make a few emotional speeches on the subject—Señor González Videla is responsible for that very crime, perpetrated against his own countrymen.

12. THE CASE OF JULIETA CAMPUSANO

During this period, thousands of men accused of being Communists have been arrested in all parts of Chile. The arrests were carried out simultaneously, as armed forces surrounded entire areas, and citizens were transported en masse to desolate regions of the country chosen at the whim of Señor González Videla's sadistic collaborator and Chief of Police, Luis Brun D'Avoglio.

The case of Señora Julieta Campusano is particularly moving.

Julieta Campusano is the First Councilwoman of Santiago de Chile; that is, she obtained the largest plurality of votes of all the members of the Illustrious Town Council of the Chilean capital.

An outstanding female leader, a woman of good and rare selflessness, she was the only woman in the entourage of Señor González Videla's presidential campaign; they traveled, without respite, to every corner of the country. As a consequence of this prolonged drain on her energies, Señora Campusano's health was seriously impaired.

Can you imagine the surprise, then, when Señor González Videla's police, serving an arrest warrant against her, entered Señora Campusano's bedroom at four in the morning and dragged her to a jail cell, in spite of the fact that she was in an advanced stage of pregnancy. Hours later, still in police custody, the councilwoman, who had so generously and untiringly accompanied the incumbent President of the nation during his electoral campaign, gave birth prematurely as a result of violent shock; and the consequences could have proved fatal to both mother and newborn child.

I believe that to portray the morality of the incumbent President of Chile, this one painful example makes additional commentaries unnecessary.

13. A COUNTRY UNDER A REIGN OF TERROR

Every newspaper in my country is censored. But because of this very censorship the press cannot warn the public that its publications have been brutally suppressed. The intent of the government is to simulate a state of normalcy that does not exist.

Nine provinces have been declared emergency zones and have been besieged in the same brutal manner as the coal provinces.

Meanwhile, the President of the Republic has invited foreign police and President Perón to intervene in Chilean affairs. The government has officially reported telephone conversations between the Presidents, often lasting for hours.

Three planeloads of Argentine police have been received with honors by the President of the Republic, who until the day of his election was president of the most powerful anti-Perón organization in South America.

A North American police chief, Warren Robins, has saturated the country with new FBI agents, assigning them specifically to direct repressions against the mine workers.

14.   SPANISH ÉMIGRÉS

For several years Señor González Videla held the honorable position of president of the Spanish-Chilean Anti-Franco Committee. While in this position he developed close friendships with intellectual and political Spanish refugees. And how has he honored their friendship and their shared objectives?

By the incarceration of Republican patriots, at his express order; by making use of knowledge that he himself, personally, obtained from them in the close fraternity of the struggle against Franco. Only my denouncement in the Senate has, to this time, prevented the mass deportation of Spanish refugees brought here during the administration of President Aguirre Cerda—and whose peace and tranquillity are a commitment of honor based on the right of asylum. There is no guarantee, considering the present culpable state of Chilean public life, that tomorrow the intent of the North American police will not be carried out and these political refugees be delivered into the hands of their Spanish executioners.

15.   CONCENTRATION CAMPS

Two concentration camps have been in continuous use during this war against the Chilean people.

The first was activated on Santa María Island, a rugged island in the harshest of climates. The former penal colony for incorrigible criminals was evacuated. In their place were housed more political prisoners than the buildings can accommodate. Hundreds of prisoners needing beds and rooms are being funneled onto this island.

A new concentration camp has been erected in Pisagua, on the ruins of a mining town between desert and sea. Nazi-style barbed wire surrounds this compound situated in one of the most overwhelmingly desolate regions of the planet. Numerous intellectuals and hundreds of labor leaders are imprisoned there; every day new contingents of prisoners arrive.

The mayors of Iquique, Antofagasta, Calama, Tocopilla, Coronel, and Lota have been transported to this concentration camp without the slightest regard for the fact that their positions are a manifestation of the will of the people. The town councils of the majority of these towns have been dissolved and, in their place, contemptible juntas have been formed by police agents and a few pro-Franco Spaniards.

16.   FORCED LABOR

The new labor policy of Chile, for the majority of basic industries, is a regime of slavery and forced labor in which workers are forced to work by the military.

I am reproducing the relevant military document, to expose it to all America:

> This is to notify _____ residing at _____ that he will report to his usual place of work on October 10 at 8:00 a.m. If he does not do so, he will be considered in violation of the Army Conscription Law and will be punished by the maximum sentence of three years and one day in a minimum-security prison. Official Seal. Military Command.

It is essential that every democrat in America be apprised of this shameful document, which does not bring any loss of dignity to the people of Chile but which assures that history will record for eternity the sinister figure of a pitiful demagogue transformed into an executioner.

17.   SEVERING DIPLOMATIC RELATIONS

You may ask: what reasons has the government of Chile given for its unusual decision to sever diplomatic relations, first with Yugoslavia and then with the U.S.S.R. and the Republic of Czechoslovakia?

The government has accused these remote countries of fomenting the coal strikes, with the express purpose of paralyzing the North American arms industry during a war which, according to the President of the Republic of Chile, has already broken out between those countries and the United States. That is, the government has taken advantage of a local economic condition to inflame an international situation.

In the case of Yugoslavia, the government has proceeded to expel the former monarchist Yugoslavian consul and a diplomat accredited in Argentina who was visiting this country. They were invited to a friendly meeting by the Minister of Foreign Relations. There, in addition to notifying the consul with unprecedented vileness and vulgarity of the break in official relations, he had the men arrested at the door to his office—after he had received them, and bid them goodbye with a friendly smile. From the Foreign Office they were escorted out of the country as if they were criminals. This action was taken so that the government could raid, with impunity, the office of the Yugoslavian delegation, removing documents they then altered and falsified in order to justify their villainous conduct.

In the case of the U.S.S.R., from the moment Señor González Videla ascended to the presidency—and in spite of his being the honorary president of the Soviet Institute of Culture—his government, ignoring protests from cultural institutions and the parties of the people, authorized a sordid and malignant campaign against the U.S.S.R., carried out by every Fascist sector of the population.

This state of affairs reached its nadir when, shortly before diplomatic relations were severed, the Soviet Embassy was raked with machine-gun fire from an automobile. The government made no attempt to find the guilty, who were emboldened by the success of their cowardly action. With the knowledge of Señor González Videla, and encouraged by a provocative speech by the President, they organized a campaign of aggression against the Soviet Ambassador that reached alarming proportions at an exhibition attended by the President.

Instead of offering the apologies that any government—even the chief of a primitive tribe—would make to distinguish such terrorist activities from any official action, the Minister of Foreign Relations, overnight, and by order of the President of the Republic, severed relations with the U.S.S.R. This "diplomacy" was extended to the Republic of Czechoslovakia at the exact moment that it was winding up negotiations to provide us with agricultural machinery and to install a sugar-beet factory to produce sugar in Chile. This was a cynically premeditated maneuver intended to shackle us to the existing North American monopolies.

Everything that has been said outside the country, divulged by North American news agencies and by official representatives of Chile, on the subject of those countries' intervention in the internal affairs of Chile is base slander; it is a dish of lies cooked up by our government, seasoned by the North American State Department expert, Mr. Kennan, and served to pro-Fascist imperialist reactionaries throughout America in an act of audacious and odious provocation. In Rio de Janeiro, in secret meetings with General Marshall, it was decided that Chile, as a country of democratic traditions, should initiate this maneuver, to influence the other Foreign Ministries of America.

So González Videla negotiated the surrender of the historical, legal, and moral patrimony of Chile. And he has been cold-bloodedly immoral in doing so. There is no other way to interpret his refusal to name an investigative commission—composed of persons from every party—that would examine the government's accusation of an attempted "subversive plot" by foreign nations linked to the U.S.S.R.

The following commission was proposed by the Communist Party: Arturo Alessandri Palma, president of the Senate, Liberal senator; Eduardo Cruz Coke, Conservative senator; Salvador Allende, Socialist senator; Gustavo Girón, Radical senator; Eduardo Frei, Falangist deputy; Pablo Neruda, Communist senator.

18. THE PRESENT SITUATION

The people of my country have no means by which to communicate the scorn these attitudes and these betrayals deserve. Terror, intimidation, censorship of press and radio, accusations instigated by the government, are the order of the day.

There are no individual guarantees, no freedom is respected, in the police state of González Videla. Homes are ransacked by night, their occupants thrown into prison or transported to desolate regions without being questioned, without even being charged with an offense. The press is daily forced to print lies, and an atmosphere of debasement of men and parties grows ever more dense in the circles surrounding the government of the republic.

19. THE RESISTANCE

Nevertheless, a profound malaise, a unanimous feeling of revulsion, exists in every social stratum of Chile, only barely concealed by the propaganda and lies of the office of the President.

Chile has known other dictatorial, military, and reactionary regimes, and a people of such high civic consciousness as our own is not easily deceived.

Daily, the upper echelons of the landholding and banking oligarchy officially applaud the actions of the government, but daily, too, many of its representatives reveal to us their individual disgust in the face of such disloyalty and of the common danger threatening the venerable and traditional democratic institutions of Chile. I am writing these lines at the present moment to notify you of the instability of the situation, which, because of its very abnormality, may escalate to greater violence. The Chilean people, nonetheless, are waiting calmly; because of their inherent good sense, they do not rise to the daily provocations of the government.

Speaking for myself, I want to make it clear to my many, many brothers from every American nation that there is no stain currently tarnishing the honor of my country that cannot be erased. I stand firmly resolved in my ever-increasing, indestructible love for my country and my absolute faith in my people.

This is not a call for support. It is simply a personal letter to the millions of men and women who will want to be informed about the drama of a country that once was the proudest among the champions of American freedom.

The instigators of these crimes threaten not only the freedom of Chile but the order and integrity of our forsaken Latin America.

Other governments will repeat these debilitating betrayals. The cruel and bloody dictators in some of our sister countries will today feel more firm and resolute as they tighten the noose around the necks of their peoples. Franco, through his government-controlled press, has congratulated Señor González Videla, who presided over anti-Franco activities.

A plan for the brutal domination of our continent is being implacably administered through the direct intervention of the North American government, and through its servitors.

In Bogotá, these puppets will recount how they have carried out their respective assignments. They will draw the dark net of slavery more closely around our countries. And each of these dancing dolls will hold as his Bible the *Reader's Digest* and a police code of torture, imprisonment, and exile.

But the day will come when these men must give an accounting of such ignominy to history, and to the people.

I repeat, I am not seeking support for Chile. We are aware of our duty and we will strive within our country to put an end to this state of violence, and for a return to normalcy and respect and decency, the venerable ideals that elevate my people to the first rank of Americans.

A PERSONAL MESSAGE

You will forgive me if I end on a personal note. I have had to declare a moratorium on answering the letters of countless dear friends.

My years as public servant and itinerant writer have taught me to be acutely sensitive to the sorrowful plight of the people; I have traveled to every corner of my country—pampa and cordillera, sea and plain—speaking out, asking questions, offering support. But just two months ago the leadership of the Communist Party summoned me and asked me to give more time and attention to my poetry. To this end, they offered isolation and solitude for one year, hoping particularly that I could complete my *Canto general.*

I want to attest to the largesse and affection contained in this request, that the tranquillity and legality of the path of the workers was such that the Communist Party would sacrifice the services of one of its senators for such a long time.

I was readying myself to weave again the rhythm and sounds of my poetry, I was preparing to sing again, to lose myself in the depths of my country, in its most secret roots, when the drama I have broadly outlined to you began to weigh upon the lives of all Chileans.

The betrayal of my people, their sorrow, has filled me with anguish. By good fortune, a band of Christian patriots, the National Falangist Party of Chile, currently being persecuted by the government to almost the same degree as the Communists, has given me the consolation of sharing with another group of human beings the gravity of this hour for Chile. The growing discontent of the people is manifest everywhere. The blackmail that would offer the pretext of war in order to terrorize our citizens and end our independence becomes clearer by the moment. Meanwhile, our national problems increase daily in the ferment of exploitation, speculation, injustice, and abuse. And in this climate of tyranny and corruption, false accusations run hand in hand with the clandestine transactions of persons close to the government. But as the tragedy grows, so too does the desire of the Chilean people to return to a democratic life by a sudden unmasking of demagogues and opportunists.

However, in the very events I am exposing to the American conscience lies the unpredictability of a situation carried to a state of chaos by hysterical, irresponsible, and treacherous leaders.

I hastened to leave my retreat on the coast of Chile to take my place in the front rank of the defenders of our threatened freedom. Daily, I confront the responsibilities of writer and patriot.

If, in carrying out these precious duties, anything should happen to me, I wish to say that I am proud of any personal risk suffered in this battle for dignity, culture, and freedom—a struggle all the more imperative for being tied to the future of Chile and to the unbounded love I feel for the country I have so often sung in my poetry.

That is why, through this document, I solemnly declare that, in the state of repression in which we live, I hold responsible for any threat against my person the present government of the Republic, and, personally and specifically, President Gabriel González Videla.

Santiago, November 1947

I Accuse

ON BEHALF OF CHILE'S GOOD NAME

Oₙᴄᴇ again I beg the indulgence of the Senate in these dramatic times in which our nation is living, so that I may address myself to the document I sent to many Americans in defense of Chile's good name, enabling them to make a rapid survey of our somber political panorama.

The President of the Republic has taken one more step in the unbridled political persecution that will make him notorious in the sad history of these days, by filing an action before the Supreme Court requesting my impeachment, so that from these chambers no further criticism will be heard against the repressive measures that will comprise the only memory of his passage through the history of Chile.

THE FOUR FREEDOMS

As I address the Honorable Senate today, I recall an event of extraordinary magnitude.

On a sixth of January much like today—on January 6 of 1941—a titan of struggle, of freedom, a giant of a President, Franklin Delano Roosevelt, gave his message to the world establishing the Four Freedoms—the foundation stone of the future for which the world was fighting and bleeding.

These were the rights:

This speech was delivered to the Senate of Chile on January 6, 1948

1. FREEDOM OF SPEECH AND EXPRESSION
2. FREEDOM OF WORSHIP
3. FREEDOM FROM WANT
4. FREEDOM FROM FEAR

This was the world promised by Roosevelt.

It is a different world from the one desired by President Truman and the Trujillos, the Moriñigos, the González Videlas, and the Somozas.

In Chile there is no freedom of speech, nor do our people enjoy freedom from fear. Hundreds of men who struggle so that our country might be free from want are persecuted, mistreated, insulted, and convicted.

On this sixth day of January 1948, exactly seven years after Roosevelt's declaration, I am being persecuted for being faithful to these exalted human ideals, and I find myself for the first time called before a tribunal, for having denounced to all America the contemptible violation of these freedoms in the last place in the world where this should have occurred: Chile.

ANCIENT HISTORY

This accusation being made against me today is ancient history: every country, every era, has illustrious and well-known antecedents. Is this because in every country the phenomena of treachery and treason are periodically repeated? No, I do not believe it is so. The names of those so unjustly accused are names the whole world respects today. Once beyond persecution and perfidy, some even became the leaders of their countries, and their countrymen demonstrated their faith in their honor and their ability to guide the destinies of their countries. And they bore always, as a mark of honor, the highest seal of honor, the persecution to which they had been subjected.

No, the reason must be found elsewhere. The reason was studied and lucidly expounded by François Guizot, a French historian and minister to Louis Philippe d'Orléans. I have here what he says in *Des conspirations et de la justice politique*:

> What will the government do that sees a badly administered society restless beneath its direction? Incapable of governing, it will attempt

to punish the society. The government has not learned how to discharge its responsibilities, how to use its strengths. So it will ask other powers within the government to carry out a task that is not theirs, to lend their strength to an undertaking for which it was not intended. And as the power of the judiciary is linked to society much more closely than any other, as all action leads, or may lead, to judicial decisions, it is precisely this branch of the government that will be called on to exceed its legitimate jurisdiction to become involved in areas in which the government has been found wanting . . .

Everywhere that politics has been false, incapable, and evil, the judiciary has been summoned to act in its stead, and be ruled by considerations imposed by the sphere of the government and not of laws; ultimately it must abandon its honorable seat and descend to the arena of political parties . . . Since it does not govern society absolutely, since it must endure some resistance, what will become of despotism? What will become of it, if its politics has not penetrated the chambers of the courts, and used the courts as its instrument? If it does not reign everywhere, it will not be secure anywhere. It is by nature so weak that the least attack places it in mortal danger. The presence of the smallest right disturbs and threatens it.

Here, expounded by a Frenchman of the first half of the last century, is the exact situation of the Chilean government in the year 1948. His words explain why my impeachment is being sought; and why, through the controlled press, I am being insulted from one end of the country to the other by journalists handsomely or poorly paid.

To accuse me of having damaged my country's prestige by publishing abroad the truth that inside this nation a rule of Extraordinary Powers and total censorship does not allow me to make known does not bring insult to me but, rather, to the greatest men of mankind, the Fathers of our nation. It is curious to see oneself branded as unpatriotic for having done here what was done in exile by those who gave us our independence and laid the foundation for what was to have been always a free and democratic nation. When I am besmirched as a traitor, as unpatriotic, is not the accusation being leveled against me the same that Osorio, San Bruno, and Marcó del Pont leveled against O'Higgins, against the Carreras, against every Chilean exiled in Mendoza or Buenos Aires who, after having fought in Rancagua, attacked with his pen the invaders that later he would conquer with his sword?

THE TYRANT ROSAS AGAINST SARMIENTO

The accusation being directed against me was also made by the tyrannical government of Juan Manuel de Rosas, who called himself the Illustrious Restorer of Law. This tyrant asked the government of Chile to extradite Sarmiento so he could be tried in Argentina for treason and sedition. I have in my hand a paragraph from the proud letter that Sarmiento sent the President of Chile on that occasion. It read:

> Conspiring for the right to speech, for a free press, on behalf of the needs of our people; conspiring by example and persuasion; conspiring for the principles and the ideas disseminated by the press and education; this new conspiracy, Excellency, will on my part be eternal, persevering, and untiring in every instance, as long as a drop of blood courses through my veins, as long as a moral sentiment lives in my conscience, as long as freedom of thought and the right to express that thought exist in any corner of the earth.

And Juan Bautista Alberdi, also exiled in our country, wrote:

> No more tyrants and no more tyranny. If an Argentine is a tyrant and wants to hold back progress, death to the Argentine. If a foreigner is liberal and has progressive beliefs, long live the foreigner.

Rosas never succeeded in getting either Sarmiento or Alberdi in his power. And once the tyrant had fallen, Sarmiento became President of Argentina.

It would be a never-ending task if I were to cite every free man who was forced to pass judgment on the tyrannical regime that subjugated his people, every free man who was charged with treason and lack of patriotism. Victor Hugo, from his exile in Guernsey the implacable critic of Napoleon III—Victor Hugo, the greatest of poets and selfless patriot, was accused of treachery by Napoleon III and his followers, who were preparing for France the humiliation and defeat of Sedan.

BILBAO

The unshakable certainty, the conviction that makes the persecuted sense, even in moments of torment, his infinite superiority over his persecutor; the strength of conviction that one is fighting for a good cause, which allowed Giordano Bruno to exclaim as he was condemned to the stake, "I am more tranquil in the dock than you"— pointing to his ecclesiastical judges—"who condemn me to death"; the commitment to a justice that separates good faith from bad, and the just cause from the unjust, were expressed by our compatriot Francisco Bilbao in unparalleled majesty during his trial. He said:

> Here, two names—that of accuser and that of accused. Two names linked by the chance of history, names that will echo down through the history of my country. We shall see, Señor Prosecutor, upon which of the two the blessing of posterity will fall. Philosophy, too, has its Code, and this Code is eternal. Philosophy will call you the reactionary. Yes, I am the innovator; you are the reactionary.

And in reference to Bilbao's case, José Victorino Lastarria says:

> The prophecy cannot but be fulfilled, for the wrathful outbursts of hatred of the servants of the old regime have always fashioned a glorious future for the victims of that wrath and have contributed to the triumph of truth and liberty with almost greater efficacy than the efforts of the brave men who sustain those values. Posterity will honor and glorify the author of *Sociabilidad chilena*.

Even so, Francisco Bilbao was convicted on charges of immorality and blasphemy, and saw his work burned at the hands of his executioner. I myself do not aspire either to acclaim or to reward. But I am absolutely certain that sooner or later—one would wish sooner—the iniquitous political trial to which I have been subjected will be judged on its merits, and its instigators and perpetrators labeled as they must be if the government is to be freed of the blunders it has committed and does not know how to rectify.

A JURIST WHO CONTRADICTS HIS OWN WORK

I want now to discuss the observations that my person, my work, and my attitude in the present situation elicited from the Honorable Senator Don Miguel Cruchaga Tocornal during last year's session of December 23. The Honorable Senator Cruchaga is not only a distinguished member of this august body but an illustrious son of Chile; his work as a legal scholar, diplomat, and Minister of Foreign Affairs has earned him an outstanding reputation abroad. His name is cited as an irrefutable authority on international matters, and his judgments carry great weight and value. As to his prestige within the country, it would be superfluous even to refer to it, as he is known by all. It is sufficient to call to mind that Señor Cruchaga Tocornal, after brilliantly discharging the important duties of Minister of Foreign Affairs for the nation, served during very difficult times as president of this body.

It is for these reasons that I note with a certain alarm, in the observations the Honorable Senator directed against me, an evident lack of clarity not only in his opinions but in the strictly legal bases of his arguments. His unquestioned prestige as a jurist seemed to be suffering an attack from the least expected quarter, from himself. How much better to have debated with me openly, with the generosity and equity one reserves for a compatriot and colleague; how much better to argue on the basis of the Christian principles that compel us to study, analyze, and research a matter before delivering against our neighbor the kind of judgment the Bible calls "rash"; how much better to maintain the serenity and impartiality that must govern the actions of every legal expert if he is to avoid falling into dangerous accusations and, what is more serious, allowing his accusations to stand in irrefutable contradiction to what he has maintained in his universally acclaimed writings. If, in a word, overnight he becomes a detractor and critic of the very work that is the basis for his fame as an expert in international affairs.

I seek the indulgence of the Honorable Señor Cruchaga and this august body for such irreverent apprehensions. But, in truth, I cannot explain within the universally accepted norms of public law the serious charge uttered against me by the Honorable Señor Cruchaga when he stated:

The Senate has had the sad privilege of witnessing one of the most unusual events in the history of Chile. In the course of a diplomatic dispute between our Republic and a foreign government, a member of this body did not hesitate to turn against his own nation, attacking the Executive and making himself an ardent defender not of Chile but of the aforesaid foreign government.

For the moment I do not choose to address the personal, impassioned, and subjective portion of the statement I have quoted. Whatever distaste it may cause me, especially in view of the fact that it is rash and unjustified, is surpassed by my disquietude as I imagine the expressions of astonishment and incredulity that must have crossed the faces of Chilean and foreign admirers of Señor Cruchaga Tocornal; indeed, that still must dominate their emotions.

"It isn't possible," they must be thinking, "that this serene and circumspect jurist has abandoned his usually scrupulous legal vocabulary to fall into such an arbitrary and vulgar confusion of words, each of which has a very clear meaning indeed; and, in the end, for what? To reach a conclusion that does not become a scholar. Can it be that, in his role as senator, Señor Cruchaga Tocornal is devoting himself to the destruction of Señor Cruchaga the international expert?"

But an even more serious matter remains. As a Chilean—that is, as a citizen of a country that has fought and will continue to fight to spread democracy and freedom within its own land, across the continent, and throughout the world—and as a senator—that is, as a member of one of the houses of Congress, which is one of the basic branches of the government—I can do no less than call to your attention the extremes to which political passion may lead, even in the case of a man of the maturity and renown of the Honorable Señor Cruchaga Tocornal. I find myself obliged to protest energetically the debased, sordid, unworthy role that in Señor Cruchaga's view the Senate must play. This august body was indeed, if I may use the words of the Honorable Señor Cruchaga, witness to a "sad privilege." But this was not the "privilege" he indicates: rather, one far worse, that of seeing itself denigrated and slandered, unjustly censured, in evident ignorance of history; that of witnessing an attempt to silence and dishonor a senator who was openly proceeding in his charge as representative of the people, fulfilling his mission as senator. This *is* sad and denigrating; this *is* to be lamented, and it clouds our reputation as a democratic nation. The Honorable Senator Cruchaga

Tocornal is entitled to make a judgment in favor of or against the Executive; he is entitled to judge me, with acrimony or benevolence; he is entitled to any and every opinion. But he is not entitled to diminish in doctrinaire fashion the lofty functions that befit a senator; and he is not entitled to condemn a member of this chamber as unpatriotic solely because he is acting as a loyal Chilean, a true patriot, and a senator who holds high the independence of the greatest of the three branches of government: the Legislative.

I have stated that I admire Señor Cruchaga's international reputation, but I also recall that for one reason or another many before him have enjoyed similar fame—among them, the historian Paolo Giovio, who was courted and praised by the monarchs of Europe. Giovio said that he used two pens when he wrote history: a gold pen for his supporters, and an iron pen for his detractors. It is apparent that in his speech the Honorable Senator used both: a gold pen for the Executive branch—*which he arbitrarily and mistakenly interprets as one and the same as the nation: an act I protest as a citizen, a senator, and even in the name of the law of whose statutes the Honorable Señor Cruchaga should be the most zealous defender*—and an iron pen against me and, strangest of all, against himself and his own magnum opus.

THE CHIEF EXECUTIVE IS NOT THE NATION

I do not believe that anyone in this august body—I do not believe that even the Honorable Senator himself—would now dare to state in cold blood that I, in criticizing the acts of the Chief Executive, openly, in this chamber, and in fulfillment of the charge entrusted to me by a portion of the people of this nation, in proceeding in accordance with the standards of the Constitution, in stating my opinions and exposing facts related to matters on which the Senate must act—I say that no one could state that *I have turned against the nation*. The Chief Executive is not the nation, and to criticize his actions, or to differ with them, is not to turn against the nation.

To turn against the nation is to accept submissively, to remain silent, to defend indefensible acts. It is to accept without protest the fact that in the development of one individual's policy—neither justified nor explained in spite of long speeches and confusing quotations —injustices and blunders have been committed that shame us in the eyes of the civilized world.

THOSE WHO ARE AGAINST CHILE

To turn against the nation is to accept that internal political maneuvering shapes international policy. *This* is to betray and attack the nation. If the nation is not a capricious and self-interested concept, if it is something pure and not bound to material interests, something just and beautiful, its ideals are those of Truth, Justice, and Liberty. Only in this way are those concepts defended for which so many men through so many centuries suffered and died; one attacks the nation when one hopes to use it as a tool for personal politics, when one wants to meld the nation—which is the sum of all Chileans, present, past, and future—into a single person. Worse still: into the short-lived policies of a single individual who in the course of a political career marked only by contradictions has shown a total absence of any honest and consistent political philosophy.

THE WORD AND THE TRUTH

I reject, therefore, not insofar as it affects me personally, but in my role as senator, the unacceptable judgment, insulting to our dignity as representatives of the people, that if here in the Senate, openly, we criticize the actions of the Executive, we turn against the nation. I lament the insult to my integrity made in the Senate of Chile, but this does not move me to describe the Honorable Senator in the same arbitrary and unjust terms he used against me. There is a difference between us: for him, it seems to have been an inconsequential matter to state before the Senate that one of his colleagues had "turned against his nation." He knew very well that this insult was an affront against the Senate, against Chile, and against justice as well, as the charge is not true. Nevertheless, he made it, and in so doing demonstrated that he has more interest in and loyalty to the word "nation" than to the nation itself. I, on the other hand, profoundly lament the unwarranted offense committed against our body and our democracy; I lament it, perhaps because I am a realist, an attitude scorned by the Honorable Senator, and I prefer to sacrifice myself and dedicate myself totally to the nation as it is in reality, rather than subordinate it to the level of a mere word. This is not the first time that idealists and anti-materialists like the Honorable Senator have assumed a paradoxical position: they, creatures of high and noble thoughts, selfless, idealistic gentlemen, mistakenly regard a transitory political authority—for what else is the Chief Executive?—as the nation, which surpasses us in time and space; they subordinate the high principles of justice and the Constitution to mere political slogans subject to the interests of the moment.

POLITICAL BETRAYAL

It has been suggested that my letter to my friends in America, listing the acts of the Chief Executive, whom the Rules of Procedure prevent me from naming here, might be classified as slanderous. Those acts were: political betrayal; abandonment of the 4th of September Platform, sworn to and signed with solemnity on July 21, 1946, the very day on which the heroic peoples of La Paz hanged from a lamppost the tyrant Villarroel and the Secretary General of the government, Roberto Hinojosa; persecution of the Communist Party, which was the decisive factor in his presidential election, as he was then opposed by the principal political colleagues who now form his "Court of Miracles"; disloyalty to the people of Chile, who voted for him in the faith that he would implement to a greater degree the sociopolitical process initiated by our great President Pedro Aguirre Cerda in 1938, and which in its basic outlines was not modified by Juan Antonio Ríos, Aguirre Cerda's successor; the insulting rebuff to the peoples of America, who have always seen in Chile the vanguard of all our peoples; the desertion, in sum, of the great ideals that a progressive humanity hoped to effect in this post-war era, as filled with hopes as with obstacles, with affirmations as with apostasies, with examples of civic heroism as with the most repugnant personal opportunism.

WE VOTED FOR A PLATFORM

It will do little good to maintain that at the time of the last presidential election the people of Chile voted for a platform and not for a person; the people voted for principles and not for flags stained by the commerce of electioneering; the people voted for the sovereignty of the nation and for economic independence, not for subjugation and surrender to foreign imperialism.

HIS OWN WORDS CONVICT HIM

To corroborate the destructive political action of which I have accused the Chief Executive, I shall call upon his own words and declarations. Reading them here will prove that I have not voiced insults and slander against him, that I am not interested in his personal life, but in his role as a politician and his acts as a leader. Furthermore, I shall establish the inconsistency between his promises as candidate and his conduct as President.

One of his biographers, his colleague Januario Espinosa, records portions of an address that González Videla delivered exactly one month after the triumph of the Popular Front, at a political celebration in honor of President-elect Don Pedro Aguirre Cerda—an event organized by the Radical Party and held in the Municipal Theater of Santiago. On that occasion Señor González Videla said:

> We do not want the participation in this government, or in any public administration, of the Judases who would sell us out, or to deal with traitors who in vicious battles of conflicting interests secretly serve the cause of the imperialism, the monopolies, the economic policy that has permitted taxation to be removed from the shoulders of the wealthy and placed on the shoulders of the poor.

And he added, addressing himself to Señor Aguirre Cerda, who one month later was to assume the leadership of the nation:

> Every sovereign must beware of the adulation of the all-too-numerous philistines who would disguise themselves in brightly colored feathers and at times of difficulty and vacillation furtively sing into the sovereign's ear criticism and betrayal of the men and the parties that first anointed him candidate and then President of the Repub-

lic. When these birds of counterfeit and changeable feathers come to roost in the eaves of the venerable mansion that has seen such struggle, I beg of his Excellency Don Pedro Aguirre Cerda, on this solemn night when we feel the presence of the spirits of Matta, of Gallo, of Mac Iver and Letelier, that he remember the sorrow of an entire people, who, in spite of having suffered such betrayal, with a faith and loyalty unparalleled in the history of America have designated him to be Leader of the poor, the poorly housed, the abandoned.

A few years later, in the last days of October 1945, before leaving on the obligatory trip every candidate for the presidency must make to the United States, he stated to a newspaper under his ownership, the *ABC* of Antofagasta:

A government of the left must have sufficient vision and responsibility not to allow itself to be used by the anti-labor factions in our country, which are successfully conspiring against the unity of the left, and whose most sensational triumph would be to use radical Ministers as instruments of repression against the working class.

Foreign interests are replacing their former negotiators and intermediaries, who had influence on the right, with persons cunningly selected from the ranks of the left, who continue to act and work within the left while in constant communication with members of the Parliament and the government.

THESE WERE HIS WORDS

In the Senate session of February 2, 1946, on the subject of the events at the Plaza Bulnes, Señor González Videla, among other incisive statements, expressed the following point:

I, in the name of Chilean radicalism, want to establish that the persons responsible for these events, whoever they may be, can in no way compromise the Radical Party, since its principles, its tradition, and its doctrine, so clearly delineated in the Convention of Valdivia, repudiate all acts of violence and repression in the resolution of social problems.

And to make himself absolutely clear, he added:

Unfortunately, the negation of the people's civil rights and the repression by arms of their peaceful demonstrations, to the point of using them as an excuse for a massacre, compromise the basic stability of our democratic regime, especially in this post-war period, which is witnessing the emergence of a revolutionary world.

And looking ahead to events in which he would play an active part, he said in this same speech: "These public tragedies are caused when political pygmies manage to climb to power. They, more than anyone, are responsible for the political and social upheavals rocking our country today."

I would exhaust the Senate's patience if I were to quote passages from the many speeches González Videla delivered as a candidate for the presidency of the Republic, or those that as President-elect he directed specifically to the Communist Party, swearing that he would never betray it; but I must recall again the words he spoke in the Plaza Constitución, warning of the dangers that lay along the road of anti-Communism:

> This is what the disguised Fascists we all know in this country want, my friends. And—because I saw them in action in noble France—I fear more deeply the treacherous Lavals of the left than any man of the right.
>
> The basis of the anti-Communist movement is the persecution and liquidation of the working class.
>
> When Hitler's forces crossed the border into France and captured Paris, the Nazi soldiers didn't bother to ask workers for their Communist identification; to belong to a union, to have any connection with a union, was sufficient cause to be persecuted, imprisoned, and sentenced to forced labor.
>
> This is the intent of the people who exploit fear of Communism: to intimidate the producing classes of this land; they hope to persecute the working class, to dissolve the unions, to prevent the workers from organizing or claiming their civil rights, which I continue to respect as I always have.

JUDGE NOW

Could anyone deny the case for political betrayal, or, at least, for a lack of consistency between promises and the way those promises have been translated into action?

The way a policy is administered is as important as its consequences. Well, what have been the consequences of Señor González Videla's policies for Chilean democracy?

Let the Conservative Deputy Enrique Cañas Flores speak for the President. According to news reports, this recent guest of Franco, acting as Chile's representative, stated: *"Chile is following Spain's lead in regard to Communism."* Does this mean that our country has become a satellite of the Fascist Axis and a threat to international peace and democracy?

How can this behavior be described? Should we be surprised by the unenviable fame we are acquiring abroad, represented as anti-Communist and anti-Soviet, transformed into a colony of imperialism and a focal point for international intrigue?

The Chilean people continue to be faithful to the platform and to its principles and to its best democratic and anti-imperialist traditions, they have not changed; it is the President of the nation who has made an abrupt about-face, now adoring what once he claimed to abhor.

In response to my measured observations based on facts *that have neither been debated nor disproved*, my accusers have chosen to resort to diatribe and bombastic accusations, rather than reason and discussion. Throughout our land, the radio and press have capitulated, and are waging an inflammatory campaign to defame me.

A DEFENDER ASHAMED

The Honorable Senate is well aware that because of the Extraordinary Powers, which were too freely conceded and are being exercised to a degree beyond the memory of any of us here, freedom of speech and the press does not exist today in Chile. The press that would maintain the standards of truth—the only press that supported the incumbent President of the Republic during his presidential campaign—has been suppressed and censored. A humorous broadcast was censored for comparing the Chief Executive's tourist travels to those of the Wandering Jew, and for commenting that "Hope Tonic, the only edible remedy offered to the people of Chile in compensation for rising prices, is out of stock even in the pharmacies." Citizens have been arrested, exiled, or relocated. The President of the Republic, in a statement to railroad management which was widely disseminated by the radio and press, *revealed the existence of an unconstitutional ideological persecution, confirming that railroad em-ployees who have been removed from their jobs were removed not for any offense but because they were Communists.* Thus, the equal-ity of all Chileans before the law, freedom of belief, freedom of assembly, and other freedoms, has been abolished. To silence any lawmakers who dare disagree with the government and make facts public which it wants kept in strict secrecy, an action of impeach-ment has been brought against me. The reasons are not to be found in the accusations that have been made *but in the unpardonable fact— unpardonable to the government—that I revealed to the nation and to the world those acts the Chief Executive wished to cloak in dark shadow, while shackling the country by use of his Extraordinary Powers, censorship of the press, and mass arrests.* Thereby, the Chief Executive presents us with a curious situation. On the one hand, he says he is defending our tranquillity, the country, and its citizens by strict compliance with the law; he says he arrests only disloyal citi-zens and those who would destroy the government; he maintains that he has saved Chile from the gravest international danger. But, on the other hand, he is annoyed—indeed, irritated to a paroxysm of anger— every time his "defending" activities are made public. The country is, in truth, finding it difficult to explain how the President of the Re-public can be both proud of his activities and ashamed and fearful that they will become known.

BUT THE TRUTH IS BECOMING KNOWN

Witness the campaign of defamation that a totally submissive press has undertaken against a member of this Honorable Senate; they seize from us the means by which we may defend ourselves; they seek to silence us even in this chamber that some have called a tribunal; but by word of mouth the truth is becoming known and the whole world will be guided by it. It is true, of course, that illogic and injustice are wont to cause men, even the most equanimous, to band together too tightly and to lose sight of our highest national and individual inter-ests. The concepts of country and nation cannot be separated from the fundamental concepts on which free and democratic coexistence is based. When they are in opposition, then there is no doubt at all: the concepts have been poorly presented, and self-interested individuals are wrongly using these sacred ideals of nation and patriotism as a cloak for behavior that cannot stand the light of day; when an oath is not kept; when one man governs for a few; when people are hungry; when freedom is suppressed; when the press is censored; when a man fears that his activities will become known; when he works against everything that sustained him; when he abandons his friends; when he is inferior, grossly inferior, to the task of governing which he has assumed; when he establishes concentration camps and piece by piece hands over the nation to foreigners; when he tolerates the certain, ever-increasing invasion of technical specialists, G-men, FBI agents, to meddle more and more in our internal affairs, then the word "nation" is debased, and it becomes necessary to raise it high again, as men without fear, to return things to their rightful places, and restore true meaning to the word.

AND THEN?

I am accused of having disclosed what is happening in Chile under the leadership of His Excellency Señor Gabriel González Videla, who governs by means of Extraordinary Powers and censorship of the press; they charge me with having spoken against my country because I did not agree with decisions taken by this same Exalted Leader. This argument is truly pitiable. If to disagree with His Excellency Señor González Videla is to turn against the nation, what can we say when we recall that Señor González Videla, as president of the Committee for Aid to the Spanish People, supported and defended *the rights of expatriate Spaniards to attack from exile the same Franco government with which he is now on such good terms?* Did he not authorize for those Spaniards, whom he called his friends and whose support he sought, the freedom that through an act of impeachment he is now attempting to deny me, the former head of his presidential campaign and a senator of the Republic?

THE TRUTH IS NOT SLANDER

I want to turn now to the charge that I slandered the President of the Republic. My attorney Carlos Vicuña, in the brilliant defense of my cause that he made before the plenary session of the Court of Appeals, argued that if I made political charges against the President of the Republic, these charges cannot be considered slander because, among other reasons, they are perfectly true and are fully known by every Chilean citizen and all foreigners who concern themselves with these matters. In my personal letter to millions, for which I am being attacked, no one, not even a judge of the Inquisition, could perceive anything but a great and pure love for my country—to which, within the limits of my capabilities, I have brought some measure of renown; and I can affirm without false modesty that my contribution is purer, more selfless, more noble, and greater than any of His Excellency Señor González's political and diplomatic accomplishments.

HAPPY NEW YEAR! AN EXCEPTION!

Just this New Year, I compared the messages the leaders of the nations of America sent to their peoples. In every country, even those known for tyrannical and unjust regimes, there were at least a few words of fraternity, of peace and hope, for the people. In every country, this solemn day that perhaps heralds a historic cycle for humanity was welcomed with prophetic words of harmony and respect.

There was a single exception. This was the message of His Excellency González Videla, saturated with hatred and intended to foment division and persecution among our people.

I AM PROUD

I am proud that this persecution has fallen on my shoulders. I am proud, because a people who suffer and endure may thus have an opportunity to see who has remained loyal to his public obligations and who has betrayed them.

ONLY CHILE

At this historic moment, in this New Year vibrant with portents, Chile is the only country on our continent with hundreds of political prisoners and exiles, with thousands of people forced from their homes, sentenced to permanent unemployment, to poverty and anguish. Chile is at this moment the only country where the radio and press have been gagged. Chile is the only country on the continent where strikes are settled by crushing underfoot the Labor Code and firing en masse presumed political opponents of the government.

I charge His Excellency Señor González Videla with the responsibility for these shameful occurrences in our democracy.

WHO IS RESPONSIBLE FOR OUR LOSS OF PRESTIGE?

In the accounts of a servile press, and in the action brought by the President of the Republic, an attempt is made to impute to me the lowering of my country's prestige. Those who commit these reprehensible actions, those who have cruelly stained the prestige of Chile throughout America, are attempting to take the offensive by assuming the role of defenders of our national prestige.

Those responsible for shackling, crushing, gagging, and dividing our nation are claiming the flag of prestige that they themselves have trampled in the dust.

When the persecutions and mass dismissals of the nitrate-salt workers were begun, the companies had in hand previously prepared lists in accordance with a preconceived plan of repression.

IN PISAGUA

A woman is being detained in Pisagua for having in 1941 initiated a work stoppage in the kitchens. This woman's magnificent action—demanding higher-quality foodstuffs in the general stores—was the only political act of a lifetime. It happened in 1941. She is in Pisagua now.

A Spanish Republican from Casablanca who was deported from Chile told us that the only political act of his life in Chile had been to contribute the modest sum of a hundred pesos to Señor González Videla's campaign.

DO NOT HAVE CHILDREN

To head the lists prepared by the copper and nitrate companies for mass dismissals, arrests, and deportation, the companies chose the workers with the largest families, in order to save thousands of pesos in family allowances.

According to these opportunists of terror, the more children Chilean workers have, the more Communist they are.

And so, when the trains and trucks carrying their immense cargoes of human anguish arrived at their destination, only one sound was heard. It was the weeping of hundreds and hundreds of children who, clinging to their mothers, wept and wailed, distilling in their tears all the sorrow of persecution and helplessness.

MY SENTENCE

At the present time there is no tribunal in which to impeach the President of the Republic for the calamitous events that have taken place in our country.

But I bequeath to him as an implacable sentence, a sentence he will hear all his life, the heartrending weeping of those children.

I Accuse the President of the Republic from this forum of resorting to violence to destroy the unions.

I Accuse the President of the Republic—during his candidacy, president of anti-Franco organizations in Chile—of having ordered, as President of the Republic, our delegation at the UN to vote against severing relations with Franco, and at the same time, in Chile, of imprisoning and exiling the Republicans who were members of the very organizations over which he formerly presided.

I Accuse Señor González Videla of having been, during his candidacy, vice president of the world organization for a Jewish Holy Land and president of that association in Chile, and, as President of the Republic, of having ordered our delegation in the UN to abstain, and to silence Chile's voice on the question of creating a Jewish state.

I Accuse Señor González Videla of having headed the anti-Perón organizations in Chile during his candidacy, and then, as President— as has been announced by the Secretary General—of having coordinated, in long conversations with Señor Perón, repressive measures against those people's organizations in Chile and Argentina.

I Accuse the President of the Republic of having denounced a Yugoslavian Communist plot against the Argentine government—

based, according to him, in Chile and in the city of Rosario in Argentina. The fantasy of these claims is underscored by the warm telegram published in the press the day before yesterday, in which General Perón cordially congratulates Marshal Tito of Yugoslavia and proposes an even closer friendship between their peoples.

I Accuse Señor González Videla of the incompetent administration of our foreign affairs, which have become a continental example of superficiality and inconsistency.

I Accuse the President of the Republic of responsibility for the present disorganization and decline in productivity, as the result of the massive removal of thousands of experienced workers from the most difficult jobs in our industries.

I Accuse the President of the Republic of ordering the armed forces to assume police duties, of setting them against the working people. I accuse him of wasting in these activities, which are alien to the army, hundreds of millions of pesos that could have been spent on improving outdated weapons systems and on acquiring modern arms, especially for the Air Force. These same opinions have been published in the army's own publications and have caused the abrupt discharge of senior officers.

I Accuse the President of the Republic of maintaining on our territory, in peacetime, foreign military bases with uniformed officers and troops.

I Accuse the President of the Republic of authorizing, even as I speak, the aerial photographing of our territory by foreign military pilots.

I Accuse Señor González Videla of engaging in a futile and sterile war against the people and popular philosophy of Chile, and of attempting to create artificial divisions among Chileans.

I Accuse Señor González Videla of attempting to suppress freedom of opinion, as in the case of my impeachment action, and by means of the most brutal censorship, and by using police and financial pressures, of attempting to silence the newspaper *El Siglo*, the official organ of his candidacy and the fruit of many years of struggle by the Chilean people, as well as *El Popular* and six other newspapers.

I Accuse the President of the Republic of lack of faith in his country; I accuse him of soliciting foreign loans, of pursuing the "chimera of gold," even at the cost of humiliating the nation, instead of formulating a distinguished, dignified, and diverse policy that would create jobs for Chilean workers and business for our nation's industries. One finds one's resources in the heart of the country; Chile does not want to be a beggar nation.

I ask the Honorable Senate: Where will it end? It is highly possible that the abnormal and anguished state of our country may continue. Every day the mercenaries of a certain press applaud what they call a reign of "social peace." But are there no sensible persons left to realize that social peace is precisely what we do not have, that we are living on the rim of a volcano, that this hatred nourished daily from the Office of the President of the Republic cannot constitute any possible base for our nation's conduct?

Where does Señor González Videla hope to lead us? Will the rule of Extraordinary Powers continue, will the excesses continue, will the mass dismissals continue, will the law of the garrote continue to substitute for the law of work, will censorship continue to reign supreme, will the dissolution of the unions continue, will the concentration camps of Pisagua continue, will persecution and betrayal continue, telephone censorship, the servility of the newspapers aligned with the government continue? Will prices continue to rise, dispossessions, the negotiations the press does not report? Mutely, will we continue down this uncontrolled path toward a dictatorship directed not only against Communists, Falangists, and all democrats, but against new sectors as well, while persons like myself—who explain to the nation and to friends abroad that these events do not compromise the dignity of the nation but rather betray the incompetence of our leaders—are accused of treason.

How long, every Chilean is asking, in this Senate and beyond it, in every walk of life, in every corner of our beloved country. How long will this nightmare continue? Workers, professional men, intellectuals, industrialists, politicians are wondering—men of the city and of the country.

Must we not check this headlong course, the warping of our public and political lives? Is not the need to return to fairness and decency evident to millions of Chileans?

The Honorable Senate must be aware to what degree the authorities must respect the residences of senators. Yet last night there was an attempt to burn down my home. The fire succeeded only in destroying part of the front door. As my telephone has been monitored by the government, I was not able to communicate with the police—which, in any case, would have been futile.

My house was built under great difficulty, but what would pain me particularly would be to see the destruction of the collections of rare books and art, which years ago I earmarked for the museums of my nation.

The trail of this outrage is easy to follow. It leads from the same cave where the criminal persecution of Julieta Campusano originated, the cave of those who robbed and destroyed the papers and type-writers of the Committee for the Defense of Public Liberties.

If this kind of attempt should succeed, and if my family and I are able to escape the flames, I shall not seek justice, but on the ruins of my burned books I will leave this placard: "Example of democracy during the presidency of González Videla."

A POLITICAL JUDGMENT

I have been accused of slandering and defaming the President of the Republic.

I reject, and shall continue to reject, those charges to the end of my days.

I have rendered a political and historical judgment of a politician who sat beside me in this body and who was elected by the same votes that elected me. When he left this chamber to run for President, the nation knows the efforts my party made to win for him a victory that would bring liberty, honor, and progress to our country.

If I wanted to defame the President of the Republic, I could do so in my writing. And if I find it necessary to refer to his conduct in the vast poem entitled *Canto general de Chile* which I am presently writing, singing of our land and the episodes that formed it, I will do so with the same honor and purity I have dedicated to my political acts.

The President of the Republic, in his writing, which I have no desire to assess here, asserts that my personal letter is the satanic work of the Communist Party, which chose a politically naïve person to sign it. My political naïveté was proved when I directed the publicity for his presidential campaign.

I am responsible for my words, but there is no doubt that the clarity and truth with which they were spoken are charged with the militant spirit of the great, the heroic party of Recabarren.

To all the Communists of Chile, to the women and men who have been mistreated, harassed, and persecuted, I salute you, and I say, "Our party is immortal. It was born from the suffering of the people, and these attacks only ennoble it and swell its ranks."

Last night I listened to the sentence handed down by the Court of Appeals, a woeful victory for the Executive, confirming my impeachment. Pressure has been exerted on the Judiciary, to the extent of minute instructions issued in the commercial columns of *El Mercurio*, and by the entire venal press and radio.

With the honorable exception of a few Ministers, the Court of Appeals has forgotten that the passions of politics must not intrude upon it, that its duty is not to cloak the arbitrary actions of a President of the Republic, but to protect its citizens from attack and abuse.

But who now recalls the decision of the Court in the trial of the subversives of 1920, when it ruled in error on the question of the Peruvian gold? Where is the Peruvian gold today? These judges have poor memories.

So, too, I am sure, this sentence of the Court of Appeals will be buried in oblivion.

No one but the people can impeach me.

When these days of opprobrium for our nation have passed, I shall go to the nitrate pampas. I shall say to the men and women who have witnessed such exploitation, such martyrdom, such betrayal:

Here I am. I promised to be loyal to your life of pain. I promised to defend you with my intellect and with my life if that were necessary. Tell me if I have fulfilled my promise, and either condemn me, or grant me the only mandate I need in order to live with honor— that of your confidence, of your hope, of your love.

And with them once more beneath the sun of those pampas, beneath the sun of Recabarren, I shall sing our National Anthem, because only its words and the struggle of the people can erase the ignominy of these sad days:

> *Sweet land, hear the vows*
> *Chile swore on your altar,*
> *Chile will be a tomb for free men*
> *or an asylum against oppression.*

Letter to His Excellency
Don Carlos Ibáñez del Campo

In my capacity as president of the Society of Chilean Writers, and in defense of the interests and rights of the creators and upholders of Chilean culture, I was pleased to accompany the Governing Board of the Society of Chilean Writers to present before Your Excellency some of the problems of our guild. I had no doubt that we could count on your consideration of initiatives that dignify the practical lives of writers in this land of Gabriela Mistral.

But there was one matter I did not bring up before the honorable President of the Republic—a political and personal problem that has concerned me deeply—since I was charged to speak on matters of great importance and gravity. I scrupulously refrained from mentioning this political matter, in order to keep it separate from my involvement as president of the Society of Chilean Writers, an exclusively cultural organization.

The case is, Your Excellency, that I do not consider myself—nor for practical purposes am I—a citizen of the Republic of Chile, and, therefore, I should not have been granted an interview with Your Excellency or with any other government authority. As my name has been removed from the lists of registered voters, I must be considered an invisible man. As a result, I have serious reservations about my very existence as a citizen. If I am denied the right granted even debased criminals in my country, not to mention our most practiced exploiters, how am I to present myself before a President? And may a President consider the petition of a man who is denied the exercise of his citizenship, which is respected and held sacred even in the most backward nations?

Mr. President, I have been honored in every country I have visited, and I do not wish to recall this recognition except to say that I believe it was awarded directly to my people and my nation. When Maria Casarès and Jean-Louis Barrault gave an emotional reading of my poetry at the Sorbonne in France, or when the town councils of Venice, Turin, Geneva, Naples, and Florence received me in full assembly, I knew that those honors reflected on the name of my distant country. When the mantle of the International Peace Prize and Chile's National Prize for Literature fell on my shoulders, I knew that these distinctions belonged to my people. When my books were translated into almost every language spoken and written in the world today, I thought with pride that through them the history, struggles, thought, and beauty of our country would become better known.

But by none of this, Mr. President, have I been deemed worthy of the vote in Chile. And a delegation of the men who in our nation represent a return to colonialism and unconscionable greed has dared to come before you to ask that I and thousands of citizens be kept in limbo, in the obscurity they demand, in the medieval shadows they desire for all Chileans. These usurpers of old have decided that we shall have no part in the coming elections; they intend to enslave the government of the Republic in order to reinstate, and prolong at any cost, their reign of ignorance and misery.

I want to make it clear, Excellency, that I do not ask for privileged status, and if only my rights as a citizen are reinstated, I will not accept them. This is not the reason for this letter, nor my final aim.

Instead, I dare to ask of Your Excellency that you return our rights as citizens and Chileans to all of us who were unconstitutionally removed from the voting lists. We were deprived of the privilege of participating in the life of the nation by a President to whose election we contributed substantially but who subsequently betrayed all his principles, causing the greatest affront to the freedom and dignity of Chile in this nation's history.

The process of history is so convoluted that it is now my responsibility to ask a President to whose election I did not contribute to rectify these monstrous wrongs. But in spite of this strange turn of events, nothing could be more monstrous than this odious discrimination against the rights of the citizenry, exercised in this instance for the purpose of separating Chilean from Chilean, dividing them, so as to exploit the entire nation.

And nothing could be more reassuring for the continuance of democracy and freedom in our country than immediate action—which today is up to you—to restore the inalienable rights of thousands of patriots, among whom I have the honor and pride to count myself.

May I reiterate my most cordial greetings to the President of the Republic.

Sincerely,

PABLO NERUDA

1958

With the Academy, Yes.
With Imperialism, No.

January 15, 1968

*D*ear Mr. Neruda:

I have the honor to inform you that the members of the American Academy of Arts and Letters and the members of the National Institute of Arts and Letters have elected you to honorary membership in both organizations. Honorary membership in the Academy and in the Institute is reserved, under their By-laws, to artists, writers, and composers, not citizens of the United States, whose services to the arts are gratefully acknowledged by their colleagues in this Republic. I trust we may have the pleasure of conveying to the membership of both bodies your acceptance of their invitation.

We are mailing you under separate cover a copy of the Yearbook of the Academy and of the Institute and a brochure which will explain the function and purposes of these organizations and the rights and privileges of honorary membership.

On receipt of your acceptance of this invitation, the Academy and the Institute will endeavor to arrange through the Department of State for the presentation of the insignia and citation of honorary membership by the American Ambassador.

With assurance of our personal respect, I am,

Faithfully yours,

GEORGE F. KENNAN
President
American Academy of Arts and Letters
National Institute of Arts and Letters

March 12, 1968

Most Esteemed Mr. Kennan:

I deeply regret the delay in replying to your letter of January 15. I was out of Chile during the month of February, and upon my return I hasten to attend to your important communication.

You inform me that the American Academy of Arts and Letters and the National Institute of Arts and Letters have elected me an honorary member of both organizations. I fully understand that this distinction, reserved for foreign artists, writers, and composers, is a great honor and recognition for those who receive it. One has only to read some of the names among the former and more recent honorary members to be fully aware of that fact. I feel, then, both uneasy and honored to find myself and my modest poetry included among such illustrious figures of the past and present as Braque, Chagall, Isak Dinesen, T. S. Eliot, Gide, Malraux, Matisse, Miró, Henry Moore, Nehru, Orozco, Bertrand Russell, Bernard Shaw, Schweitzer, Shostakovich, Villa-Lobos, and H. G. Wells.

I also appreciate the fact that as your members honor me in this way, their recognition, by extension, falls on my country, its culture, and its people. I recognize, too, that the criteria by which the Academy and the Institute select their foreign members have particular significance in the present times. I see this as a reflection of North American thinking, manifested recently in the opposition to the war in Vietnam, which is consistent with the high cultural values of your nation, values exemplified in your institutions.

As I accept this honor, I must make clear my sympathy for the protest of so many North American intellectuals, whose opposition and attitudes I share: in this I represent the majority of the writers, artists, and composers of the Latin American continent.

The earth-shaking events of our age are inseparably bound to our own moral and aesthetic preoccupations, casting a pall over our lives. But the fact that the dignity of intelligence is rising up against aggression on the very site where it was born can only be an inspiration for those who, like myself, uphold reason and humanism over injustice and violence.

Thus, as I accept this high honor from the American Academy and Institute, I must point out that I could not accept either the insignia or the citation from the hands of any ambassador of the United States, or in any office that represents your government.

I would feel deeply honored to receive the citation from the hands of the president of your institutions, or any of their members, among whom I count personal friends I sincerely admire, such as Malcolm Cowley, Arthur Miller, Robert Lowell, and many others. But if this change in the normal procedures of your institutions should create any difficulty, I would be pleased, if that be the case, for you to consider my name for this great honor on a more favorable occasion.

In the meantime, I send heartfelt thanks to the president and the members of the American Academy and National Institute of Arts and Letters, with gratitude for their generous proposal.

With all good wishes.

PABLO NERUDA

March 26, 1968

Dear Mr. Neruda:

I was pleased to receive your letter and your acceptance of honorary membership in the American Academy and the National Institute of Arts and Letters. However, I understand and respect your feelings for not accepting the citation and insignia from our Ambassador to Chile. This does not in any way negate your election.

If you are planning to be in the United States any time in the near future it would be my pleasure to present the insignia and citation to you. If, however, you should be in another country, as near as Mexico, for instance, I might be able to fly down to make the presentation to you there.

Very Sincerely Yours,

GEORGE F. KENNAN

On May 28, 1968, at the annual Ceremonial of the American Academy of Arts and Letters and the National Institute of Arts and Letters, Pablo Neruda was inducted, in absentia, as an Honorary Member, in recognition of his contribution to poetry.

Oh, Springtime, Let Me Be Again among My People

MY beloved fellow citizens:

Let me begin by telling you of my latest travels.

Europe is a contradictory structure whose culture appears to have survived time and war. More than anywhere, I felt welcomed in France, with its eternal example of reason and beauty. Need I say that tears came to my eyes when the King of Sweden, that wise king who has lived ninety years, bestowed on me his golden salute, a medal destined for you, for all Chileans. Because my poetry belongs to my country.

But, in spite of my prolonged travels, it is here, among this multitude of Chileans, that I want to make my confession, which is at the same time a declaration of my confusion.

With your help I want to reason out the cause of this confusion. You are here, supposedly, to receive me, and greet me, and welcome me. And I thank you for it, yes, many thanks, many times over. But the fact is, I feel as if I had never left Chile, as if I had never been away, as if nothing had ever happened to me anywhere but here in this land. My happiness and my sorrow originated here, and remained here behind me. It is as if the wind of this land, the wine of this land, the struggles and dreams of this land reached me where I worked in Paris and there enveloped me night and day—more beautiful than the cathedrals, taller than the Eiffel Tower, more abundant than the waters of the Seine. In short, you are witnessing the return of one who never left Chile.

This speech was delivered at the National Stadium in November 1972, on Neruda's return to Chile after receiving the Nobel Prize

There is a little of everything in this world. There are people born to stay, and others born to go away. There are some who leave because they have a faraway love, or because they like a street, a library, a laboratory, in some other part of the world. I do not criticize them. There were others who felt their pocketbooks were in danger, who fled because they feared an earthquake would strike their bank accounts. I don't criticize them. They will not be greatly missed.

But, for one reason or another, I make a sad exile. In some manner or other, our country goes with me when I travel; the geographical essence of the land lives with me while I am away.

I was born in the heart of Chile; I was raised on the frontier; I spent my youth in Santiago; Valparaiso conquered me; the desert and the pampa opened to me, giving me the oxygen and space my soul required; I traveled the vineyards of the central valley, the sands of Iquique, the valleys of Patagonia, the savage coast of lonely Aysén; and the illustrious cities of Chillán, Valdivia, Talca, Osorno, Iquique, and Antofagasta hold no secrets for me, nor do sleepy towns like Chanco and Quitratué, or Taltal and Villarrica, or Lonquimay and El Quisco. Learning to know my country, singing of it, traveling across it in our struggle, I have divided and multiplied myself while carrying my poetry the length and breadth of our land, to the high country and the lowlands, to the past and to the future we are building.

Many great and small affairs of Chile came to my attention during my two-year absence. Among the most serious was the crushing weight of the cross of foreign debts bequeathed to us by previous governments. And then the defense of our copper, which I was called upon to direct from our Embassy in Paris, against the international pirates who hoped to continue plundering our riches.

But not only great causes and great events touch the heart of one who is far from home. Other things, too, like congratulatory messages from hundreds of friends, known and unknown. The pile of cables and telegrams was so large that I have yet to answer them all. Then there was the package I received from Chile, from a country-woman whom I had never met, containing a *mate* gourd, four avocados, and a half dozen green chili peppers.

During this period the name of Chile has been magnified to an extraordinary degree. The world now sees us as a nation that exists, where formerly we passed unnoticed among a multitude of under-developed countries. For the first time we have a face of our own, and no one in the world dares ignore the magnitude of our struggle to build a national destiny.

France, the whole of Europe, is passionately interested in our affairs. Meetings of the people, student gatherings, books appearing every week in every language: they study us, examine us, analyze us. Every day I must restrain the newspapermen who—and only in the line of duty—want to know everything, or, preferably, more than that. President Allende is universally known. The discipline and strength of our working class are praised and admired. Our armed forces, with their renowned concept of duty, astonish observers of the Latin American scene.

This warm sympathy felt for Chile by foreign nations has been greatly increased as the result of the conflicts over the nationalization of our copper deposits. The world has realized that this is a gigantic step in our nation's new independence. Everyone had been asking how a sovereign nation could place the development of its natural resources in the hands of foreigners.

Without subterfuge of any kind, the Popular Government, in reclaiming our copper for our own nation, established our sovereignty beyond question of doubt.

When a North American company attempted an embargo against Chilean copper, a wave of emotion spread across the whole of Europe. It wasn't only the newspapers, television, and radio that evinced their concern, lending us their support; once again, we were defended by the conscience of a popular majority.

We received many testimonies of loyalty during those difficult times. Let me tell you about three of them that movingly demonstrate the extent of Europe's emotion. You already know that the stevedores of France and Holland refused to unload copper in their ports, as a symbol of their opposition to the aggression against us. This magnificent gesture moved the entire world. Indeed, such acts of solidarity teach us more about the history of our times than lectures at a university: these are the people communicating, coming to know and defend one another. Our defense occasioned even more emotional outpourings: the second day of the embargo, a humble Frenchwoman sent me a 100-franc bill, the fruit of her savings, to aid in the defense of Chilean copper. And a letter from a small town in France was typical of the warm loyalty aroused by Chile's cause. The letter was signed by every inhabitant of the town, from the mayor to the parish priest, all the workers, the athletic teams, and the students of the community.

So, then, the radiance of Chile has followed me, enfolded me, enveloped me. For myself, I have never felt fear before any adversity or pride in any prizes that have come my way. But I have felt fear and pride as they affected the image of my country. As I felt proud, so far away, of the importance we were acquiring in European eyes, I also feared the lack of understanding, the actual menace, that lurks both inside and outside our nation.

I know that there are Chileans who want to draw us toward a confrontation, toward civil war. And although it is not my purpose in this place and at this time to enter the arena of politics, I have a duty as a poet, as a politician and patriot, to warn all Chile of this danger. As writer and citizen, my role has always been to unify Chileans. But now I am saddened to see you intent on harming one another. If Chile, if the body of Chile, were wounded, my poetry would bleed. It cannot be.

While in France, I read in a newspaper that a certain politician, an ardent advocate of civil war, had uttered this memorable phrase: "It won't matter if we have to rebuild Chile beginning from zero." This bizarre man plans to spill everyone's blood, the blood of all Chileans except his own, in order to begin from zero and see that others—not he—rebuild his private fortune. But civil war is a grave matter. We must take measures to insure that the agitation that sets brother against brother does not grow or prosper. Orderly progress often imposes serious sacrifices: but this is the traditional, if revolutionary, road of our history, and we will follow it. The struggle for justice does not mandate spilling blood on our flag.

I witnessed one civil war, and it was a struggle so cruel and so painful that it marked my life and my poetry forever. More than a million dead! Blood spattered the walls of my home; I saw bombed buildings collapse, and, through shattered windows, saw men, women, and children mangled by shrapnel. I have seen men kill men who were born to be their brothers, men who spoke the same tongue, who were children of the same land. I do not want this destiny to befall my nation.

That is why I want to call upon the sanest and most humane Chileans to band together to put straitjackets on the mad and inhumane men who would lead us into civil war.

You have seen how foreign interests intrigue and bring pressure outside our country to belittle the triumphs of our Popular Government. You must realize that the threads of any international conspiracy woven by these same powerful interests pass through our land. We now know that the assassination of a glorious soldier, General Schneider, was plotted outside our country. To our shame, the hands of the assassins were Chilean hands.

Eighty years ago, the powerful European companies that dominated Chile in that era provoked a civil war. They fanned to the point of frenzy the dissent between the Parliament and the President. Among the victims of that war is counted a great and generous President, José Manuel Balmaceda. He was mocked, threatened, ridiculed, and insulted, until he was driven to suicide. Although history then was written by the enemies of Balmaceda, his name has since been washed clean by the people of Chile, and he has been restored to his rightful place as a visionary leader and patriot.

I believe that the present stage of our history resembles others in our past. We will live difficult hours in Chile, President Allende has said, as we undertake this arduous journey to affirm before the entire world our sovereignty and our principles.

Similarly, after 1810, after we proclaimed our national independence, Chile had to survive great and small problems as well as the attacks of those who hoped to return to Spanish colonialism. But the Republic asserted itself under the leadership of O'Higgins, Carrera, Manuel Rodríguez, Freire, Camilo Henríquez, and the ragged, barefoot patriots who fought at Rancagua, Chacabuco, Maipo, on the roads, on the seas, and in the cordilleras of Chile.

History teaches us that we are marching forward, that the liberation of the people is being fulfilled, in spite of everything.

I want to end my remarks by thanking the Vice President of the Republic for his welcoming words, and for his presence here; General Prats has greatly honored me. I do not find it strange that a soldier and a poet should stand before the people in this huge open-air ceremony. It is known at home and abroad that our Vice President guarantees the security of our constitution and our national self-respect.* But his strength and his nobility go beyond these concepts:

---

* Pablo Neruda's faith in General Carlos Prats's strong support of democratic institutions was later validated by history. Shortly before the military coup against the constitutional government of Salvador Allende, and under pressure from those who conspired against that government, General Prats resigned his position. Neruda wrote him the following letter:

Isla Negra, August 31, 1973

Most esteemed General:
  You may have resigned, but for the great majority of Chileans you will always be General in Chief and an exemplary citizen.
  The incitement to crime and sedition is rooted in the distant past of Chile's history. When the Republic was still in swaddling clothes, in 1811, the traitorous Tomás de Figueroa rose up in arms against our newborn Republic. The descendants of his supporters still venerate his memory: a street in Santiago, in Las Condes, bears his name. This says it all.
  One cannot watch without anguish the blind persistence of those who want to lead us to the disaster of a fratricidal war with no goal other than the conservation of feudal privileges exhausted by history, and by the irreversible course of human progress. This progress is the hope of Chile and of the world.
  As, with the sacrifice of your brilliant career, you confronted the possibilities of a civil struggle, you have underscored not only the nobility of your character but the depths of your patriotism. Accept the salutation, admiration, and loyalty of

                                                        PABLO NERUDA

General Prats responded:

Santiago, September 4, 1973

Most distinguished Don Pablo:
  A thousand thanks for the encouragement and support expressed in your letter of August 31, which strengthened the tranquillity of conscience I feel now that I have become an ordinary citizen; my decision was made in reaction to the baseness and moral cowardice which, it is to be regretted, have come to be the basis for the acts of those who hope to repeat in Chile the story of *The Leopard.*
  I shall remember as one of the most edifying moments that destiny has afforded me the invitation by the President of the Republic to represent our nation's sentiments at the homage rendered our great Chilean poet, honored with the Nobel Prize for Literature.
  I want to express my best wishes for a speedy recovery of your health,

his morality is the basis of our affection for the armed forces of Chile, for those on land, sea, and in the air who bear, along with the intense colors of our flag, the peaceful continuity of a glorious tradition.

In my poems I celebrated the heroes who with bloody willows wove the cradle of the nation. I sang of their deeds, their impassioned, often sorrowful, lives. Blended in my poetry are love for our land and reverence for those who with their valor and sacrifice established the bases for our Republic. And I recognize in this General in Chief of the Republic, as in all the armed forces of Chile, the grandeur of our historic past and the incorruptible loyalty with which they have defended the lawful processes of our sovereignty and our democracy.*

The soldiers of Chile are present in this great stadium. They are identified with the geography of Chile, and on mountain and highway, in the cities and on the frontiers, in rain, sand, desert, and in danger, they are the eternal guards of the endeavors and tranquillity of every Chilean.

And delegations of the people are here today. My greetings to each and every one: the petroleum workers from Magallanes, the construction workers from Santiago, the nitrate miners from Tarapacá, the stonemasons from Coquimbo, the copper miners from Antofagasta, the textile workers from Concepción, the merchants from Valparaiso, the grape growers from Curicó, the sugarcane growers from Linares, the fishermen from Chiloé, the bargemen from Maule, the dairy workers from Osorno, and our comrades from Polpaico.

To the women who have come here bearing testimony of their

---

because Chile needs—towering above the political trenches—the force of intellectual values you symbolize, so that reason and sanity will once again reign in this beautiful nation, so that its people may achieve the social justice they so richly deserve.

I repeat my gratitude for your loyalty, and want to express my deep personal appreciation.

CARLOS PRATS GONZÁLEZ

After the military coup, General Prats was driven from Chile, and on September 30, 1974, he was assassinated in Buenos Aires.

* Until the coup of September 11, 1973, Neruda's perception of "the incorruptible loyalty" of the armed forces of Chile was shared by the vast majority of the population.

tenderness, you have the homage of a poet who owes to you the inspiration for each of his books.

To the young people who have lent color, liveliness, and joy to this marvelous celebration, I give this message: I have sung the praises of our nation. Your task is to sustain and ennoble it, to make it more just, more generous, and more beautiful every day.

To the children who have come by the hundreds to this stadium: since I cannot give you a star, I leave a kiss for every one.

Not a few poets have received distinctions such as National Prizes, or even the Nobel Prize. But perhaps none has received this supreme laurel, this crown to his work—the delegations of a whole nation, a whole people. Your attendance not only moves me to the bottom of my heart, it indicates that I may not have been mistaken in the direction of my poetry.

Years ago, while far from Chile in an enforced exile, desolate over the distance that separated me and with no hope of returning, I wrote these lines:

> *Oh, Chile, long petal*
> *of sea and wine and snow,*
> *oh when*
> *oh when and when*
> *oh when*
> *will I be home again?*
> *The sash of your*
> *black-white foam will encircle my waist*
> *and my poetry*
> *will flood your land.*
>
> *My people, truly, in the springtime*
> *does my name echo in your ears,*
> *do you recognize*
> *in me a river*
> *flowing past your door?*
>
> *I am a river. If you strain*
> *to hear beneath the mines*
> *of Antofagasta, to*
> *the south of Osorno*
> *or the cordillera in Melipilla,*

in Temuco, in a night
of dewy stars and rustling laurel,
if you place your ear to the ground
you will hear me flowing,
submerged and singing.
October, oh springtime,
let me be again among my people!

What shall I do if I cannot see
our men and women,
if I cannot bear on my shoulders
my share of hope?
If I cannot carry the flag
handed down from man to man
in our long struggle,
finally to reach my hands?

Oh patria, patria,
oh native land, when
and when and when,
when
will I be home again?

Even far from you
I am still
part of you, your son,
and today, again, it's springtime.
But I have crowned myself with your flowers,
I go forward with your victory on my brow,
in you my roots are growing still.

Oh when
will the green thunder of your ocean
wake me from my dream?
Oh when, patria, at election time
will I go from house to house
leading timid freedom by the hand
to shout in the middle of the street?
Oh when, my native land,
will you be wed with me,

with sea-green eyes and snowy gown,
when will our numberless children
bequeath the earth to those who hunger?

When, oh native land, new-clad,
when, oh springtime,
oh when and when
will I waken in your arms,
sea-sprayed and wet with dew?
When I stand beside you,
when I take you by the waist,
no one will harm you,
I will defend you,
singing,
when I walk with you, when
you walk with me,
ah, when?

Well, my fellow citizens, my friends, my comrades, all these things have come to pass—my return, all the verses of "When."

I will go from house to house in the March elections.

This morning I was awakened by the marine thunder of Isla Negra.

The land has passed from the hands of the glutted to the hands of the hungry.

In this ceremony with its whistles and drums I seem once again to have wed my native land. And you must not believe that this is a marriage of convenience. It is a case of love, the great love of my life.

My thanks, men and women of Chile, companions, friends: thank you for your friendship, for your affection, for the recognition you will in time give to poets to come.

Because life and struggle and poetry will live when I am but a tiny memory in the radiant history of Chile.

Thank you, because you are the people, the best of the world, the salt of the earth.

Thank you.

A Few Words among Friends

Esteemed candidate of the people:

I have delivered many speeches in the North, South, East, and West of Chile on behalf of your candidacy, on behalf of the ideas and ideals that give it meaning, direction, goals. I have spoken before miners, farmers, and citizens of every walk of life.

Today I want to say a few words among friends, a conversation in the bosom of the family.

For the first time, we writers and artists will have a true friend—no, more, a close relative—in the presidential palace. Somewhere in that building, according to the propaganda of another candidate, sits an empty chair, a kind of throne that according to his publicity awaits him. In general, we writers and artists, we so-called intellectuals, have been isolated from the presidency of the Republic; we have likened that office to an empty throne, a seat without an occupant. Occasionally, we thought we glimpsed a human being, a Chilean with a real and profound concern for Chile. But quickly we'd see that it was the same old face of indifference, superficiality, and cruelty. I do not intend to name names. Our purpose is not to point to a vacuum but to evoke hope.

This hope is not excessive, it is not blind hope, it threatens no one. We merely ask that we be considered, that our right to exist, to grow, and to create, be recognized. Small countries, tossed by geography into the most remote convolutions of the planet, have a single destiny with which to combat misfortune, and this destiny is bound

---

Written during the presidential campaign of Salvador Allende

to their spiritual creation, to the strength of their culture. This is their great weapon.

Currently, a huge mass of iron and steel is being dismantled without ever having been used to fire on, to exterminate anyone in the defense of our flag. The most powerful weapon in the history of Chile was considerably less expensive and of considerably less tonnage: it was a small and fragile woman bowed down by concerns of intelligence and existence; her name was Gabriela Mistral.

I know that Gabriela, even after she received the Nobel Prize, lived in fear and trembling for her post, victimized by the Ministry of Culture, awaiting the slash of the claw, attack, reprisal. This permanent loss of confidence affected her personality, it changed her, made her reticent, like those wind-buffeted trees of Patagonia that she wrote about in her poetry—to a degree, drawing her self-portrait.

We do not expect preferential treatment. We do not contemplate a court of crowned thinkers, favored by dynamic intellectual power. But in full awareness of the contribution that artists and writers make to the development and the honor of our nation, we demand consideration of our lives and our problems, assurance that the young may continue their creative development without opposition. But we know—and that is why we are here—that, first and foremost, our people must be elevated to the life of human dignity they deserve. And in this struggle, in this aggressive conviction, we feel we are represented by Salvador Allende.

Salvador, I accompanied you on your tour of the hamlets of the North. Together we ate bread baked for you by the countrywomen of Paihuano. We were together in Monte Grande, where the valleys of the Elqui join together. Farther up are shards of stone, walls of rock and thorns. Farther down, the waters sing and buds are beginning to stir.

But more imposing than nature, more promising than the green, warm, silent valleys, are our people, our Chilean men and women, our forsaken farmers and miners of Norte Chico. You will never forget, Salvador—nor can I—the people who came down from the mountains carrying small flags to greet you, the thousands of women and barefoot children who filled the plaza in Vicuña that night. They had come long distances to gather there—sure, strong, symbols of the neglect, but also of the hope, of our people. As solemn as statues there beneath the trees of the plaza of Vicuña, they represented the strength and tenderness of Chile.

We asked one another that night, looking at those young barefoot girls in the land of their birth, how many Gabrielas, how many, must there be here and in other cities, towns, mountains, and ports of our nation?

We artists and writers have much to ask of, much to say to, the new President of Chile. We have work to do, and we do not want to leave it to him, nor do we want him to leave it to us alone. Some problems are vital to us, problems of conscience. These are the problems of our nation, and they come before those of our profession.

First, we must wipe out illiteracy! We don't want to continue to write for a people that can't read. We don't want to feel the shame, the ignominy, of a static and vulgarized past. We want more schools, more teachers, more newspapers, more books, more magazines, more culture.

This regime of lords surrounded by servants and pedants and the poor cannot continue. The crisis is upon us; this way of life is outmoded in the world. We know that there are parties that want to conserve the old ways, and they are, cynically, called conservatives, or, deceptively, liberals. But we are prepared for a battle to the death with the past—not the illustrious past whose continuity we represent; no, we will preserve the best of the past, but we will kill the canker of the past, and that canker is called ignorance, backwardness, neglect.

We believe—and when I say we, I mean all the forces that sustain this hope—we believe passionately in the creative potential of the people of Chile. We believe in the intelligence of the people, in their skill, in their uprightness, in their courage. The people of Chile represent a boundless terrain whose fertility and flowering we must hasten.

President-to-be of Chile: I hope that you will often call on writers and artists, and that once in power you will talk with us, and listen. You will always find in us the greatest loyalty to the destiny of our nation, and the greatest selflessness.

We have a single interest, shared by you: to give dignity to our people. In this context we say to you that this struggle you head today is older than Chile: it is the glorious battle of the Araucan

Indians against the invaders; it is the thought that inspired the flags, the battalions, the declarations of our Independence; it is movement for the advancement of the people led by Francisco Bilbao. And even closer to us, Recabarren was not only the greatest proletarian of the Americas, he was also a writer of plays and pamphlets.

The intellectuals of Chile have been witness to the drama, the tragedies, and the victories of our people.

We stand beside you on this occasion, and we proclaim you our candidate for the presidency of the Republic of Chile, because we believe, firmly and joyously, that you will never abandon this path.

In victory, standing beside you, will be all those who fell: infinite sacrifice and bloodshed, agony and sorrow, that could not deter our struggle. Standing beside you, too, is the present—a broader and more secure awareness of truth and history.

And last, also by your side, are the impressive victories already scored, and the inevitable liberation of all peoples.

Pablo Neruda Speaks

The Poet Is Not a Rolling Stone

THE Rector has spoken magnificently, and I want to reiterate what he said about the relationship of the poet to his people.

I am, once again, that poet.

I say once again, because throughout history it has been the duty of poets to insure this relationship. To fulfill it with devotion, with suffering, with joy.

The first stage of a poet's life must be devoted to absorbing the essences of his native land; later, he must return them. He must restore them, he must repay them. His poetry and his actions must contribute to the maturity and growth of his people.

The poet cannot be torn from his land except by force. Even in these circumstances, his roots must stretch across the ocean deeps, his seed follow the flight of the wind, again to become flesh in his homeland. He must be rationally and reflexively national, maturely patriotic.

The poet is not a rolling stone. He has two sacred obligations: to leave and to return.

The poet who leaves and doesn't return becomes a cosmopolite. As a cosmopolite he is scarcely a man, he is barely a reflection of a dying light. Above all in solitary lands like our own, isolated in the wrinkles and folds of the planet, as indispensable witnesses to the emergence of our people, all of us, from the most humble to the most proud, have the good fortune to attend the birth of our nation—each of us in a small way father to it.

I have collected these books from the world's cultures, these sea-

This speech was delivered at the dedication ceremonies of the Pablo Neruda Foundation for the Study of Poetry at the University of Chile, Santiago, June 20, 1954

shells from all the oceans, and I give this seafoam from the Seven Seas to the university as an act of conscience, as well as to repay to a small degree what I have received from my people. This university was not founded by decree, but was born of man's struggle; and its tradition of progress, renewed today by its Rector, Gómez Millas, comes from the upheavals of our history and is the star of our flag. This progress will continue. Some future day, as a consequence of long-awaited changes, it will be an expansive university of the people. I have gathered these books from everywhere in the world. They have traveled as much as I, but many have lived four or five centuries longer than my own fifty years. Some were given to me in China; I bought others in Mexico. I found hundreds in Paris. Some of the most valuable come from the Soviet Union. All of them are a part of my life, of my personal geography. It was a work of long patience to search for them, an indescribable pleasure when I found them, and they have served me well with their wisdom and beauty. From now on they will serve many more, demonstrating the generous nature of books.

When in the course of time someone reads these titles, he will not know what to think of the person who collected them, nor will he be able to decide why many of them were added to the collection.

Here is a small *Almanach de Gotha* from the year 1838. These Gotha almanacs kept current the titles of senile aristocracies, the names of royal houses. They were the catalogues of Vanity Fair.

I have the book because of one line, lost in the tiny print, which says: "12th of February 1837. The Russian poet Alexander Pushkin dies as a result of a duel." This line stabs me like a dagger. World poetry still bleeds from this wound.

Here is the *Romancero gitano* inscribed by another murdered poet. Federico wrote its magnanimous dedication in my presence, and Paul Eluard, also dead now, left his signature on the first page of this book.

They seemed eternal to me. They seem eternal. But they are gone.

One night in Paris I was being entertained by my friends. That great French poet came to the party bearing treasures in his hands. One was a clandestine edition of Victor Hugo, persecuted in his time by a petty tyrant. And he brought me something else, perhaps the most precious thing I have—two letters in which Isabelle Rimbaud, writing from a hospital in Marseilles, tells her mother of her brother's death.

These letters are the most heartrending testimony I have ever known. Paul said to me as he gave me the letters: "See how the last words are missing; it says only, 'What Arthur wants . . .' and the part that follows has never been found. And that was Rimbaud. No one will ever know what he wanted."

Here are the two letters.

Here, too, is my first Garcilaso, which I bought with unforgettable emotion for five pesetas. The date is 1549. Here is a magnificent edition of Góngora from the Flemish publisher Foppens, printed in the seventeenth century, when poets' books were incomparably majestic. Although it cost only a hundred pesetas in the Madrid bookshop of García Rico, I paid for it in monthly installments of ten pesetas. I still remember the expression of astonishment on García Rico's face—that wondrous bookseller who looked like a peasant from Castile—when I asked him to sell me the book on time.

And here are two first editions of my favorite Golden Age poets: *El desengaño de amor en rimas* (*Love's Lost Illusions in Verse*), by Pedro Soto de Rojas, and the nocturnal poetry of Francisco de Latorre:

> *Bright lights of heaven, bright*
> *eyes in the awesome face of night,*
> *bright crown, bright Cassiopeia,*
> *Perseus and Andromeda . . .*

So many books! So many things! The past will live on here. I remember when we lived with Rafael Alberti in Paris, beside the Seine. We were discussing once how ours is the age of realism, the age of fat poets.

"Enough of thin poets, anyway!" Rafael declared in his cheerful Cádiz voice. "Romanticism produced more than enough skinny poets."

We wanted to be fat like Balzac and not thin like Bécquer. On the ground floor of our house was a bookshop, and there, pressed against the shop window, were the complete works of Victor Hugo. When we went out, we'd pause at the window and measure ourselves.

"How fat are you?"

"About as fat as *Les Travailleurs de la mer*. And you?"

"No bigger than *Notre Dame de Paris*."

Some will also ask one day why there are so many books on animals and plants. The answer is in my poetry.

Besides, books on zoology and botany have always fascinated me. They have kept me a child. They brought to me the boundless world, the infinite labyrinth, of nature. These books on exploring our earth have been my favorites, and it is rare that I go to sleep without gazing at plates of glorious birds or dazzling insects as intricate as clockwork.

But it is little that I am giving, that I am returning, that I place in the hands of the Rector and, through him, bequeath to the patrimony of the nation. These gifts are, in short, personal and universal fragments of knowledge captured in my voyage through the world. I give them to you. I am not of those families that preach pride of lineage on all sides and then auction off their past.

The splendor of these books, the oceanic flora of these seashells, everything I amassed in my lifetime, despite poverty and by constant hard work, I give to the university—that is, to everyone.

One word more.

My generation, in reaction against the decadent exquisiteness of the moment, was anti-book and anti-literature. We were sworn enemies of vampirism, of the night world, of spiritual opiates. We were children of nature.

Nevertheless, nature reflects the unity of knowledge; intelligence reveals the most remote or simple relationships among things; and then unity and relationship, nature and man, are translated into books.

I am not an intellectual, and these books reflect more reverence than investigation. I have collected the beauty that dazzled me, and the subterranean labor of conscience that led me to the light. But I have also loved these books as precious objects, sacred foam of the course of time, essential fruit of man. Now they will belong to countless new eyes.

Here they will fulfill their destiny of giving and receiving light.

It Is Worthwhile to Have
Lived, Because I Have Love

M ANY years ago, walking in the wilderness along Lake Ranco, I thought I had come upon the source of this land of mine, or the sylvan cradle of poetry, attacked and protected by all nature.

The sky was sharply outlined against the towering treetops of the cypresses, the air stirred the balmy fragrance of the forest depths, everything had a voice—the whisper of hidden birds, falling fruit and branches that disturbed the foliage—but for a moment everything stopped in an instant of silent, secret solemnity; everything in the forest seemed to be waiting. A birth was imminent, and what was being born was a river. I don't know its name, but its headwaters, virgin and dark, were barely visible, feeble and silent, searching for an outlet among the great fallen tree trunks and colossal rocks.

A thousand years of leaves had fallen at its origin, all the past tried to hold it back, but merely perfumed its flow. The new river dissolved the old dead leaves and thrived on the nurturing coolness it would spread along its path.

And I thought: this is how poetry is born. It comes from invisible heights, it is secret and dark in its origins, solitary and fragrant, and like the river it will assimilate whatever falls in its current; it will seek a route between the mountains, and its crystalline song will ripple through the meadows.

Poetry will water the fields and give bread to the hungry. It will meander through the ripe wheat. Pilgrims will slake their thirst in it, and it will sing whenever men struggle and when they are at rest.

This speech was delivered at the University of Chile on the poet's fiftieth birthday, July 12, 1954

And then it will unite them, and it will flow among them, founding peoples. It will hew valleys, carrying to roots the propagation of life.

Poetry is song and fertility.

Poetry emerged from its secret womb and flows, fertilizing and singing. It kindles energy with its swelling waters, it works at milling flour, tanning hides, cutting wood, giving light to cities. It is useful, and awakens to find banners along its banks: festivals are celebrated beside the singing water.

I remember one day in Florence when I visited a factory to read my poems before a group of workers. I read with all the modesty a man from a young continent may experience beneath the shadow of the sacred presence hovering there. After my reading, the factory workers gave me a gift. I have it still. It is a 1484 edition of Petrarch.

The waters of poetry had flowed, had sung, in that factory, and had flowed through the workers' lives for centuries. Petrarch, whom I always imagined hooded like a monk, was but another simple Italian, and the book I took in my hands with such reverence acquired a new prestige in my eyes. It was a divine tool in the hands of man.

So I think that if many of my countrymen and some illustrious men and women from other nations have come to attend these ceremonies, they come to celebrate in my person the responsibility of poets and the universal growth of poetry.

I am content simply that we are gathered here. It pleases me to think that what I have done and what I have written has brought us closer together. It is the first duty of the humanist and the fundamental task of intelligence to ensure knowledge and understanding among men. It is worthwhile to have struggled and to have sung, it is worthwhile to have lived, because I have love.

I know that in this land isolated by an immense sea and deep snows you are not honoring me but rather a victory for man. Because if these soaring mountains, if once these pitiless waves of the Pacific tried to prevent my nation's voice from being heard in the world, if they opposed the struggle of the people and the universal unity of culture, now these mountains and this great ocean have been conquered.

In this remote nation, my people and my poetry have fought for communication and friendship.

And this university that greets us in fulfillment of its intellectual responsibilities consecrates a victory of the human community and reaffirms the honor of Chile's star.

Rubén Darío lived beneath our Antarctic star. He came from the marvelous tropics of our Americas, and perhaps on a blue and white winter's day like today he reached Valparaiso, to renew Spanish-language poetry.

On this day my thoughts and my respect are with his starry magnitude, with the crystalline magic that will never cease to bedazzle us.

Last night, among my first gifts, Laura Rodig brought me a treasure I unwrapped with intense emotion. It was the first draft of Gabriela Mistral's *Sonetos de la muerte* (*Sonnets of Death*), written in pencil in 1914 and covered with corrections in her powerful handwriting.

I believe that these sonnets rise to the heights of the eternal snows, and rumble beneath the ground, echoing Quevedo.

I remember Gabriela Mistral and Rubén Darío as Chilean poets, and as a poet reaching his fiftieth year, I want to recognize in them the ageless eternity of true poetry.

I am indebted to them, and to everyone who wrote before me in every language. To list them would take too long; their constellation fills the sky.

Greetings, and Let the Dance Begin

My dear young people gathered here from every nation.

Allow me to present to you the games and dances, the sad and happy songs, the impishness and essence, of the American peoples.

The Aztecs left us their seed, their harvest songs, their war hymns, their rituals of peace. The Mayans planted their flowery fire across the slender waist of Central America.

The Araucans danced beneath their protective trees.

The Spanish left a ribbon of sighs, the happy tunes of mountainous villages, and the language in which for centuries the struggles, illusions, and dark dramas of our people, their unbelievable stories, have unfolded.

In Brazil roared the most powerful rivers of the continent, singing and telling stories. Men and women hummed to one another and danced beneath the palm trees. From Portugal came honey-sweet sounds, and the voice of Brazil was steeped in jungle depths and citrus blossoms by the sea.

These are the songs and dances of America.

On our continent, hope was often submerged in blood and shadow; the people seemed drained, their hearts shattered by waves of terror; still, we sang.

Lincoln was assassinated, freedom seemed to die with him; still, black men sang along the banks of the Mississippi. Theirs was a song of sorrow that has not yet ended, a profound song, a song with roots.

This message was sent to a youth festival in Warsaw, July 22, 1965

In our South, on the great pampas, only the moon lighted the prairies, the moon and the guitars.

In high Peru, the Indians sang like rushing mountain streams.

On all the continent, man saved his songs, protected them with the strength of his arm, the peace of his pleasures; he kept alive the ancient traditions, the radiance and gentleness of his festivals, the testimony of his sorrow.

I present to you the treasure of our people, their grace, all they have preserved in spite of terrible trials, abandonment, and martyrdom.

The happiness, songs, and dances of all America shine in this festival of youth and peace, along with the joys, the songs, and the dances of other peoples.

From the most distant of America's countries, from Chile, separated from the world by the towering Andes and joined to all countries by its ocean and the history of its struggle, I bring greetings to the young people of the festival and I say to them:

Our songs rose higher than our mountains, and they will be heard here; our dances were more persistent than the ocean waves, and will be presented here. Let us defend this delicate strength, let us defend the unity of love and peace that kept them alive. This is the duty of all men, the central treasure of peoples, the light of this festival.

Greetings, and let the dance begin.

A Guest in Caracas

I never dreamed so great an honor might be conferred on my poetry, on this wanderer's songs. As these celebrated Venezuelan prizes are being awarded, I am grateful for such a distinction. The honor is made even greater by the words of the renowned poet Juan Liscano. I will not try to protest the dithyramb of a brother. I will treasure it, examine myself in its mirror and continue to be true to the dignity of poetry and the inseparable struggle of the people.

This morning I drove down from Mount Avila. High above Caracas lies the city's green crown, its dewy emeralds, but the city itself had disappeared. It had been obliterated by a conjurer's veil of powdery flour, vapor, and heaven's handkerchiefs, and we were forced to search for the lost city, to enter it from the skies, and find it finally amid the mists clinging to the cordillera—a city of tall buildings, intricate, tentacular and noisy, a buzzing beehive erected by the will of man. The eagle eyes of its founders chose this wrinkled valley in which to establish the springtime of Caracas. And then time brought as well the beauty of houses whose wrought iron preserves silence, along with buildings of pure geometry and light, where the future resides. A true American, I first salute the glittering city, then, with equal warmth, the hills of the people, the alleyways colorful as flags, the avenues opening to every highway of the world. And I salute its history, never forgetting that from the womb of this city surged the torrential and heroic waters of the river of American independence.

I salute Caracas, a city of strong and enduring peoples, of heritages

---

This speech was delivered before the Town Council of Caracas, February 4, 1959

340

so powerful they are constantly renewed, city of liberation and intelligence, city of Bolívar and Bello, city of martyred lives and new beginnings, city which on a January 23 recently harvested from the grains of time shone like the dawn across the Caribbean, for all our beloved and sorrowing America!

But all this beauty and history, the laurels and the archives, the windows and the children, the blue buildings, the cherry-colored smile of a beautiful city—all this can disappear. A handful of infernal essence, of unchained energy, can demolish its buildings and lives and reduce them to ashes, a handful of atoms can destroy Caracas and Buenos Aires, Lima and Santiago, a powerful New York, a silvery Leningrad.

Descending from the peaks and contemplating the throbbing beauty of the city that now confers on me the honor of being its friend, I thought of the destruction that threatens us. That threatens everything created by man, and whose accursed stigma will hound his descendants, and I thought that as the town councils of America were the cradle of our liberty, it is they that now or in the future should sound the warning against nuclear death, and thus protect not only our city but every city, not only our lives but man's survival on the earth.

Once again, I thank the Town Council of the city of Caracas for its fraternal welcome. Thank you, because your approval authorizes me to continue on my course of defending love, clarity, justice, happiness, and peace—that is to say, poetry.

The Nocturnal Washerwoman

I may be fulfilling the dream of all poets of all times. They have hoped to join and be joined with, to embrace and to address, women more than men.

This is something every poet has wanted—Greek, Italian, German, Norwegian, Persian, Spanish, or French. And fate has disposed that I, a humble poet from the far ends of the earth, in a single day, in a single hour, be together with more women than all those poets combined had dreamed of.

My brother poets, die with envy!

Especially because we are talking about my intelligent, gracious, patient, spirited, and beautiful compatriots, Chilean women. And as you have done me the honor of coming to listen to my verses and my words, I count myself favored by good fortune, but not unworthy of it.

I accept the honor of being a prophet in my own country, although I wished no more than to be a poet of my land and my people.

But I say with all sincerity that it was not I who produced this miracle: history produced it, the changing times, the inexorable advance of humankind. This rendezvous of a poet with the women of Chile could not have taken place before. It is a sign of the times.

From the most remote ages, women have listened to men's secrets: warriors, governors, rebels, great and tormented artists, conquerors and conquered, heroes and villains. The prayers of priests sought a

---

This speech was delivered before a women's congress held in the Caupolicán Theater in Santiago

woman's intercession to reach heaven. Musicians, sculptors, painters, and writers verified the incomparable beauty, the sublime maternity, the love, sorrow, and heroism of our beloved companion. But through centuries of praise, woman continued in the dark ages, exploited, martyred, and forgotten by a harsh and brutal society that even debated in council whether or not a woman had a soul.

The truth is that woman's soul had long illuminated the world.

This was a tragic period of bloodshed and violence, of incense and basilicas, of wars in which men fought one another like larvae. Conquest, invasion, conflagration filled the Middle Ages. The chivalric romance made of woman a gilded myth, an untouchable star that knights-errant must conquer by dint of sword and poetry. Woman was unattainable, alien to reality and truth.

This repression lasted for centuries, and was overcome only to the degree that woman began to take part in men's struggles, placing herself at his level, even surpassing him in self-denial, in valor, in greatness.

History has proved that the struggle is the same for men and women, for black and white, for believer and nonbeliever. It is a universal struggle to improve the human condition so that justice will be within the grasp of all the exploited. Naturally, then, woman shares in this universal struggle.

The mother is the first stage in the future of the child. At the beginning, mother and light are a single entity. The child's life, the man's life, is but a continuation of that light.

I had not one but two mothers. I have recounted on other occasions how my mother died shortly after giving me life. She died in Parral, of tuberculosis. She was a schoolteacher. My father, a railroad man, married again. So I had my own, and a second, mother.

But the world we live in needs more than selfless and long-dead mothers like the one I resurrected from the depths of my heart in order to feel her presence in this room.

This important woman is nameless except to a very few. She is unknown, but her name is "mother." Enveloped in silence, she is called "wife," and later, "grandmother"—never known except to those who had that honor and that love, that unrecognized honor and that often poorly repaid love. Because women know ingratitude as the sailor knows the sea and the farmer knows the land. And as in the case of the sea and the land, ingratitude is always unexpected: just when every possibility has been foreseen, one more blow falls— storm or earthquake.

Years ago, when we were living in Santiago, Matilde and I used to sit at night looking out over the city from above. Below our house— in a neighboring street of which we had only a partial view—every night, as if a participant in some rite, a washerwoman appeared with two candles and a tub. Punctually, from nine until late at night, that woman scrubbed and scrubbed her washing. We were never able to see her face. She was a silhouette stooped beneath the night, beneath the weight of the night, between the flames of two tiny flickering candles. If I had been one of the poets of the past who loved beauty for beauty's sake, and art for art's, I would have celebrated that ritual washerwoman in the figure of a priestess presiding over her temple of foam, her vestments, and religious veils.

But I, a poet of our times, saw in that washerwoman not a ritual but a sorrowful reality, the lives of millions of women of our enormous, forsaken America. The same candles, at the same hour, winter or summer, might also be lighting the harsh duties of a mother in Ecuador, Bolivia, or Venezuela. From the Orinoco to Patagonia, from the sumptuous volcanoes that were nature's gift to us, to the gigantic thorny cactus of the Mexican plateau, that washerwoman, that nocturnal woman washing clothes while her children slept, was for me the dark heroine of our people. I never met her, and perhaps she never knew I watched her from the darkness of my home. To her I dedicated these lines:

> From the garden, high above,
> I watched the washerwoman.
> It was night.
> She washed, she splashed,
> she scrubbed,
> for a moment her hands
> glittered in the suds,
> then
> disappeared in shadow.
> Seen from above
> in the light of her candle

she was the only living thing
in the night,
the only thing alive:
something
shuddering
in the suds,
arm-deep in washing,
movement,
untiring energy:
up and down
movement,
falling, rising
with celestial precision,
submerged hands
up and down,
hands, old hands
washing in the night,
late into the night,
washing
other people's clothes,
hands in the water
removing the signs
of work,
the stain
of bodies,
the ground-in memory
of weary feet,
of worn-out
shirts,
of faded
shorts,
she washes,
washes
in the night.

From time to time
the nocturnal
washerwoman
lifts
her head

and stars blaze
in her hair;
the shadow
blurred
her head,
it was the night, the sky
of night
the washerwoman's
hair,
her candle
a tiny
star
that set afire
the hands
that lifted,
swished
the clothes,
rising,
falling,
hoisting
air
and water,
glowing soap,
magnetic suds.

I couldn't hear,
couldn't hear
the whisper
of the clothing in her hands.
My eyes
in the night
saw only her,
alone,
a planet.
She blazed,
the nocturnal
washerwoman,
washing,
scrubbing
the clothes,
working

in the cold,
the harsh night air,
washing in nocturnal winter silence,
washing, washing,
poor
washerwoman.

Poetry Is Rebellion

I have never known, Señor Rector, how to be eloquent in my appreciation. The world's magnitude, knowledge, acknowledgment, the joy of a gift received, smooth as a comet's passing, all this and much more is contained within a single phrase. When one says thank you, many other words are included that come from times long past or present, from as far away as the origins of man, from as near as the secret beating of one's heart.

So it is that with my thanks I want to express and encompass the movement, the surroundings, the unmarked roads, perhaps the inevitability, that causes me to return continually in my life and in my poetry to these frontiers in the rainswept South, to these great rivers of my homeland, to the generous silence of these lands and these men.

If I learned a poetics, if I studied a rhetoric, my texts were the mountainous solitudes, the pungent aroma of the undergrowth, the pullulating life of the golden carabus beneath fallen tree trunks in the forest, the dense thickets where the copihue dangles the jade capsule of its fruit, the ax ringing on the rauli beech, the roof leaking on the poverty of my childhood, the moon-filled love, the tears and jasmine of my starry adolescence.

But life and books, journeys and war, goodness and cruelty, friendship and menace, changed a hundredfold the vestments of my poetry. It has been my fortune to live at every latitude and in every clime, my fortune to suffer and to love like any man of our time, to love and

---

This speech was delivered at the University of Concepción in 1968

to defend noble causes, to suffer my personal sorrows and the humiliation of our peoples.

Perhaps the duties of the poet have been the same throughout history. Poetry was honored to go out into the streets, to take part in combat after combat. When they called him rebel, the poet was not daunted. Poetry is rebellion. The poet is not offended if he is called subversive. Life is more important than societal structures, and there are new regulations for the soul. Seeds spring up everywhere, all ideas are exotic, every day we await momentous changes, we are experiencing the excitement of a mutation in the human order: spring incites rebellion.

We poets hate hatred and make war on war.

Only a few weeks ago, in the heart of New York, I began my reading with some verses of Walt Whitman. Only that morning I had bought still another copy of his *Leaves of Grass*. When I opened it in my hotel room on Fifth Avenue, the first thing I read were these lines, which I had never particularly noticed before:

> *Away with themes of war! away with war itself!*
> *Hence from my shuddering sight to never more return that show of*
> *blacken'd, mutilated corpses!*
> *That hell unpent and raid of blood, fit for wild tigers or for lop-*
> *tongued wolves, not reasoning men.*

These lines brought an instantaneous response. The public that overflowed the auditorium stood and applauded wildly. Unknowingly, through the words of the bard Walt Whitman, I had touched the anguished heart of the North American people. The destruction of defenseless hamlets, napalm burning entire villages of Vietnamese —all this, through the words of a poet who lived a hundred years ago, condemning injustice with his poetry, was palpable and visible to those who were listening. Would that my poems were so lasting, the poetry already written, and the poetry still to come.

I don't remember the title of the first verses of mine published in the noble review *Atenea*. But I do remember, despite the passing years, the emotion of seeing my black strophes filling the white pages of *Atenea*. I remember the weight and the scent of the paper, and how I carried that journal under my arm to show it proudly to all my friends. It seemed to me that the fragrance of the southern forests that issued from those pages was the fragrance of my austral birthplace recognizing me as its child, and giving me, as today, my words.

Honorable Rector: I am still that proud adolescent, and my gratitude has brought me back to these shores, where a great and serene river bears in its moving mirror the creative image of history and intelligence.

And for the honor of being named and remembered by your university, Señor Rector, my friends, professors, students, fellow poets, my friend the Bío-Bío, I have but a single phrase, no less encompassing, no less true, for being oft repeated. A single, well-worn phrase, but one that shines like a rare coin: Thank you!

Latorre, Prado, and My
Own Shadow

LITTLE accustomed to academic ceremonies, I cast about for a theme for my address, and among suggestions from my friends emerged the names of two illustrious writers, both former members of this faculty, both long absent from this world of earthly cares: Pedro Prado and Mariano Latorre.

These two names awakened different, widely divergent echoes in my memory.

I never enjoyed a close relationship with Mariano Latorre, and it was only through reasoning and understanding that I learned to appreciate his stature as a great writer associated with the description and formation of our nation. A genuinely national writer is a true hero, and no people can afford the luxury of ignoring such a person. This fact is independent of contemporary reactions, of the value placed on his work, of the hurried, obligatory disinterest of new generations, or the malice, self-interest, or superficiality of the critics.

The only thing I knew well about Latorre was his cold, sharp-featured face, and, I confess, I was not among those spared the sting of his scorpion tail. But only the most unyieldingly bitter man takes seriously petty tales, quarrels and squabbles, street-corner and café gossip, when summing up the actions of a great man. For Latorre was a great man. It takes an encompassing heart to absorb all the resounding names and the fragrant diversity of our nation.

Mariano Latorre's shining virtue was his admirable intent to turn us

---

This speech was delivered on the occasion of Neruda's installation as an Academic Fellow of the Faculty of Arts and Letters at the University of Chile, March 30, 1962

back toward the ageless essence of our land. Though I viewed society from a different perspective and had a very different orientation toward writing and the soul, though I am myself far removed from the method and expression of Mariano Latorre, I can do no less than revere his unambiguous work, the eternal crystalline shadow over our formative years, the patrician reed woven into our nation's cradle.

An entirely different matter was Pedro Prado's profound influence. Prado was the first Chilean in whom I recognized the mark of intelligence unobscured by the provincial modesty to which I was accustomed. Thread by thread, from allusion to a presence, a person, a custom, tales, landscapes, reflections, everything was woven together in Prado's conversation; nothing deflected his narrative line, and sensitivity and depth were the magic foundations of the ever-changing, never-finished, enchanted castle he built throughout his lifetime.

I had come from the rains of the South, from the monosyllabic speech of those cold lands. My adolescence was an apprenticeship in taciturnity, and Prado's conversation, the delightful maturity of his infinite comprehension of nature, his perpetual philosophical musings, taught me the possibilities of human association and society, and the communication of intelligence.

My southern timidity was based on the indivisibility of solitude and speech. My people, my parents, neighbors, aunts and uncles, my companions, spoke only when necessary. My poetry had to be kept secret, rigidly separate from its origins. Beyond the immediate demands of everyday life, the youth of the South could not allude in their conversations to the possibility of shadow, mysterious trembling, or fleeting perfumes. I kept all that in a locked compartment intended for my transmigration, that is, for my poetry, provided I could keep it alive in those lethal compartments isolated from human communication. Naturally, the climate, the region, the vast, sparsely populated expanses, were not solely to blame for my retarded verbal development; there was the devastating barrier of class distinction. It is possible that in Prado was distilled the sorcery of an active and original thinker on the nature of the upper middle class. What I know is that Pedro Prado, the leader of an extraordinary generation, was for me, much younger than he, a superb bridge between my unyielding solitude and the undreamed-of delights of the intelligence Prado displayed at every hour and in every place.

Even so, I didn't appreciate every aspect of Prado's creation, or of his usually virtuous personality. None of my literary companions, nor I myself, wanted to play the facile role of literary cutthroat. The iconoclast had become passé by the time I began my career, though no doubt he will be resurrected many times more. The role of assassin will always be attractive to the collective vanity of writers. Every writer has wanted to be the lone respected survivor in the midst of the assembly of the goddess Kali and her murderous cult.

The writers of my generation owed very real debts to the masters who preceded us, because undivided generosity was the order of the day. In my own books are entered large and unpaid accounts owed to three great men of our literature. Before any other, Pedro Prado wrote a serene and masterly page about my first book, *Crepusculario*, that was as charged with feeling and vision as the dawn at sea. Our national master of criticism, Alone, who is also our master of contradictions, lent me, without really knowing me, the money to rescue my first book from the clutches of the printer. And as I've recounted more than once, it was Eduardo Barrios who personally delivered, and so fervently recommended, my *Veinte poemas de amor* to Don Carlos George Nascimento that Don Carlos called me to announce in these sober words that I was a publishable poet: "Very well, we will publish your little work."

My disagreements with Prado were almost always based on a different view of life, on the extraliterary planes that were always more important to me than some static problem. A great many of my generation placed their true values above or beyond literature, relegating books to their proper place. We preferred the streets, or nature, the smoke-filled shepherd's hut, the irresistible fascination of the port of Valparaiso, the turbulence of IWW union meetings.

Prado's defects were, for us, the remoteness from life, the interminable meditation on the essence of life that overlooked its throbbing immediacy.

As a youth I loved extravagance, and detested the forced austerity of poverty. But we sensed in Prado a conflict between an austere equilibrium and the inciting temptations of the world. If anyone ever served at the altar of an exalted spiritual life, that man was, without doubt, Pedro Prado. And as we are not sufficiently acquainted with the intimate details of his life, nor desirous of intruding on his secret existence, we cannot imagine his personal torments.

In his literature, his dissatisfaction took the form of a passive restlessness that led almost always to a persistent metaphysical questioning. In those days, influenced by Apollinaire, and by the earlier example of the salon poet Stéphane Mallarmé, we published our books without capital letters or punctuation. We even wrote our letters without punctuation of any kind, hoping to go the French one better. One can still find copies of my *Tentativa del hombre infinito* without a single period or comma. Actually, I'm amazed to see so many young poets in 1961 practicing a faded French mode. As punishment for my own cosmopolitan past, I propose to publish a book of poetry in which I eliminate words, leaving only punctuation.

In any case, the new literary waves wash by without disturbing the tower of Pedro Prado, a tower of the twenties, adding his values to those of others—and we already know he was worth ten of them. Except for that trace of interior coldness, a reclusiveness that does not enrich his writing, but rather impoverishes it.

During the same period, Ramón Gómez de la Serna, the Picasso of our maternal prose, is stirring up things on the peninsula and generating an Amazon-like current in which entire cities are swept along toward the sea, carrying relics, wakes, preambles, antiquated corselets, grandees' beards—all the affectations of an instant that this magus captures in a fulminating flash.

Then Surrealism arrives from France. It's true that this movement doesn't offer a single whole poet, but we hear the howling of Lautréamont in the hostile streets of Paris. Surrealism is fertile and deserves the deepest and most reverential bows for having, with such cataclysmic audacity, torn the statues from their pedestals, punched holes in bad paintings, and painted a mustache on the Mona Lisa, who, as everyone knows, needed one.

But Surrealism does not lure Prado back to life. He digs ever deeper into his well, and its waters grow dark and murky. At the bottom of the well he will not find the sky, or the splendor of the stars, only earth. Earth lies at the bottom of every well, as it is also the end of the journey for the astronaut who must return to his land and his home in order to be a man again.

The last chapters of Prado's great book *Un juez rural (Country*

Judge) are submerged in this well, and are darkened not by the movement of the water but by nocturnal earth.

Speaking in the most general terms, we can see in our poetry a tendency toward the metaphysical, which I neither reject nor give undue importance. My point of departure is not a critical-aesthetic point of view but my own creative and geographic situation.

We see this hemispheric solitude in many of our other poets. In Pedro Antonio González, in Mondaca, in Max Jara, in Jorge Hubner Bezanilla, in Gabriela Mistral.

If this is an escape from reality, from the retrospective repetition of already elaborated themes, or from the dominant influence of our geography, our turbulent volcanic and oceanic configuration, it will be thoroughly debated and discussed, since critics lie in wait for us poets with telescope and shotgun.

But there can be no doubt that we are semi-solitary actors, oriented or disoriented, in vast, barely cultivated terrains, in a semi-colonial society, our voices muted both by the amazing vitality of our nature and by the familiar isolation to which we are condemned by the cities of today and yesteryear.

This language and this attitude are still being expressed by those of the highest worth in our nation, with regular irregularity, with a kind of anger and sadness and rage that know no resolution.

If this literature does not resolve conflicts of such magnitude, it is because it does not confront them, and if it does not confront them, it is because it is ignorant of them. This is the reason for the restlessness that is rather formal in Pedro Prado, enchantingly effective in Vicente Huidobro, and harsh as the cordillera in Gabriela Mistral.

From all these defects, all these contradictions, experiments, and obscurities—if the proper mixture of necessary clarity is added—a national literature is formed. It is the thankless role of Mariano Latorre, master of our letters, to blind us with his clarity.

In a country in which all the marks of colonialism persist, in which the culture breathes and perspires through European pores as much in the plastic arts as in literature, there is no alternative. Every attempt to exalt the nation is a process of rebellion against colonialism, against the incrustations that tenaciously and unconsciously preserve our historical dependence.

Our first novelist was a poet: Don Alonso de Ercilla. Ercilla is a refined love poet, a Renaissance man bound with all his being to the vibrant Mediterranean foam from which Aphrodite has just re-emerged. But his mind, enchanted by the rebirth of this great treasure, by the dazzling light that burst victoriously across the shadows and stones of Spain, finds in Chile nourishment for his ardent nobility, as well as pleasure for his ecstatic eyes.

In *La Araucana* we see not only the epic development of men locked in mortal combat, not only the courage and agony of our fathers embraced in mutual extermination, but the pulsating natural catalogue of our patrimony. Our birds, plants, and waters, our customs and ceremonies, languages and races, arrows and aromas, snows and tides—all these things were given names, finally, in *La Araucana*, and once named, began to live. This sonorous legacy was ours to revive, ours to preserve and defend.

But what did we do?

We lost ourselves in incursions into the universal, in the world's mysteries, and that cohesive treasure revealed to us by the young Castilian has been dwindling in its reality and faltering in its expression. The forests have been burned, the birds have abandoned the original lands of their song, the language has been altered by foreign sounds, the old way of dress hidden in closets, the traditional dance replaced by another.

Suddenly, one summer evening, I felt an urge to talk with Prado. I was always captivated by the flow of his reasoning, to which he occasionally added some mote of his personal interests. His store-house of direct observations on humans and nature was prodigious. Perhaps this is what wisdom is, and Prado is what most closely approached my adolescent definition of "a wise man." But there is more superstition than truth in this, since later I was to know more and more wise men who were almost all gifted with special talent and passion, tinged with rebellion, and forged in the crucible of human struggle. But no one since has had quite the same effect on me, given me quite the same impression of being in the presence of an unparalleled intellect. Not even André Malraux, who more than once traveled with me the weary roads between France and Spain, the electricity of his Cartesian fanaticism shooting off sparks.

Much later, one of my wise friends was to be the great Ilya Ehrenburg, also dazzling in his incisive knowledge of causes and creatures, ardent and adamant in his defense of the Soviet nation and universal peace.

Another of the great lords of knowledge whose close friendship life has granted me is the Frenchman Aragon. The same torrents of reasoning, the most precise or the most impetuous analyses, the flights of a cultivated and audacious intelligence: tradition and revolution. Over some point or other, but inevitably, Aragon erupts, and the explosion reveals the scope of his belligerence. Aragon's sudden anger transforms him into a magnetic pole charged with the most dangerous electrical storms.

So then, among my friends who were wise, the Pedro Prado I knew in my youth lingers in my memory as the calm image of a great blue mirror eternally reproducing an essential landscape of reflections and light, a serene, always overflowing goblet of reason and equilibrium.

On that evening I crossed Matucana Street and took the rickety trolley to the dusty suburb in which the venerable ancestral home of the writer was the only decent building. Everything surrounding it was poverty. As I walked through the grounds and saw the main fountain filling up with fallen leaves, I felt I was being enveloped in the allegorical atmosphere, the deserted splendor of the master. Adding to that feeling was a penetrating aroma whose source Prado always guarded with a mysterious smile, and which only later I discovered was produced by the herb called *varraco* grass, an aromatic plant that grows in Chilean ravines and which would quickly lose its perfume if we called it *verraco* (wild-boar) grass, something we'd expect to find at the taxidermist's. Already confused and consumed by the ambience, I knocked at the door. The house seemed deserted, inhabited only by silence.

The heavy door swung open. In the half shadow of the entryway, I couldn't see anyone, but I thought I could hear the clear sound of dragging chains. Then from among the shadows appeared a masked figure that pointed a long threatening finger at my forehead, compelling me to walk in the direction of Prado's great hall and drawing room; I knew the room, but it seemed totally transformed. As I walked, a second, much smaller figure, covered completely by a tunic and mask, and bowed beneath the weight of a shovel piled high with earth, followed behind me, scattering dirt over each of my footsteps. I came to a halt in the middle of the great room. Outside, dusk was falling, the strange light of that abandoned park in the crumbling suburbs of Santiago.

In the almost empty room I could see lined up against the walls a dozen or more throne-like chairs and, squatting in them, more of the turban- and tunic-clad creatures staring at me, unspeaking, from behind frozen masks. Minutes passed, and in that fantastic silence I began to believe that I was dreaming, or that I had entered the wrong house, or that there must be some miraculous explanation.

Fearful, I began to retreat, but at last I spotted one face I recognized, that of the irrepressibly mischievous poet Diego Dublé Urrutia, maskless, staring at me, his features contorted in a grimace accentuated by the pressure of his right index finger against his upturned nose.

I realized that I had stumbled into one of those secret ceremonies always being celebrated someplace, somewhere. Here magic seemed the norm, and it seemed only normal that its practitioners, its dreamers, should meet in the depths of a deserted park to practice it.

Trembling, I left the house. The onlookers, surely filled with pride over having sustained such unusual poses, allowed me to leave, while the rotund hobgoblin figure, whom later I identified as Acario Cotapos, followed me to the door with his shovel, sprinkling dirt over my departing footsteps.

I can never speak of Prado without recalling that unforgettable ceremony.

To the benefit and boon of his writing, the bitter struggle for bread was unknown to the illustrious Pedro Prado, thanks to his birth into an exclusive class that until then, and during the lifetime of our companion and master, suffered no upheaval. For many years the dusty street that led to the ancestral home of Pedro Prado would serve as the unbreached barrier to his lofty thought.

But perhaps it would be to his hidden and unvoiced satisfaction that in my infrequent returns to that out-of-the-way spot I found the iron railings removed, and saw hundreds of the poor children from neighboring streets invading the manorial rooms, which serve today as a school. We must never forget this Pedro Prado, a steadfast traditionalist, bowed before the tomb of Luis Emilio Recabarren, leaving as still another floral offering of his bountiful philosophy a clear homage to the ideas that in his conservative innocence he thought to be unattainable utopias.

A third possibility for this speech would have been a critical self-examination of the forty years of my literary life, an encounter with my own shadow. In fact, as of last spring, forty years have passed, blending into the fragrance of the lilacs, the honeysuckle, of 1921, and of the Selecta publishing house on the Calle San Diego where I was suffused in the penetrating odor of ink as I entered and left carrying my first little book—booklet, really—*La canción de la fiesta*, printed in October of that year.

If I were to try to classify myself within our literary fauna and flora or within the fauna and flora of countries other than our own, I would have to declare at customs, as well as here in this Central Hall of Education, my lasting deficiencies in dogma, and my very vulnerable reputation as a maestro.

Maestros are not uncommon in literature and the arts. Some have a lot to teach, and some are dying to influence people, simply for the sake of influencing. From the little I know about myself, I believe I can say that I don't belong to either group, but rather to the common multitude always thirsting for knowledge.

I do not say this in deference to a sense of humility I do not possess but to the leisurely conditions that determined my development through the long years, of which I must on this occasion leave some testimony.

Can anyone doubt that a sense of superiority and a compelling drive for originality play a decisive role in writing?

Such motives have become greatly aggravated in our time, though they did not exist during the laborious emergence of civilization, when in America tribes raised their sacred stones, and in the East and the West the needles of pagodas and the Gothic arrows of basilicas reached toward God, unsigned by any man.

I have known not only men but entire nations which, before a product was developed, before the grapes ripened and the casks were filled, while the empty bottles stood waiting, had already advertised the name, the quality, and the inebriating effect of that still-unseen wine.

The ignored writer driven to the wall by the financial conditions of a cruel time has often gone to the market square to compete with his wares, setting free his doves in the midst of the strident crowds. He has despaired in the deathly light between nightfall and the bloody dawn, and he has striven to shatter the threatening silence. "I am first," he has cried. "I am the one and only," he has repeated with untiring and bitter self-idolatry.

This daring and audacious prevaricator has dressed himself as a prince, like D'Annunzio, constantly astounding the stupefied schools of elegant fish along the shore. In our untamed Americas the elegant Vargas Vila rose up against the bristling tyranny of lawless dictators and brutal colonists, and shrouded with his courage and his coruscating poetic prose an entire autumnal epoch of our culture.

And others, many others, proclaimed themselves.

Actually, we are not concerned that the chaos of this tradition of egocentricity goes beyond writing. We are concerned only—vitally concerned—with the anguished writer who finds himself before an unyielding city wall, one he wants to tumble with the blast of his trumpet in order to see the angels of light crowned; and to make sure that their light illuminates more than the rapturous pride of the work he has built to last through eternity, and that it call attention, even if painfully—and, occasionally, accompanied by the ultimate explosion of suicide—to the actions of a spirit wounded by a heartless society.

Many writers of great talent, even in my generation, were forced to choose the road of torment, along which the poet crucifies himself, destroyed by his role as messiah.

Fully aware of these atmospheric currents, I felt swirl about my head the winds of our inhuman condition. We had to choose between appearing to be masters of things we didn't know, in order to be believed, or condemning ourselves to the perpetually obscure lot of common laborers, shapers of clay. This crossroads for poetry led to major disorientations. And those who are just beginning to feel perplexed between the flame and the ice of true poetic creation may still be diverted from their path.

Apollinaire, with his telegraphic genius, expressed it perfectly:

Among us and for us my friends
I mediate this long debate between tradition and imagination
Between Order and Adventure

You whose mouth is made in the image of God's
Mouth which is order itself
Be compassionate when you compare us
To those who were the perfection of order
We who seek adventure everywhere
We are not your enemies
We want to bring to you the vast and exotic domains
Where mystery flowers for one who will gather the blooms
New fires are burning and unknown colors
A thousand imponderable phantoms
That we must make real
We want to pursue virtue a purview where all is silence
Confront time ours to banish or call back again
Have pity on those who carry the battle to the frontiers
Of the infinite and the future
Have pity on our errors have pity on our sins

As for me, I took refuge in my senses and confidently set about sorting and weighing my materials for a task of building that I must have thought then, and can now confirm, would last to the end of my days. I say "confidently" even though one cannot foretell his own future, and he who does so is condemned, his insincerity known far and wide. Perhaps it is sincerity—this modest, old-fashioned word, so trampled and scorned by the resplendent entourage that is the erotic companion to aesthetics—that best defines the acts of my lifetime. Though sincerity does not imply a simplistic surrender of emotion or knowledge.

When first by vocation, and then by choice, I fled the role of literary master—all the dubious superficiality that had left me in a perpetual crisis of externalizing, rather than constructing—I somehow understood that my work should be of a form so organic and whole that my poetry would be like the very act of breathing, the measured product of my existence, the result of natural growth.

Therefore, if any lesson is to be derived from work so intimately and obscurely bound to my being, this lesson might be found beyond my acts and activities, only through my silence.

During those years I went out into the streets, prepared to defend the solidarity of men and peoples, but my poetry could not be taught to anyone. I preferred that it filter down over my country like the rains of my native land. I did not urge its acceptance in societies or academies, I did not impose it on passing youth; concentrated in it was the essence of my own experience, of my senses, forever opened to the expanses of ardent love and the spacious world.

I do not claim for myself the privilege of solitude: I was never lonely except when that terrible condition was imposed upon me. And so I wrote my books as I wrote them, surrounded by a loving throng, by the infinitely rewarding multitude of man. Neither solitude nor society can alter the needs of the poet, and those who argue exclusively for one or the other falsify their role as bees who for centuries have been building the same fragrant cell, with the same necessary nourishment for the human heart. But I condemn neither the solitary poets nor those who broadcast the collective cry: silence, sound, the separation or joining together of men—everything is material for poetry, precipitating the combustion of an unquenchable fire, of an inherent communication, of a sacred inheritance that for thousands of years has been translated into words and elevated into poetry.

Federico García Lorca, that great enchanting enchanter lost to us forever, was always very curious about my work, about anything I was in the throes of writing or about to finish. I felt the same curiosity about his extraordinary creation. But any time I began to read one of my poems, halfway through he would raise his arms, shake his head, cover his ears, and cry, "Stop! Stop! That's enough, don't read any more, you'll influence me!"

As I had been educated in the egoistic tradition of American letters, in which we hurl Andean boulders at one another or find stimulation in mutually exaggerated praise, I found this great poet's modesty delightful. I remember, too, that he used to bring me whole sections of his books, bountiful bouquets of his unique blossoms, and ask me to think up titles. I did this more than once. And once, too, Manuel Altolaguirre, both a poet and a person of heavenly charm, suddenly pulled an unfinished sonnet from the sheaves in his pocket and said, "I can't get the last line, write it for me." When he marched away, he was very smug about the line he had extracted from me. A generous man. The world of the arts is one great workshop in which we all work and in which everyone helps his fellow, though he may not know or believe it. And, most important, we are aided by the

work of those who came before us: we know there can be no Rubén
Darío without a Góngora, no Apollinaire without a Rimbaud, no
Baudelaire without a Lamartine, no Pablo Neruda without them all.
And it is out of pride, not modesty, that I proclaim all poets my
masters, for what would I be without the years I spent reading everything that had been written in my country and in every universe of
poetry?

I remember as if I still held it in my hands a book by Daniel de la
Vega; it was a white-covered book with an ocher title that someone
had brought to my aunt Telésfora's house one summer many years
ago, in the country near Quepe.

I carried the book to a sweet-smelling bower. There I devoured *Las
montañas ardientes (Blazing Mountains)*, for that was the book's title.
A wide stream rushed by the great round boulders where I sat reading. The tangled branches of the powerful laurel and the curling
coigue rose overhead. Everything smelled of green, and secret water.
And there, in the heart of nature, crystalline poetry raced with the
sparkling waters.

I am sure that some drop of those verses still flows in my own
stream, and though later other drops, electrified by greater discoveries
and extraordinary revelations, were added from an infinity of roaring
torrents, I have no reason to erase from my memory that celebration
of solitude, water, and poetry.

In an era of militant intellectualism we have become discriminating
about the past, favoring those who foretold changes and established
new dimensions. This is to falsify oneself by falsifying one's prede-
cessors. Reading many of today's literary reviews, we note that some
have chosen Rilke or Kafka as their uncles or grandfathers—that is,
writers whose secrets now hold no mystery, who are clearly labeled,
and fully visible.

As for me, I was influenced by books that are now out of vogue,
such as the sensual, funereal books of Felipe Trigo, steeped in that
somber lust that seems always to have been a part of Spain's past,
reflecting its sorcery and blasphemy. And the rapiers of Paul Feval,
swordsmen whose weapons glinted beneath a feudal moon; the illustrious world of Emilio Salgari; the fleeting melancholy of Albert
Samain; the delirious love of Paul and Virginie; the tripetal bells
Pedro Antonio González raised in an Oriental accompaniment to our

poetry, for a moment transforming our poor mountainous terrain into a great carpeted and gilded hall. A world of all temptations, all books, all rhythms, all languages, all bees, all shadows—a world, in short, of all poetic affirmation—saturated me to such a degree that I was successively the voice of all those who taught me a particle, passing or lasting, of their beauty.

But for me the largest, the most expansive, book has been this book we call Chile. I have never ceased to read the mother country, never taken my eyes from my nation's long outlines.

I have been virtually incapable of loving, of understanding, other lands.

In my travels through the Far East I understood very little. The violent color, the sordid atavism, the emanations of the crisscrossed jungles whose beasts and plants somehow threatened me. These were the enigmatic places that to this day are indecipherable to me. Similarly, I never totally understood the arid hills of mysterious, metal-rich Peru, or the argentine expanse of the pampas. As much as I have loved Mexico, I probably have not understood her. I felt alien in the Ural Mountains, in spite of the fact that I found justice and truth there. In a Paris street, immersed in the overwhelming atmosphere of the most universal of cultures and the most extraordinary multitudes, I felt as solitary as those little trees in the South that rise half blighted from the ashes. Here it has always been the opposite. My heart is still moved—after all this time—by those wooden houses, those run-down streets, humming like guitars in the wild winds, that begin in Victoria and end in Puerto Montt. Houses where winter and poverty inscribed hieroglyphs that I can understand, as I understand the sunset in the pampas of northern Chile, seen from Huantajaya, when the hills take on the flashing, dazzling, iridescent, resplendent, or ashen colors of the wild dove's throat.

As a child I learned to read the backs of the lizards that sparkled like emeralds on the rotted tree trunks in the forests of the South. And I have never forgotten my first lesson in the constructive intelligence of man—a viaduct, or bridge, soaring high above the Malleco River, a delicate network of iron as sleek and vibrant as the most beautiful musical instrument, each of its strings gleaming in the fragrant solitude of that transparent region.

I am a poet patriot, a nationalist of Chilean clay. Our beloved land!

In books it is sometimes difficult to glimpse her snow and seafoam image through the thick martial boughs. The aureole of battle first depicted by our Alonso de Ercilla, that diamantine father who descended upon us as from the moon, has clouded the image of our more intimate and humble realities. Intent on our multi-volume histories of the nation, we neglected our black pottery, the child of the clay and hands of Quinchamalí, and the baskets woven from the stalks of the copihue. In the face of all the legends, the heroic truth, and the aggression of those centaurs who came from Spain to thunder across our land, we forgot, in spite of *La Araucana* and its mournful pride, that our Indians are to this day illiterate and without land or shoes. That nation of scars and tatters, that infinite region that everywhere defines us with its poverty, is, with its fertile, rain-soaked mythology, an overflowing storehouse of creative possibilities.

I've talked with people in the country stores of San Fernando, Rengo, Parral, and Chanco, where advancing dunes are obliterating their homes; I've talked vegetables with farmers in the Santiago valley, and recited my poems in the Central Plain before the members of a union of common laborers, men whose clothes consisted of a gunnysack tied around the waist.

Only I can know my emotion as I read my verses in a forsaken, nitrous flatland where men wearing the ancient *cotona*—the cotton undershirt typical of the mines—stood listening beneath a boiling sun, rooted in the sand like sun-baked statues. The hovels of the port of Valparaiso, of Puerto Natales and Puerto Montt, the factories of greater Santiago, the mines of Coronel and Lota and Curanilahue, have seen me come and go, meditative and silent.

This is a wanderer's profession, and everyone knows—and I take pride in the fact—that wherever I go I'm greeted not just as a Chilean, which is no small thing, but as a true brother, which is a great thing indeed. This is my *ars poetica*.

I saw my first automobile in Temuco, and then my first airplane, the flight of Don Clodomiro Figueroa, who lifted off the ground like an unlikely kite, with no kite string but the solitary will of this, our first cavalier of the air. Since those days, since the southern rains of my youth, everything has been transformed, and that "everything" includes the world, the earth that geographers now tell us is not as round as we thought—perhaps not convincing us completely, since we know that men were also slow to believe it rounder than had been thought.

My poetry changed as well.

Wars came; we had known wars before, but now they brought new and more devastating cruelties. From the sorrows that stung and tortured me in Spain I saw Picasso's *Guernica* born—a painting of the magnitude of the *Gioconda*, but at the opposite pole of the human condition: one represents the most serene contemplation of life and beauty; the other, the destruction of stability and reason, man's panic about man. So painting, too, changed.

Among the discoveries and disasters that shook the stones beneath our feet and the stars above our heads, there emerged, from the middle of the last century to the beginnings of this century, a generation of extraordinary fathers of hope. Marx and Lenin, Gorki, Romain Rolland, Tolstoy, Barbusse, Zola emerged as momentous events, as new leaders of love. They worked with deeds and words, and left for us on the world's table a bundle containing a bountiful inheritance for all to share: intellectual responsibility, eternal humanism, and a plentitude of conscience.

But then came men who despaired. Once again they projected on the leaf screen of generations the spectacle of terrified men without bread or stone—that is, without food or defense—reeling between sex and death. The twilight glowed black and red, veiled in blood and smoke.

Yet great human causes were revitalized. Because man did not want to perish, he again realized that the fountain of life must remain intact, untainted, and creative. Men of advanced years, like the illustrious Lord Bertrand Russell, like Charles Chaplin, Pablo Picasso, North America's Linus Pauling, Dr. Schweitzer, and Lázaro Cárdenas, in the name of millions opposed the threat of atomic war, and suddenly a man could see that all men were represented and defended, even the simplest of them, and that intelligence would not betray humankind.

The Black Continent, which had supplied slaves and ivory to imperial greed, shuddered on the map and twenty republics were born. Tyrants trembled in Latin America. Cuba proclaimed its inalienable right to choose its own social system. Meanwhile, three smiling young men—two Soviets and one North American—ordered strange suits and took off for a leisurely outing among the planets.

A long time has passed since I so reverently stepped into the ancestral home of Pedro Prado for the first time, and since I bid farewell to the remains of Mariano Latorre in our overgrown Cementerio General. I bid that master goodbye as if I were bidding goodbye to the Chilean landscape. Something went with him, something inseparably bound to our past.

But my faith in truth, in the continuity of hope, in justice and poetry, in man's perpetual creativity, comes from that past, accompanies me in the present, and is here with us in this fraternal gathering.

My faith in all the future's harvests is affirmed in the present. And I declare, though it is a commonplace, that poetry is indestructible. It may shatter into a thousand fragments, but it will become crystal again. Poetry was born with man and will continue to sing for man. It will sing. We will sing.

Throughout this long memoir that I have delivered before the university and the Faculty of Arts and Letters that welcomes me, presided over by Juan Gómez Millas and Eugenio González—friends to whom I am linked by the oldest and most emotional ties—you have heard the names of the many poets who permeate my writing. Many I did not name also form a part of my song.

My song will not end. Others will renovate the form and the sentiment. Books will tremble on the shelves, and new and unheard words, new signs and new seals, will rattle the doors of poetry.

My Burning Faith in Peace

M Y first words today are for Frédéric Joliot-Curie. The renown of this medal is too great for the chest on which it rests, as is the honor you confer on me.

Never have creative energy and the dignity of intelligence been raised to such heights as in Joliot-Curie. He became the exemplar of our era, because we know that he moved within the labyrinths of science with the ease of one who knew the entrances and exits of unexplored highways. And when in his laboratory this discoverer harvested the fruits of the trees of good and evil, he emerged to warn humanity that the fruit he had just plucked contained the seed of a new hell and of total annihilation.

Our master Joliot-Curie is not only a major hero of the world of the intellect, but he is also for me a memory whose outlines can be traced only by tenderness. He seemed so fragile, this indomitable man. His face was lined by the intense discipline of wisdom, his eyes wearied by the subterranean radiance of knowledge; everything about him indicated that in this incredible struggle against terror and for man's survival on earth, he would be felled, exhausted by its consuming demands. When he died, he bequeathed to us the dual inheritance of his scientific achievement and his humanity. Joliot-Curie did honor both to science and to conscience. His example became a standard and a way of life.

We, too, and our peoples, must choose between opposing paths. We bow in greeting and then engage in battle. But we must choose

---

This speech was delivered when Neruda received the Joliot-Curie Medal at the Municipal Theater in Santiago, April 8, 1968 between creation and destruction, between love and the void, between peace and war, between life and death. Never has the power of death been greater, and never has humanity been more fully warned of the danger. As a consequence, our duty has never been more imperative: no one can evade that duty, it is the mandate of our time.

Present here are Latin American friends who have chosen to congregate around the portrait of that master of peace to reaffirm, once again, the ties that unite us. I know almost as well as they the misfortunes, the underdevelopment, the poverty of each of our nations. I know, too, the struggle, the joy and the songs, the capacity for endurance, the heroism of all of our peoples. I greet each and every one of them in my embrace, in the brotherhood that recognizes no differences among our origins or our future.

Señor Votshinin has made a difficult journey from the Union of Soviet Socialist Republics, paying us great honor, representing the greatest inspiration known to contemporary man. This inspiration is the existence and the persistence, the unparalleled triumphs, of the Soviet people and their great Revolution. His presence in this hall is further testimony that that vast nation, governed by a classless society, invariably joins in every movement for peace and liberation manifested anywhere on our planet.

As I greet him, I pause to commemorate two moments of mourning.

Comrade Votshinin: we know that there are still tears in the eyes of the Soviet people following the tragic death of the supreme hero of land and sky, Yuri Gagarin.

His name was both legendary and familiar to all Chileans. His feats did more than unite reality and fantasy, our planet with other planets, man with the mysterious universe. This young hero had other virtues: he unified the most far-flung peoples, for his encounter with the cosmos was an act of reconciliation among all peoples. In his flight he represented the very heart of humanity, the restlessness of all men, the audacity of all races, the incredible miracle of all human beings.

Every people considered him their own, he represented all humanity, from its most primitive advances, from the obscurity of its origins and its painful march toward progress, to the discovery of all possibilities.

We know that the Soviet Union is a formidable seedbed of modest but illustrious heroes. The world still thrills at the memory of its glorious defense of peace and liberty in crushing the threat of Hitler. Those were somber and bloody days, and all humanity recognizes its immeasurable debt to the Soviets.

Gagarin was the son of light. He was the luminous archangel of our age. He is close to all nascent life. His heart has been stopped, but his memory will flower with every spring, in every gaze, in every child who for the first time contemplates the stars.

A second sorrow, more personal, is with me tonight, because I feel sure that my beloved friend Ilya Ehrenburg would have been present on this occasion.

We all know that the World Council of Peace considered him among its most energetic founders. I will always remember him— unruly locks, ancient eyes, a trace of a smile—at the exhausting meetings, conferences, and congresses of peace.

This overburdened man, whose inviolable intelligence made him seem as old as the world, always set an example of active intelligence and unbelievable powers of endurance.

This great master of universal literature accepted the humble as well as the distinguished tasks that were part of his role as the major ambassador of the Peace Movement. With his unforgettable brisk steps he hurried down hallways, took part in commissions, took his place on platforms, convincing, developing, clarifying, explicating, lending to the cause of peace and friendship among peoples the full capacity of his boundless intelligence. One day would find him in the palace of Belgium's Queen Mother, that great lady, benefactress of music and truth. Another evening would find him in the seldom-entered fortress of Pablo Picasso, and he left for the airport bearing a new dove that took flight from his hands. In Finland or Italy, in his adored Paris, in Japan or Chile—every nation, every airport, saw this gray-haired man in wrinkled trousers expending his strength and intelligence in the battle against terror and war.

With his death, I lost one of the men I have most admired and respected. He honored me by counting me his friend, and we worked and traveled together, sharing dreams and hopes that are still alive. Because, in spite of the death of these two Soviet heroes of peace, in spite of the painful shadow cast by their absence, our struggle for brotherhood, peace, and truth will live on, nourished in the sanctuary of our duty and fortified by their memories.

Romesh Chandra: you have undertaken this long journey to Chile, to this country that lies at the very ends of the earth, to bring this medal. I knew your country, India, when I was very young. I lived in the labyrinths of its great cities, I entered its temples, I lived among its ancient, sacred dreams, with the millenary suffering of its people, with the awakening of its independence. I was a rebellious youth who had come from the student rebellion of 1921, and gravitated quite naturally toward the brotherhood of revolutionary Hindus. The awakening of all Asia originated in your nation, and the winds that later were to demolish the walls of the Empire were rising there, in the shadow of the world's most ancient gods. How slow the road seemed to me. The era of colonialist servitude seemed as if it would never end in those interminable regions containing enormous continents and thousands of scattered islands. Yet our century has witnessed the crumbling of those empires that had seemed indestructible because of their façades of steel, stone, and mud. The most powerful of arms was raised against them: human intelligence, the human action that turns the wheels of history. It is in the name of that intelligence, of that faith in an ever-finer, freer, more liberated destiny of man that you have come from such a great distance. I thank you.

Subsequently, we have lived through the agony of a second world war. We have seen the messianic masks of warriors drop away, and we have seen the true face of war. The gallows and the gas chambers erased forever the legend of the knight who went forth to do battle for his God, his King, and his Lady. Following the surrender, thousands of living specters gave horrifying testimony to the lengths of human cruelty. Many of the monsters were punished. But, terrified, we ask ourselves whether such an inconceivable horror might again befall history.

More recently, we have seen how peace, a peace so tragically obtained, has been betrayed. One state more powerful than the rest has carried death and destruction to lands far distant from its territory.

With ferocious violence it has destroyed the cities, the cultivated fields, the buildings, and the lives of a small nation whose people, proud of their ancient culture, had only recently burst free from their colonial chains.

Genocide has been practiced in a frightening form. Napalm, with fearsome efficiency, has blasted lives, seeds, and books. But a new epic, worthy of history's greatest, has moved all humanity.

Because Vietnam has risen a thousand times from its ashes: seemingly dead, it has risen with a grenade in its hand. Reason seemed routed before the cold dementia of the invaders, but Vietnam, with an extraordinary offensive, is closer than ever to a timeless victory.

And the peoples of Latin America know that this victory is indivisibly bound to our destinies. The aggressive powers that currently dominate the government of the United States have shown no intention of respecting the independence of our nations and our inalienable right to defend the systems of government that are most appropriate and fair for ourselves.

The recent aggression in the Caribbean and the embargo imposed on Cuba by the North Americans and by reactionary forces in Latin America are proof of the intolerance and error of this policy of aggression.

But the times are changing. In the very cradle of the aggressor have been raised the voices of its most distinguished intellectuals. Students and citizens at every level of North American life have energetically and courageously denounced the North American invasion of Vietnam. Thousands of youths have burned their draft cards, and the number of deserters is increasing daily.

The death of Martin Luther King, cruelly and coldly murdered, has filled the world with mourning, and the United States with shame. We have always been moved by this extraordinary figure, defender of his race and leader of his people. He was killed by abominable, seemingly powerful forces. From the unjust war in Korea to the disgraceful assault against the independence of Vietnam, these forces have been unleashed in North America as a poisonous by-product of war. It is in official violence that we must seek the origin of these crimes. Two wars have taught thousands of young men the practice of killing and burning, and total disregard for human life. Racism, delinquency, perversion, and cruelty have been aggravated to such a degree among North Americans that a fearful mankind contemplates a retrogression to the primal laws of the jungle, to brutality and force. To fly the national flag at half-staff above the White House is a sad and pitiful gesture, because we know that that same flag flies in Vietnam above the worst atrocities the world has known. It is in war, in that war, that we must seek the origins of crime. In that war is fermenting the yeast of many additional horrors that will befall North America.

The heroism of the Vietnamese, world denunciation, and the fiery protests of his own people have caused President Johnson to announce that, in the near future, he will bring his sorry political career to an end.

One wishes he would make his resignation effective before the next elections. The man has already lost the election before the tribunal of history, which brooks no appeal.

The American republics are children of the anti-colonial struggle and international solidarity. Horsemen of our glorious, verdant Colombia galloped across the sands of Peru carrying the banners of liberation. Argentines crossed the highest peaks and one hundred and fifty years ago, here in Maipú, only a few kilometers from this theater, covered themselves with blood and laurels. Chileans under the command of a Scots admiral set sail to liberate the Pacific Ocean. Napoleonic soldiers of France and battalions of black Africans fought for the independence of Chile. Our America has not been able to send men to Vietnam, but it has made known to the world, from Havana and Mexico to polar Patagonia, its unanimous sentiment of solidarity, and its faith in the victory of the aggrieved.

But we must speak a bitter truth. We have not done enough. We could have done much more, we shall do much more. Why have some of the governments of our republics remained silent about the war in Vietnam? Amid world accord and discord, can this timid silence that has every appearance of complicity be tolerated?

Every day, a powerful Soviet Union has spoken out. General de Gaulle, a proud and independent man, has more than once indicated his dissatisfaction with North American policy.

Our Latin American governments have different tones, colors, perspectives, and origins. Some are impetuous in their reaction; others regard the future with timidity; some cultivate fear in their people; others make clear their desire to assure the forward progress of our poor unfortunate America.

We will not discuss those tendencies now. But we have the right to demand of these nations that they declare themselves in regard to the most important issue of our age: peace or war, life or death.

The government of the United States of North America, with its evil and bloody action in Vietnam, has lost every vestige of prestige in this civilization. At this moment it is negotiating its material and moral destruction. The periodic repetition of such adventures has been tragically characteristic of our powerful neighbor.

Latin American governments must hear the voice of their peoples, and tip the scales in favor of peace and independence. It is the hour to prove that, born out of anti-colonial fervor, our nations reject this new colonialism that seeks to establish itself with its inhuman cruelties.

I know that many will smile at the idea of asking certain governments to participate in this call for peace, since many times they have in their own nations violated the ideals of liberty and justice. Even so, in this hour of crisis I demand a united effort, a union of the good and the bad, of those who are governed and those who govern, a union of the just and the unjust, in order to put an end to the greatest depravity of our time: the invasion and destruction of Vietnam.

This is a moment of crisis in which Latin American nations, who must call on justice in their own defense, must support the cause of justice before all the world.

We believe in peace, and we will knock at every door to achieve its sovereignty. We thirst for peace among men, as pilgrims thirst for water to sustain their strength along the way. I have entered every house that would open its door to me.

I have tried to speak with all men, unafraid of contamination from the adversary, the enemy. I will continue to do so. I believe that the dialogue cannot die, that no conflict is a sealed tunnel, that the light of understanding can penetrate at either end.

As I accept this magnanimous distinction, I want to avoid any personal sentiment. Instead, I believe that friends from neighboring and distant countries have gathered here on this occasion to give testimony to their burning faith in man, in life, in truth and liberty: that is, in peace. That is enough, and I thank you for the recognition, for your expression of brotherhood that does not honor me but my nation and my people.

The Murdered Albatross

I⊤ has been my fate during a lifetime of wandering to attend a number of rather strange meetings, but a few days ago I was present at one that turned out to be the most mysterious of all the gatherings I have ever attended or taken part in. I was sitting there with some of my compatriots; facing us, in a circle that seemed enormous, sat men responsible for the worlds of finance, banks, and treasuries, representing the many countries to which my own, it seems, owes a great deal of money.

There were but a few of us Chileans, and our illustrious creditors, almost all the large nations, were many, some fifty or sixty. We were there to renegotiate our National Debt, our Foreign Debt—greatly increased, in the half century we have had such a debt, by previous governments. In this period of time, men had reached the moon, bearing penicillin and television. In war, napalm had been invented in order to democratize with purifying fire some of the planet's inhabitants. During these fifty years, the North American PEN Club has labored nobly on behalf of understanding and reason. But, as I could see in that implacable assembly, it was the *standby* that threatened Chile with a garrote of the most modern design. In spite of half a century of intellectual understanding, the relationship between the rich and the poor, between nations that lend crumbs and other nations that are starving, is still a relationship composed of anguish and pride, justice and the right to life.

In a sense, I have come here to clarify my relationship with you,

---

This speech was delivered on April 10, 1972, at a dinner in New York marking the fiftieth anniversary of the founding of the PEN American Center

the writers of the United States and the older world of Europe. It is important in this company that we know what we owe one another. We must constantly renegotiate the internal debt that weighs on us writers everywhere. We all owe something to our own intellectual tradition, and something to what we have taken from the world's treasury. We, the writers of the American continent to the south, came of age knowing and admiring, in spite of the difference in languages, the amazing growth of North American letters. We were especially impressed by the astonishing flowering of the novel, which from Dreiser to the present demonstrates a new, convulsive, and constructive strength whose greatness and passion are unequaled in the literatures of our time—unless it be in that of your dramatists. Not a name has escaped our attention. It would be as impossible to list them as it would be to catalogue the heights they reached and the violent depths they revealed. The hard, often cruel, disillusionment of your literature represents the unique testimony of great and noble writers confronting the conflicts resulting from your vertiginous capitalist expansion. In these exemplary works, nothing has been exempt from the truth and the souls of multitudes and of individuals have been bared—the powerful and the insignificant, crowded together in cities and suburbs, drops of the blood of your national arteries, of your individual and collective lives. These elements can be perceived even in the detective novel, frequently a more faithful testimony of truth than has been acknowledged.

As for myself, now a man of almost seventy, I was barely fifteen when I discovered Walt Whitman, my primary creditor. I stand here among you today still owing this marvelous debt that has helped me live.

To renegotiate this debt is to begin by making it public, by proclaiming myself the humble servant of the poet who measured the earth with long, slow strides, pausing everywhere to love and to examine, to learn, to teach, and to admire. That man, that lyric moralist, chose a difficult road; he was a torrential and didactic bard. These two qualities seem antithetical, more appropriate for a caudillo than for a writer. But what really matters is that the professor's chair, teaching, the apprenticeship to life held no fear for Walt Whitman, and he accepted the responsibility of teaching with candor and eloquence. Clearly, he feared neither morality nor immorality, nor did he attempt to define the boundaries between pure and impure poetry. He is the first absolute poet, and it was his intention not only to sing but to impart his vast vision of the relationships of men and of nations. In this sense, his obvious nationalism is part of an organic universality. He considers himself indebted to happiness and sorrow, to advanced cultures and primitive societies.

Greatness has many faces, but I, a poet who writes in Spanish, learned more from Walt Whitman than from Cervantes. In Whitman's poetry the ignorant are never humbled, and the human condition is never derided.

We are still living in a Whitmanesque epoch; in spite of painful birth pangs, we are witnessing the emergence of new men and new societies. The bard complained of the all-powerful European influence that continued to dominate the literature of his time. In fact, it was he, Walt Whitman, in the persona of a specific geography, who for the first time in history brought honor to an American name. The colonialism of the most brilliant nations created centuries of silence; colonialism seems to stultify creativity. I have only to mention that in three centuries of Spanish domination we had no more than two or three outstanding writers in all America.

The proliferation of our republics produced not only flags and nationalities, universities and small, heroic armies, and melancholy songs of love, but a veritable eruption of books, which sometimes formed an impenetrable thicket with many blooms but little fruit. But with time, and especially today, the Spanish language shines through the writing of American authors, who from the Rio Grande to Patagonia are inundating with magical tales and tender, desperate poems a dark continent walking the stormy path toward a new independence.

Today we see other new nations, new flags, and new literatures appearing with the abolishment—total, we may hope—of colonialism in Africa and Asia. Overnight, the world's capitalists fly the new standards of peoples we have never known, but who are beginning to speak out in the clumsy, painful voices of the newborn. Black writers in Africa and America are beginning to communicate the true pulse of their hapless, long silent, race. Political struggle is an integral part of poetry. Man's liberation often flows in blood, but always in song. And human song is every day enriched in our great era of martyrdom and liberation.

I must humbly ask you to forgive me if I again turn to the problems of my country. The whole world knows that Chile is undergoing a revolutionary transformation within the framework of the dignity and stringency of our laws. And a great many people are offended by this process. Why don't these Chileans throw someone in prison, why don't they shut down the newspapers, why don't they shoot the opposition?

Our road is one we have chosen for ourselves, and we are determined to follow it to the end. But secret enemies are supplying themselves with every type of weapon in order to deflect the course of our destiny. And as in this kind of warfare cannons seem to be outdated, they employ an arsenal both ancient and modern. From it they can choose dollars, arrows, telephone and telegraph industries—anything is fair as long as it defends the old, irrational privileges. That is why, in that meeting where we were renegotiating Chile's Foreign Debt, I was so vividly reminded of *The Rime of the Ancient Mariner*.

Samuel Taylor Coleridge based his desolate poem on an incident that took place at the southern tip of my country, recounted by Shelvocke in his travel diaries.

In the cold seas of Chile we have every breed, genre, and species of albatross: wandering and gigantic, gray and lofty, they fly like no other bird.

That may be why our nation has the elongated shape of an albatross with extended wings.

And in that for me unforgettable meeting about a Foreign Debt we were trying to renegotiate with equity, many of those who were most implacable seemed to aim their weapons against Chile in hopes that the albatross would no longer fly.

I don't know whether it would be an indiscretion on the part of a poet who has been an ambassador only one year to say to you that perhaps, of all the financial representatives with all their official papers, it was the North American delegate who was most ready to point his crossbow at the heart of the albatross. I must admit, however, that this financier has a delicious name that brings a fitting end to a banquet: Mr. Hennessy.

But if Mr. Hennessy would give himself the pleasure of reread-ing a venerable poet, he would learn that in *The Rime of the Ancient Mariner* the sailor who committed that crime was condemned to carry the heavy weight of the murdered albatross around his neck for all eternity.

My dear friends:

With interest and emotion I have read the history of these fifty years of the United States PEN Club. It has been a half century of great hopes and magnificent deeds: a noble and honorable achievement that we must celebrate thoughtfully and with joy. We writers are easily individualistic, we are less readily collectivist. We carry a sub-versive germ that is a profound part of our expression and our being, and our rebellion often turns against our own kind. We look for the enemy closest to us, and, mistakenly, we find him among those who most closely resemble ourselves. To bring us together is the task of giants. And to bring us together despite political, linguis-tic, and racial differences is a great undertaking. Honor is due those who have made possible a sense of unity among writers of all nations, without sectarian rejection of their inclinations or their beliefs.

I am sure that you have received me and my debts, not as an implacable tribunal, but as a generous and fraternal association. I have said that it is necessary to recognize what we have learned from the few and from the many. In this way we establish our security; that is, the awareness of an uninterrupted and universal community of thought.

In this way we continue to work with the past, secure in the fruition of its beauty, and, still on this same path of honor, secure in the works that other writers will write for men who have not yet been born.

The Invisible Presence

W<small>E</small> have come from afar, from our own internal or external realities, from opposing, disparate languages, from countries that love one another. And we have found ourselves here on this central and universal night, having come from chemistry, microscopes, cybernetics, algebra, barometers, and poetry to join together. We have emerged from the darkness of our laboratories to face a light that honors us—even, for a moment, blinds us. For us, the laureates, it is joy and agony.

But before responding, before taking a breath, I must gather my thoughts, allow me, I live a long way from here, allow me, to return to my country, allow me, and I thank you.

I return to the streets of my childhood, to winter in southernmost America, to the lilacs of Araucan lands, to the first María I held in my arms, to the mud of streets that never knew pavement, to mourning Indians bequeathed us by the Conquest, to a country, a dark continent that sought the light. And if that light beams from this festive hall and reaches across earth and sea to illuminate my past, it is also illuminating the future of American peoples who are defending their right to light, to dignity, to liberty and life.

I am a representative of the past, and of the present struggles that fill my poetry. Forgive me if I have directed attention to personal concerns, to the earth's forgotten, who on this joyous occasion seem more real than my writing, loftier than my cordilleras, broader than the ocean itself. I am proud that I belong to all humanity, not to a few but to many, and that here I am surrounded by their invisible presence.

These comments were made in the name of all the 1971 Nobel laureates

Poetry Shall Not Have
Sung in Vain

M Y remarks will trace a long voyage, a personal journey through far regions in the antipodes whose remoteness does not lessen their resemblance to the landscape and solitudes of the North. I am speaking of the extreme south of my country. We Chileans retreat farther and farther until we come to the boundaries of the South Pole that is the source of our similarity to the geography of Sweden, whose head brushes the snowy northern pole of the planet.

There in the remote wilderness of my native land, where I found myself because of a series of events now forgotten, if one must—and I had to—reach the Argentine frontier, one must first cross the Andes. In those inaccessible regions one travels through great forests as if through tunnels, and along that dark and forbidden route there were very few recognizable landmarks. And yet, in this land where there were no tracks, no trails, I and my four companions, in a snaking cavalcade—overcoming the obstacles of imposing trees, impassable rivers, enormous outcroppings of rock, desolate snows—had to seek —more accurately, to reckon—the route to my freedom. The men accompanying me knew the direction we must travel, the potential routes through the heavy undergrowth. But to be more certain on their return—after they had abandoned me to my fate—from their horses they slashed at the bark with their machetes, blazing a trail on towering trees.

Each of us rode forward awed by that limitless solitude, that green and white silence, the trees, the huge climbing vines, the humus de-

This lecture was delivered on the occasion of Neruda's acceptance of the Nobel Prize for Literature, December 13, 1971

posited over the centuries, the half-toppled trees that suddenly confronted us, one further barrier to our progress. Nature was bedazzling and secret, and at the same time an ever-increasing threat of cold, snow, persecution. Everything coalesced: solitude, danger, silence, and the urgency of our mission.

Occasionally we followed a faint trail left perhaps by smugglers, or possibly by outlaws, and we had no way of knowing how many of them might have perished, suddenly surprised by the icy hands of winter, by the raging snowstorms of the Andes that can smother an unwary traveler, burying him beneath seven stories of whiteness.

On either side of the trail, in the midst of that savage desolation, I saw something resembling human handiwork, lengths of piled-up branches that had suffered many winters, the offerings of hundreds of travelers, tall mounds of wood to commemorate the fallen, to remind us of those who had been unable to continue and who lay forever beneath the snows. With their machetes my companions lopped off the branches brushing against our faces, boughs sweeping down from the heights of the enormous evergreens, from the oaks whose last leaves were trembling before the onslaught of winter storms. And I, as well, left on each mound a memento, a calling card of wood, a branch cut from the forest to adorn the tombs of those many unknown travelers.

We had to cross a river. Those small streams born in the peaks of the Andes rush down precipitously, discharging their violent, vertiginous force, become cascades, crush earth and rock with the energy and momentum carried from those noble heights; but we were able to find a pool, a broad mirror of water, a ford. The horses waded in till they lost their footing, then struck out toward the opposite shore. Soon my horse was almost completely swamped by water, and I began to sway, nearly unseated; my feet churned as the beast labored to keep his head above water. And so we crossed.

We had no sooner reached the far shore than my guides, the countrymen who were accompanying me, asked with the trace of a smile: "Were you afraid?"

"Very. I thought my hour had come," I said.

"We were right behind you with our ropes ready," they said.

"My father went down at this very spot," one added, "and the current carried him away. We weren't going to let that happen to you."

We rode on until we came to a natural tunnel that might have been carved in the imposing rock by a roaring, long-since-disappeared river, or possibly an earth tremor had created in those heights the rocky channel of hewn-out granite into which we now penetrated. After a few yards, our mounts were slipping and sliding, struggling to find a foothold on the rough stone; their legs buckled beneath them, their hoofs struck sparks; more than once I found myself lying on the rocks, thrown from my horse. My mount was bleeding from the nostrils, his legs were bloody, but doggedly we continued along the unending, the splendid, the arduous road.

Something awaited us in the middle of that wild forest. Suddenly, as in an extraordinary vision, we came to a small, gleaming meadow nestled in the lap of the mountains: clear water, a green field, wild flowers, the sound of rivers, the blue sky overhead, munificent light uninterrupted by foliage.

There we paused, as if within a magic circle, like visitors at a holy shrine; and the ceremony in which I participated had even greater overtones of holiness. The cowboys dismounted. In the center of the enclosure was set—as if for some ritual—the skull of an ox. One by one, my companions silently walked forward and placed a few coins and scraps of food in the openings of the skull. I joined them in that offering destined for rough, wandering Ulysseses, for fugitives of every ilk, who would find bread and assistance in the eye sockets of a dead bull.

But that unforgettable ceremony did not stop there. My rustic friends took off their hats and began a strange dance, hopping on one foot around the abandoned skull, retracing the circle left by the countless dances of others who had come this way. I had some vague comprehension then, standing beside my taciturn companions, that there could be communication between strangers—solicitude, pleas, even a response—in the farthest, most isolated solitudes of the world.

Farther along, very close now to crossing the border that was to separate me for many years from my country, we were navigating by night the last ravines of the mountains. Suddenly we saw a light, a sure sign of human habitation, but as we rode nearer, we saw only a few ramshackle structures, a few rickety sheds, all seemingly vacant. We entered one, and in the light of a great fire saw tree trunks blazing in the center of the room, the cadavers of giant trees burning there day and night, whose smoke escaped through the chinks in the roof to drift through the shadows like a thick blue veil. We could see great wheels of cheeses piled there by those who made them in this high country. Near the fire, clumped together like burlap bags, lay several men. From the silence we heard the chords of a guitar and the words of a song which, born of the glowing coals and the darkness, carried to us the first human voice we had heard in our long trek. It was a song of love and far horizons, a lament of love and of longing for the distant spring, for the cities from which we had come, for the boundless infinity of life. They had no idea who we were; they knew nothing of a fugitive; they did not know my poetry or my name. Or did they know it, know us? What mattered was that we sang and ate beside their fire, and then we walked through the darkness to some very primitive rooms. Through them ran a thermal stream, volcanic water in which we bathed, warmth released from the cordillera, which gathered us to its bosom.

We splashed like happy children, sinking into the water, cleansing ourselves of the burden of that long ride. When at dawn we set out on the last kilometers of the journey that would separate me from the eclipse fallen over my beloved land, we were refreshed, reborn, baptized. We rode away singing, filled with a new spirit, with a new hope that propelled us toward the great highway of the world awaiting me. When (I remember vividly) we tried to give those mountain men a few coins in payment for the songs, the food, the thermal bath, for the roof and bed, that is, for the shelter we had so unexpectedly stumbled upon, they refused our offer expressionlessly. They had done what they could, that's all. And in their "that's all" was deep, unspoken understanding—perhaps recognition, perhaps the same dreams.

Ladies and gentlemen, I never found in books any formula for writing poetry; and I, in turn, do not intend to leave in print a word of advice, a method, or a style that will allow young poets to receive from me some drop of supposed wisdom. If in this address I have recounted certain events from the past, if I have relived a never-forgotten adventure on this occasion and in this place so remote from that experience, it is to illustrate that in the course of my life I have always found the necessary affirmation, a formula, awaiting me, not to become enshrined in my words, but to lead me to an understanding of myself.

I found in that long journey the prescription for writing poetry. I was blessed by gifts from the earth and from the soul. I believe that poetry is a solemn and transient act to which solitude and unity, emotion and action, one's private world, man's private world, and the secret revelations of nature contribute in equal measure. I am similarly convinced that all this—man and his past, man and his commitment, man and his poetry—is preserved in an always expanding community, in an activity that will someday integrate reality and dreams, for this is how they are united. And I tell you that even after so many years I do not know whether the lessons I learned as I crossed a dizzying river, as I danced around the skull of a steer, as I lay in the purifying waters that flowed from the highest mountains— I tell you I do not know whether that experience originated in me, to be communicated later to other human beings, or whether it was a message sent me by other men as a demand and a summons. I don't know whether I lived it or I wrote it, I don't know whether the poems I experienced in that moment, the experiences I later sang, were truth or poetry, ephemera or eternity.

From such things, my friends, comes the kind of enlightenment the poet must learn from his fellow men. There is no unassailable solitude. All roads lead to the same point: to the communication of who we are. And we must travel across lonely and rugged terrain, through isolation and silence, to reach the magic zone where we can dance an awkward dance or sing a melancholy song; but in the dance and the song are consummated the most ancient rituals of awareness—the awareness of being men, and of believing in a common destiny.

The fact is that if some, or many, have thought that I was a sectarian, unable to break bread at the table of friendship and shared responsibility, I will make no attempt to justify myself. I do not believe that there is room for accusation or justification among the duties of the poet. After all, no one poet has administered poetry, and if one paused to accuse his fellows, or if another chose to waste his life defending himself against reasonable or absurd recriminations, I am convinced that only vanity leads us to such extremes. I say that the enemies of poetry are not to be found among its practitioners or patrons but in a lack of harmony within the poet. Thus it follows that no poet has a more fundamental enemy than his own inability to communicate with the most ignorant and exploited of his contemporaries; and this applies to all times and all nations.

The poet is not a "little god." No, he is not a "little god." He is not chosen for some cabalistic destiny superior to that of persons who perform different duties and offices. I have often said that the best poet is the man who delivers our daily bread: the local baker, who does not think he is a god. He fulfills his majestic yet humble task of kneading, placing in the oven, browning, and delivering our daily bread, with a true sense of community. And if a poet could be moved in the same way by such a simple conscience, that simple conscience would allow him to become part of an enormous work of art—the simple, or complicated, construction that is the building of a society, the transformation of man's condition, the simple delivery of his wares: bread, truth, wine, dreams. If the poet becomes part of the eternal struggle, if each of us places in the hands of the other his ration of commitment, his dedication and his tenderness toward the labor shared every day by all men, then the poet will be part of the sweat, the bread, the wine, the dream of all humanity. Only on this not-to-be-denied road of accepting our role as ordinary men will we succeed in restoring to poetry the amplitude chiseled away from it in every age, chiseled away by poets themselves.

The errors that have led me to relative truth, and the truths that have often led me to error, never permitted me—not that I ever attempted it—to define, to influence, or to teach what is called the creative process, the peaks and abysses of literature. But I have learned one thing: that it is we ourselves who create the phantoms of our own mythification. From the very mortar with which we create, or hope to create, are formed the obstacles to our own evolution. We may find ourselves irrevocably drawn toward reality and realism —that is, toward an unselective acceptance of reality and the roads to change—and then realize, when it seems too late, that we have raised such severe limitations that we have killed life instead of guiding it to growth and fruition. We have imposed on ourselves a realism heavier than our building bricks, without ever having constructed the building we thought was our first responsibility. And at the opposite extreme, if we succeed in making a fetish of the incomprehensible (or comprehensible to only a few), a fetish of the exceptional and the recondite, if we suppress reality and its inevitable deterioration, we will suddenly find ourselves in an untenable position, sinking in a quicksand of leaves, clay, and clouds, drowning in an oppressive inability to communicate.

As for the particular case of writers from the vast expanses of America, we hear unceasingly the call to fill that enormous space with creatures of flesh and blood. We are aware of our obligation to populate this space, and at the same time we realize our fundamental, our critical obligation to communicate in an uninhabited world which is no less filled with injustice, punishment, and pain because it is uninhabited. We also feel the obligation to revive the ancient dreams slumbering in our stone statues, in our ancient, ruined monuments, in the vast silences of our pampas, in our dense jungles, in our rivers that sing like thunder. We are called upon to fill with words the confines of a mute continent, and we become drunk with the task of telling and naming. Perhaps that has been the decisive factor in my own humble career; and in that case my excesses, or my abundance, or my rhetoric, will turn out to be nothing more than the simplest acts of routine American responsibility. Each of my verses strove to be palpable; each of my poems sought to be a useful tool; each of my songs aspired to be a sign in space to mark a gathering at the crossroads, or to be a fragment of stone or wood on which someone, others, those to come, could inscribe new signs.

Carrying the duties of the poet to their logical consequences, I decided, whether correctly or in error, that my commitment in society and in life should be that of a humble partisan. I decided this even as I witnessed glorious failures, solitary victories, stunning defeats. I understood, finding myself an actor in the struggles of America, that my human mission was none other than to add my talents to the swelling force of unified peoples, to join them in blood and spirit, with passion and hope, because only from that swelling torrent can be born the progress necessary for writers and for peoples. And though my position raised, or may raise, bitter or amiable objections, the fact is that I can accept no other road for a writer in our vast and harsh landscape if we want the darkness to flower, if we are to hope that millions of men who still have not learned to read us—or even to read—who still cannot write—or write to us—will live in a climate of dignity without which it is impossible to be a whole man.

We inherited the misery of peoples who have been marked by misfortune for centuries—the most Edenic, the purest peoples, peoples who built miraculous towers from stone and metal, jewels of dazzling splendor: peoples who suddenly found their lives dashed and silenced in a terrible era of colonialism that persists to this day.

Our original guiding stars are struggle and hope. But there is no such thing as solitary hope or struggle. In every man are joined all past ages, and the inertia, the errors, the passions, the urgencies of our time, the swift course of history. But what kind of man would I be if I had, for example, contributed in any way to the continuing feudalism of our great American continent? How could I hold my head high, graced by the great honor bestowed on me by Sweden, if I did not feel proud of having played a small part in the present changes in my country? We must look at the map of America, recognize its great diversity, the cosmic reaches of the space in which we live, to understand that many writers refuse to share in the curse of opprobrium and pillaging cast upon American peoples by dark gods.

I chose the difficult road of shared responsibility, and rather than reiterate my worship of the individual as the central sun of the system, I preferred to devote my humble services to the sizable army that may from time to time take the wrong turning but which advances relentlessly, marching forward day by day in the face of stubborn reactionaries, the impatient, and the uninformed. Because I believe that my duties as a poet embraced brotherhood not only with the rose and symmetry, with exalted love and infinite nostalgia, but with the thorny human responsibilities I have incorporated into my poetry.

Exactly a hundred years ago, a poor but splendid poet, the most tortured of the damned, prophesied: "*A l'aurore, armés d'une ardente patience, nous entrerons aux splendides Villes.*"

I believe in that prophecy of the seer Rimbaud. I come from a dark province, from a country separated from others by a severe geography. I was the most abandoned of poets, and my poetry was regional, sorrowful, steeped in rain. But I always had confidence in man. I never lost hope. That may be why I am here with my poetry, and with my flag.

In conclusion, I say to all men of good will, to workers, to poets, that the future of man is expressed in Rimbaud's phrase: only with fiery patience will we conquer the splendid city that will shed light, justice, and dignity on all men.

Thus, poetry shall not have sung in vain.

Index